Public Health: Past, Present and Future

Celebrating academic public health in Edinburgh, 1902–2002

With sincere appreciation and thanks to
Professor Timothy O'Shea, Principal of
the University of Edinburgh

from

Raj Bhopal

and

John Last

Eighth of December 2004

Published by TSO (The Stationery Office) and available from:

Online
www.tso.co.uk/bookshop

Mail, Telephone, Fax & E-mail
TSO
PO Box 29, Norwich, NR3 1GN
Telephone orders/General enquiries: 0870 600 5522
Fax orders: 0870 600 5533
E-mail: book.orders@tso.co.uk
Textphone 0870 240 3701

TSO Shops
123 Kingsway, London, WC2B 6PQ
020 7242 6393 Fax 020 7242 6394
68-69 Bull Street, Birmingham B4 6AD
0121 236 9696 Fax 0121 236 9699
9-21 Princess Street, Manchester M60 8AS
0161 834 7201 Fax 0161 833 0634
16 Arthur Street, Belfast BT1 4GD
028 9023 8451 Fax 028 9023 5401
18-19 High Street, Cardiff CF10 1PT
029 2039 5548 Fax 029 2038 4347
71 Lothian Road, Edinburgh EH3 9AZ
0870 606 5566 Fax 0870 606 5588

TSO Accredited Agents
(see Yellow Pages)

and through good booksellers

Applications for reproduction should be made to

The Nuffield Trust
59 New Cavendish Street
London
W1M 7RD

www.nuffieldtrust.org.uk

First published 2004

ISBN: 0 11 703264 6

Printed in the United Kingdom for The Stationery Office

Public Health: Past, Present and Future

Celebrating academic public health in Edinburgh, 1902–2002

Edited by Raj Bhopal and John Last

The Nuffield Trust

FOR RESEARCH AND POLICY
STUDIES IN HEALTH SERVICES

DEDICATION

We dedicate this book to the memories and achievements of Professor Henry Littlejohn, the first medical officer of health in Edinburgh, and Professor Charles Hunter Stewart, the first Alexander Bruce and John Usher Professor of Public Health.

CONTENTS

THE FUTURE

FIGURES

TABLES

CONTRIBUTORS

Raj Bhopal is the Alexander Bruce and John Usher Professor of Public Health and head of the Division of Community Health Sciences, Public Health Sciences Section, University of Edinburgh, Scotland.

Sheila M. Bird is senior statistician at the Medical Research Council's Biostatistics Unit, Cambridge, England, and visiting professor at the Department of Statistics and Modelling Science, University of Strathclyde, Glasgow, Scotland.

Harry Campbell is reader in genetic epidemiology, Public Health Sciences, University of Edinburgh, Scotland.

Sarah Cunningham-Burley is reader and co-director of the Centre for Research on Families and Relationships, Public Health Sciences, Division of Community Health Sciences, University of Edinburgh, Scotland.

Peter Donnelly is director of public health for Lothian Health Board, Edinburgh, Scotland.

Gerry Fowkes is professor of epidemiology in the Wolfson Unit for Prevention of Peripheral Vascular Diseases, Public Health Sciences, Division of Community Health Sciences, University of Edinburgh, Scotland.

Anthony J. Hedley is chair professor in the Department of Community Medicine, University of Hong Kong, Hong Kong SAR, China.

John Last is emeritus professor of epidemiology at the University of Ottawa, Canada.

David M. Macfadyen is a former director of programme management for the World Health Organization (Region for Europe) and an honorary fellow of Public Health Sciences, Division of Community Health Sciences, University of Edinburgh, Scotland.

Una Maclean is a former reader in public health, Public Health Sciences, University of Edinburgh, Scotland.

Gordon D. Murray is professor of medical statistics and head of public health sciences at the University of Edinburgh.

Timothy O'Shea is principal and vice-chancellor of the University of Edinburgh, Scotland.

G. H. Palmer is professor of grain science at the International Centre for Brewing and Distilling, Heriot-Watt University, Edinburgh, Scotland.

Colin N. Ramsay is consultant epidemiologist for the Scottish Centre for Infection and Environmental Health, Glasgow, Scotland.

Margaret Reid is head of the Division of Community-based Sciences at the University of Glasgow, Scotland.

John Wyn Owen C.B., Secretary, Nuffield Trust.

Helen Zealley is a former director of public health for Lothian Health Board, Edinburgh, Scotland.

The contributors' posts are given as they were at the time of the conference in 2002.

Foreword

It is with great pleasure that we introduce you to this collection celebrating 100 years of academic public health at the University of Edinburgh. The achievements over the last 100 years, as reflected in several chapters, are reason enough to celebrate. However, the real reason to celebrate is the timeliness of this book. Worldwide, the profile of public health has never been higher. Promoting health and reducing inequalities are increasingly seen as being as important, if not more important, than fighting disease. This volume gives a clear and compelling account of what has been achieved to date and sets out a vital agenda for future work.

The Nuffield Trust welcomed the opportunity of participating in the celebration of public health in Scotland, and this volume joins a long history of the Trust's work featuring Scotland's health. The tradition of public health in Scotland has some distinctive features, not least due to the work of the Usher Institute, whose work, as displayed in this volume, we hope to open up to a wider appreciation. The influence of the Scottish tradition in public health is already global; and with devolution, there is now an opportunity to pioneer a new era in public health law internationally, with exemplar legislation for a Health of the People Act.

Edinburgh has much to be proud of for the contributions made over the last 100 years. Moreover, as brought out very clearly in this collection, we are in great shape to make continuing contributions over the coming years to research and development in the crucial area of public health. The university is committed to building on its past achievements and to making an even greater contribution in the next 100 years.

TIMOTHY O'SHEA, GORDON D. MURRAY and JOHN WYN OWEN

Preface

As editors, we have enjoyed several rare privileges. Foremost of these was the opportunity to participate in the celebration of 100 years of academic public health in the University of Edinburgh. To our knowledge, few universities anywhere can match this record, and no other in the UK. A landmark event such as this brings both opportunities and motivation for reflection on the history of the subject and on its future directions. From such reflection we draw inspiration from the work both of our predecessors and of our contemporaries. We also have an opportunity to give honour where it is due, and especially where such dues have been forgotten. The editors have a special opportunity to share intimately in this task with the contributing authors. In bringing together the diversity of contributions, the editors help shape a narrative that is more than its component parts. Our aim in this narrative is to bridge global and local, historical and contemporary public health and produce a volume that stimulates thought as well as acting as a record for our successors celebrating future centenaries.

Centenary celebrations provide time for connecting, reconnecting and cementing relationships with former and current students and colleagues. This is the time to make new friends and build relationships beyond the usual boundaries of discipline and department. The participants at the conference took such opportunities enthusiastically. As editors, we hope that this volume will continue the dialogue already started, and develop it further within the wider world of public health.

The issues raised by this volume are generalisable across eras, places and cultures. The core message is this: public health is goal driven, and strives for higher life expectancy, reduction in disease, illness and disability, and a greater well-being in the population in its entirety, while minimising inequalities. This vision of public health is global, and yet it cannot be achieved without successful local and regional infrastructures, sometimes dependent upon one or a few catalytic people, and more usually on small groups or departments. Global public health is dependent upon a myriad of such infrastructures. The history of academic public health in Edinburgh, therefore, represents a microcosm of the whole, and the lessons arising from this volume have wide implications.

The papers in this volume were presented at the Public Health Sciences Centenary Conference entitled 'Public Health: Past, Present and Future' on Friday, 1 November 2002, at the Assembly Rooms, Edinburgh. The Public Health Sciences Section of the Department of Community Health Sciences at Edinburgh University, which draws its lineage directly from the setting up of the Alexander Bruce and John Usher Chair of Public Health in 1898, celebrated 100 years of contribution to academic public health following the opening in 1902 of the John Usher Institute of Public Health. During the three days of the celebrations, over 300 people participated. Participants represented 24 different countries.

About the year 1900 the health of the people of Edinburgh was showing some improvement, due to better housing conditions in the city. Nonetheless, smallpox and other lethal infectious diseases were still seen. Epidemics of cholera and typhus disappeared sooner from Edinburgh than from any other large city in the UK, but there were many other public health and social problems, such as tuberculosis and malnutrition of children, to be tackled.

The Usher Institute of Public Health has participated in keeping Edinburgh at the forefront of public health research and education, making it one of the finest cities in Europe, and helping it to become a healthy place to live. The institute has trained undergraduates and postgraduates from all over the world and has had a global influence. The research programmes, including those on breast cancer, vascular disease, tuberculosis and health care evaluation, have enhanced Edinburgh's reputation as an international research centre for public health. The original initiative of John Usher remains vigorous and innovative, through extensive research on vascular disease, cancer epidemiology and genetics, tackling inequalities in health and developing and evaluating effective services. Education for undergraduates and postgraduates focuses on the study of the pattern of diseases on populations; the social, environmental and genetic basis of disease; and the design, delivery and evaluation of services for the prevention, control and cure of diseases.

The Usher Institute of Public Health was built with funds from Sir John Usher of Norton, of the famous Edinburgh distilleries, and provided laboratory and teaching facilities for medical officers of health and student doctors. The institute was located at some distance from the medical school and the hub of the university. The university's present Section of Public Health Sciences, the successor to the institute, is now located in the medical school complex at Teviot Place, within the main university campus. This symbolises the increasing integration of disciplines that characterises modern-day research and teaching in public health.

The conference reviewed the history of public health globally and in Edinburgh; examined trends in infectious and chronic diseases; predicted directions of inter-disciplinary public health research in the social sciences, medical statistics and epidemiology; and peeked into the future, including the development of a new public health law for the 21st century. We trust that we have captured the deliberations to the satisfaction of authors, sponsors and national and international readers alike.

1902 - 100 years of academic public health - 2002

Acknowledgements

This list of thanks is incomplete, because the number of people who helped is so great that to list them all would require many pages. These helpers will recognise their own valued input.

We thank the authors, without whose work this volume would not have been possible. We thank the Centenary Organising Committee and the History of Public Health in Edinburgh Group. In the work of these two committees, and in the many activities associated with the conference and the ensuing publication, numerous support and academic staff of public health sciences and colleagues in other departments within the University of Edinburgh and other institutions dedicated much time and energy. We thank them.

The conference that gave birth to this collection was sponsored by the University of Edinburgh, Lothian Health Board, The Nuffield Trust and The Wellcome Trust. The Chief Scientist's Office in the Scottish Executive sponsored Professor John Last's visit to Scotland in 2002. The preparation of the book has been sponsored by the Section of Public Health Sciences, and its publication by the Nuffield Trust.

THE PAST

1. Landmarks in the history of public health

John Last

Three discoveries determined the health and history of the human species. The first occurred almost a million years ago, when our hominid precursors discovered how to use fire to cook the meat they had hunted. They evidently found that cooked meat tasted better, it didn't go bad so quickly and eating it was less likely to make them ill. We've been improving our understanding of nutrition, a basic public health science, and the art of cooking ever since.

Some 12,000 years ago, as the world warmed up after the last Ice Age, two more discoveries transformed human communities forever. Our forebears, perhaps the women, learnt how to domesticate animals for food, milk and clothing. About the same time they discovered that seed grain could be planted, harvested and stored from one season to the next, as well as used to make flour and thence bread and similar high-density carbohydrate foods. These great discoveries eliminated reliance on precarious hunting and gathering, and made permanent human settlements possible. They were the indispensable basis for every human achievement since.

The secure food supply led to the first great population surge. Little settlements became villages, villages became towns, towns grew into cities. Before long, civilisations with religions, laws, history, customs, traditions and sciences arose on fertile plains beside great rivers in Egypt, the Middle East, India and China. Our ancestors had begun to climb the long road to health, towards our present situation. (We might ask, as we consider the wars, the suffering, the injustices of the world of the early 21st century, 'Where did we take a wrong turn?' But that's a story I neither have time, nor am professionally equipped, to tell adequately.)

As humans grew fruitful and multiplied, so did the variety and number of their diseases. Permanent human settlements transformed ecosystems and, abiding by epidemic theory, the probability of respiratory and faecal–oral transmission of infection rose as population density increased. Ecological and evolutionary changes in micro-organisms account for the origins of diarrhoea, measles, malaria, smallpox, plague and many other diseases. Micro-organisms evolve rapidly because of their brief generation time and prolific reproduction rates. Many that previously had lived in symbiosis with animals began to invade humans and became pathogenic. Some evolved complex life cycles involving several host species: humans and other mammals, humans and arthropods, humans and freshwater snails.

These evolutionary changes in host–parasite relationships occurred at least several millennia before we had written histories. Our oldest written records that have a bearing on health date back about 4,000 years. *The Code of Hammurabi* (*c*.2000 BCE) contains ideas indicative of insight into the effects on health of diet and behaviour. It also suggests rewards and punishments for physicians who did their jobs well or poorly.

Hippocrates, the father of medicine, was also the father of public health. He flourished in a school of medicine at the Temple of Asklepios, near Epidaurus in Greece about 450 BCE. The Hippocratic writings contain rich medical wisdom based on careful observation of sick and healthy people and their habits and habitats. *On Airs, Waters and Places* outlines environmental health as it was understood two and a half thousand years ago. The relationship of environment, social conditions and behaviour to health and sickness is made explicit in the timeless advice of the opening paragraph:

> Whoever would study medicine must learn of the following. First, consider the effect of each of the seasons … and the differences between them … Study the warm and cold winds … and the effect of water on health … When a physician comes to a district previously unknown to him he should consider its situation and its aspect to the winds … and the nature of its water supply … Whether the land be bare and waterless or thickly covered with vegetation and well-watered, whether in a hollow and stifling, or exposed and cold. Lastly, consider the life of the inhabitants – are they heavy drinkers and eaters and consequently unable to stand fatigue, or being fond of work and exercise, eat wisely but drink sparely.[1]

In short, environment and lifestyle – very modern concepts.

The 16th-century Italian monk Fracastorius recognised some ways infection can spread. His conclusion that disease could pass by intimate direct contact from one person to others was easy because he saw the dramatic epidemic of syphilis that was so obviously spread by sexual intercourse. He described this in a mock heroic poem, *Syphilis, sive morbis Gallicus* (1530),[2] about the swineherd Syphilis and how he got and passed on to others the 'French disease' then raging in Europe. His anti-hero, of course, gave us the name of the disease.

Fracastorius's other concepts – droplet spread and spread by way of contaminated articles such as clothing and kitchen utensils – were published in *De Contagione* in 1546.[3] Fracastorius is important because he made a conceptual breakthrough and brought about what Thomas Kuhn calls a paradigm shift in understanding of infection and some ways to control it.

After Fracastorius the pathfinders on the road to health became so numerous I can mention only a handful of my personal public health heroes: John Graunt, James Lind, Edward Jenner, John Snow and Louis Pasteur.

John Graunt (1620–1674), a London merchant haberdasher, was an amateur scientist and an early Fellow of the Royal Society. He was interested in the impact of epidemics, especially the plague, and how plague caused the numbers of deaths and the age at death to vary from one year to another. For over 100 years before his time, parishes had kept records of baptisms and deaths, and what was then understood about causes of death was inscribed in the Bills of Mortality. Graunt collected and analysed these Bills of Mortality.[4] He demonstrated differences between males and females, between London and rural areas, and the ebb and flow of epidemics of plague. This was the foundation for the science of vital statistics. John Graunt demonstrated the importance of gathering facts in a systematic manner to identify, characterise and classify health conditions of public health importance. The diagnostic categories in the Bills of Mortality tell us what was understood 400 years ago about the variety of human ailments and their causes.

James Lind (1716–1794) was born and educated in Edinburgh. He was apprenticed to a surgeon when he was 15 and spent nine years as a naval surgeon, during which time he saw many cases of scurvy, a disease that disabled and often killed sailors on long ocean voyages. Lind thought this disease might be caused by a diet lacking fresh fruit and vegetables. He conducted an experiment, giving different diets to each of several pairs of sailors. This was, in fact, the first clinical trial ever conducted – although the sample sizes were very small, there was no random allocation and no informed consent was obtained from the sailors. The two sailors who received fresh oranges and lemons recovered rapidly from the scurvy; the others did not. Lind also initiated the first effective measures aimed at enhancing hygiene in the British navy, but he is best known for his work on scurvy.[5] Not only was this the first reported clinical trial, it was also proof that a dietary deficiency can cause disease and that a well-balanced diet is essential for good health. Thus Lind, like Fracastorius, was responsible for an important paradigm shift in the understanding of causes and control of disease.

Edward Jenner (1749–1823) was a family doctor who practised throughout his life in the village of Berkeley, Gloucestershire. In his day smallpox was a ubiquitous threat to life and health. In severe epidemics it killed up to a quarter of all it attacked. When it didn't kill, it often left disfiguring facial pockmarks and if it affected the eyes it caused blindness.

The practice of variolation, inoculation into the skin of dried secretions from a smallpox bleb, was invented in China about 1,000 years ago and spread along the Silk Route, reaching Asia Minor in the 17th century. Lady Mary Wortley Montague, wife of the British ambassador to Constantinople, described the practice in a letter dated 1 April 1717 and imported the idea to England when she came home. By the time Jenner was a child, variolation had become popular among educated English families as a way to provide some protection against smallpox.

Jenner knew the popular belief in Gloucestershire that people who had been infected with cowpox, a mild disease acquired from cattle, did not get smallpox. He reasoned that since smallpox in mild form was transmitted by variolation, it might be possible to transmit cowpox in a similar way. A smallpox outbreak in 1792 gave him an opportunity to confirm this notion. In 1796 he began a courageous and unprecedented experiment – one that would now be unethical, but that has had incalculable benefit for humankind. He inoculated a boy, James Phipps, with secretions from a cowpox lesion. In succeeding months, until the summer of 1798, he inoculated others, most of them children, up to a total of 23. All survived unharmed, and none got smallpox.

Jenner published *An Inquiry into the Causes and Effects of the Variolae Vaccinae* [6] – perhaps the most influential public health treatise of all time – in 1798. The importance of Jenner's work was immediately recognised and although there were sceptics and vicious opponents, vaccination programmes began at once. The frequency and ferocity of smallpox epidemics began to decline early in the 19th century, but it remained a menace. In 1949 the American epidemiologist Donald Soper worked out the strategy of containment (i.e. vaccinating all known contacts of every diagnosed case). In 1966 the World Health Organization (WHO) embarked on a campaign to eradicate smallpox. The last naturally occurring case was a girl in Somalia in 1977. In 1980 the World Health Assembly proclaimed that smallpox, one of the most deadly scourges of mankind, had been eradicated. At the beginning of the new millennium, samples of smallpox virus survive in secure biological laboratories in several countries, but thanks to Edward Jenner this terrible disease need never again take a human life – unless it is used in biological warfare.

John Snow (1813–1858) was a London physician, and a founding father of modern epidemiology. (He was also a pioneer anaesthetist and invented a new kind of mask to administer chloroform, which he gave to Queen Victoria to assist at the births of her two youngest children.) Snow's work on cholera demonstrated fundamental intellectual steps that must be part of every epidemiological investigation. He began with a logical analysis of the available facts, which proved that cholera could not be caused by a 'miasma' (emanations from rotting organic matter), as proposed in a theory popular at that time, but must be caused by a transmissible agent, most probably in drinking water. He confirmed the proof with two epidemiological investigations in the great cholera epidemic of 1854. He studied a severe localised epidemic in Soho, using analysis of descriptive epidemiological data and spot maps to demonstrate that the cause was polluted water from a pump in Broad Street. His investigation of the more widespread epidemic in South London involved an inquiry into the source of drinking water used in over 700 households. He compared the water source in houses where cholera had occurred with that in houses where it had not. His analysis of the information about the cases and their sources of drinking water showed beyond doubt that the cause was water that was being supplied to houses by the Southwark and Vauxhall water company, which drew its water from the Thames downriver, where many effluent discharges polluted the water. Very few cases occurred in households supplied with water by the Lambeth company, which collected water upstream from London, where there was little or no pollution. This was a remarkable feat, completed 30 years before Robert Koch identified the cholera bacillus. Snow published his work in a monograph, *On the Mode of Communication of Cholera* (1855).[7] This book has been reprinted in modern editions and is still used as a teaching text.

Medical science advanced rapidly in the second half of the 19th century, applying the exciting discoveries of a new science, bacteriology, which transformed public health. The great bacteriologists of the late 19th century identified many pathogenic bacteria, classified them, developed ways to cultivate them and, most important, worked out ways to control their harmful effects, using sera, vaccines and 'magic bullets' such as the arsenical preparations that Ehrlich developed to treat syphilis. It would be useful to discuss each of them, but in the interests of brevity I will focus on just one figure – Louis Pasteur (1822–1895). The French chemist evolved into a bacteriologist and was a towering figure of 19th-century bacteriology and preventive medicine. By 1854 he had been appointed professor of chemistry in Lille, and was invited to solve the problem of the aberrant fermentation of beer that caused it to taste bad and made it undrinkable. He showed that the problem was caused by bacteria that were killed by heat. In this way he invented the process for heat treatment to kill harmful bacteria, first applied to fermentation of beer and then to milk – the process known ever since as pasteurisation, which has saved innumerable children from an untimely death. He went on to study and solve many other bacteriological problems in industry and animal husbandry. Pasteur developed attenuated vaccines, first to prevent chicken cholera and then, in 1881, to control anthrax, which was a serious threat to livestock as well as an occasional human disease. Before this, in 1880, he began experiments on rabies, seeking a vaccine to control the disease, which without treatment is invariably fatal.

Following the success of the anthrax vaccine Pasteur believed that an attenuated rabies vaccine could be made. This, of course, was many decades before the virus was visualised. He successfully tested his rabies vaccine in 1885 on a boy, Joseph Meister, who had been bitten by a rabid dog. Pasteur became not just a national but also an international celebrity. He visited Edinburgh, and played a part in initiating actions that led to the creation of the Usher Institute.

Pasteur, Henle, Koch, Virchow and soon battalions of bacteriologists and pathologists firmly established the fact that micro-organisms caused many diseases – the germ theory was fact, not theory. But many germ diseases require much more than germs before they can do their worst damage. Tuberculosis is caused by the tubercle bacillus acting in conjunction with poverty, ignorance, overcrowding, poor nutrition, adverse social and economic circumstances, and other enabling and predisposing factors. The diarrhoeal diseases, including cholera, are caused by various micro-organisms, but these get into the gut when ingested with contaminated water or food; that is, they are really caused by poor sanitary and hygienic practices.

By late in the 19th century, many of these factors had been clarified. The stage was set for the health reforms that included the sanitary revolution, the beginnings of a social safety net, provision of immunisations, nutritional supplements for schoolchildren, prenatal care for pregnant women and other essential public health functions that we take for granted 100 years later. It required a dedicated army of public health workers to achieve all this.

I have singled out Hippocrates, Fracastorius, Graunt, Lind, Jenner, Snow and Pasteur as public health pathfinders on the road to good health. Their patients or experimental subjects – Lind's sailors, James Phipps, Joseph Meister and all others known and unknown by name – should be remembered and honoured too.

Many others belong in their company: Ignaz Semmelweiss and Oliver Wendell Holmes both understood better than the heavy-handed Joseph Lister that clean-liness is essential to prevent childbed fever and other hospital-acquired infections; the great German pathologist Rudolph Virchow recognised that political action as well as rational science is necessary to initiate effective action to control public health problems; Edwin Chadwick and Lemuel Shattuck reported on the appalling sanitary conditions associated with the unacceptably high infant and child death rates that prevailed in 19th-century industrial towns; and William Farr established vital statistics in England as a model for other nations to follow. And so the list grows from a handful of public health pathfinders to whole armies.

More was needed than scientific discoveries, however. These had to be applied, and this often required drastic changes in the established social and economic order. So other pathfinders appear on the road to health. They included politicians, administrators, journalists, creative writers, performing artists, cartoonists. The journalists, creative writers and artists who transmit the scientific concepts of public health to the general public and to the politicians are indispensable partners in the team that makes it possible for us to advance up the road to better health.

I can identify five essential ingredients of the processes that brought about the public health reforms we call the sanitary revolution of the late 19th and early 20th century. Indeed, these five features are essential for the control of all public health problems.

1   **Awareness that the problem exists**. John Graunt began this process with *The Natural and Political Observations*. Others consolidated his conceptual breakthrough, and it was applied to great effect after the establishment of formal national vital statistics in England and Wales under the inspired leadership of William Farr. By Farr's time, widespread literacy, the proliferation of daily newspapers and word of mouth helped to enhance awareness among thoughtful people everywhere that there were massive public health problems in society at that time.

2   **Understanding the causes**. In the second half of the 19th century understanding rapidly increased as epidemiology, bacteriology and nutritional and environmental sciences explored the previously unknown landscapes of aetiology and pathogenesis. The new mass media – daily newspapers – propagated this understanding among literate people throughout the country.

3   **Capability to control the causes**. With astonishing speed once the initial breakthroughs had occurred, sera and vaccines were developed to control many of the lethal microbial diseases that had plagued earlier generations. Improved dietary practices, pasteurisation of milk, personal hygiene and, above all, environmental sanitation to rid drinking water of polluting pathogens, all advanced rapidly in the final quarter of the 19th century and the first few decades of the 20th century.

4 **The belief (sense of values) that the problem is important**. This is an essential prerequisite to determination to do something about it. It is the most fascinating and challenging aspect of the essential features. It is the moral imperative that drives public health reforms. Geoffrey Vickers described the history of public health as a process of redefining the unacceptable – an endless process of identifying conditions, behaviours and circumstances that individuals, communities and cultures must no longer tolerate. Throwing the contents of the chamber pot into the street, clearing one's nostrils on the tablecloth and coughing and spitting on the living-room floor became unacceptable in the late 19th century. Many beyond the boundaries of medical science and public health practice played a role in this process. In the era of the great reforms of the 19th century, they included social reformers like Edwin Chadwick, journalists like Henry Mayhew and Charles Kingsley, novelists like Charles Dickens, cartoonists in *Punch* and other periodicals – all of them aided by the rise of literacy in those times. Collectively they inspired a mood of public outrage that became an irresistible force for reform.

5 **Political will**. There is always resistance to change, there are always interest groups – often rich and powerful withal – who will do whatever it takes to obstruct necessary improvement. In the era of the sanitary revolution it was the owners of water companies, factories and tenement housing who resisted most vigorously. Legislation and regulation are almost always necessary, and inevitably generate opposition. But when the other four features – awareness, understanding, capability and values – are in place, the political will to bring about reforms gathers momentum and usually succeeds eventually.

These five essential ingredients required for public health reforms apply equally to other public health problems that have waxed and waned in my lifetime: tobacco addiction, impaired driving, domestic violence, child abuse, irresponsible domestic and industrial waste disposal, etc.

Mountainous barriers to health of our own making have appeared lately. The most formidable is a cluster of human-induced changes to global ecosystems and the global commons – the atmosphere, the oceans, wilderness regions, stocks of biodiversity – that threaten all life and health on earth, not just the life and health of humans.

Another is perhaps an inherent flaw in the human character that leads many individuals and national leaders to believe that disputes can be settled by violent means. Now we have so many terrible weapons that violence can and does cause immense suffering, innumerable deaths (80% or more of these deaths as well as a similar proportion of permanent maiming and disability are among non-combatants) and appalling damage to ecosystems, the environment and the fabric of society. Sadly, this is rarely recognised as a public health problem. The very first essential ingredient, awareness of the problem, is lacking. Both these massive public health problems, in my view, are linked to the insatiable human craving for petroleum fuels, an addiction far more pervasive and dangerous than addiction to tobacco. So far in our only partially sentient and insightful civilisation, this isn't even recognised as a public health problem.

A public health problem that has been recognised is a worldwide pandemic of tobacco addiction and its many adverse effects on health and long life. Another is the global pandemic of HIV/AIDS. These are both associated with modern urban life and social behaviour, including the marketing practices of trans-national corporations. Surmounting these barriers to health will require social, cultural and behavioural changes and political action.

I am an optimist. I believe that the pace of scientific advances will be maintained in the future, and that values will continue to shift in favour of essential changes towards global ecosystem sustainability. I don't know whether those who follow us will ever reach the ultimate summit of Halfdan Mahler's 'health for all' but I am confident that they will continue to climb towards it. Thereby hangs the tale to be told by someone standing here 100 years from now, at the 200th anniversary of the Usher Institute.

Notes

[1]   G. E. R. Lloyd (trans.), *Hippocratic Writings* (Harmondsworth: Penguin, 1978), p. 148.
[2]   Hieronymi Fracastorii (Fracastorius), *De Contagione et Contagiosis Morbis et Eorum Curatione, Libri III*, trans. and notes by W. C. Wright (London and New York: Putnams, 1930).
[3]   Ibid.
[4]   J. Graunt, *Natural and Political Observations Mentioned in a Following Index and Made Upon the Bills of Mortality with Reference to the Government, Religion, Trade, Growth, Air, Diseases and the Several Changes in the Said City* (London: John Martyn, 1662).
[5]   J. Lind, *A Treatise of the Scurvy* (Edinburgh: University of Edinburgh Press, 1953).
[6]   E. Jenner, *An Inquiry into the Causes and Effects of the Variolae Vaccinae* (1798) (London: Dawsons, 1966).
[7]   J. Snow, *On the Mode of Communication of Cholera* (London: Churchill, 1855).

REFERENCES

Ponting, C. *A Green History of the World: the environment and the collapse of great civilizations*. New York: St Martin's Press, 1992

Porter, R. *The Greatest Benefit to Mankind: a medical history of humanity from antiquity to the present*. London: Harper Collins, 1997

Sigerist, H. E. *A History of Medicine 1: primitive and archaic medicine*. New York: Oxford University Press, 1967

2. Some historical notes on health and public health in Edinburgh

Helen Zealley

Early Edinburgh

History shows Edinburgh in the 12th and 13th centuries to have been a small burgh stretching from Castle Hill eastwards down the High Street to Blackfriars Wynd, south to the Cowgate, north to the valley below the castle and west to the castle and the Grassmarket.

These two centuries are reputedly the happiest in Scottish history – or at least lowland Scottish history. Scotland had its own kings and avoided the introduction of feudalism imposed on England by the Norman Conquest. Relative stability allowed settlements such as Edinburgh to develop and prosper. Forts and castles provided some protection and the churches provided for the development of learning, music and the arts.

As settlements became established, trading developed – partly between the burgesses of the town and the castle and partly between the townsfolk and the surrounding country people. In addition, Edinburgh, using the port of Leith, was well placed to develop trade across the North Sea, particularly with the Low Countries, which in turn influenced the architecture of the town.

The year 1296 saw the end of this peaceful period, as Edward I of England began what was to become 300 years of recurrent invasion and attack by the English. In response to Edward's invasion a wall was built to provide protection. The first – the King's Wall – was begun in 1329. The only remaining portion of this wall can be seen below the old public health building in Johnstone Terrace. In addition, some sort of dyke was created at the east end of the valley, below the crest of the hill, in order to dam up the Tumble River and create the 'North Loch' – now the site of Princes Street Gardens and Waverley Station.

Also in 1329 the burgh was given a Royal Charter by Robert the Bruce, although it had been given an earlier charter by King David I together with a vast forest – the Borough Muir – about two miles to the south of the town.

Between 1514 and 1520 a more extensive wall – the Flodden Wall – was built around the periphery of the town; indeed it was so long that it has been argued it couldn't have been defended and that 'its main value must have been in quieting the disturbed nerves of the citizens.'[1] An alternative argument is that it was built to keep out the vagrants that were believed to carry the plague – a major public health challenge that recurrently faced Edinburgh between 1492 and 1645. This wall had six gateways, the most imposing being at the Nether Bow. Whatever its main purpose, the burgh wall, which was extended between 1620 and 1623, gave vital protection from repeated English invasions right up to the time of Oliver Cromwell. A third wall – the Telfer Wall – slightly extended the enclosed area to the south from 1636.

These walls were fundamental to the overall boundary structure of the town, which remained virtually unchanged until 1765 – almost 600 years later. However, as the town prospered the population increased from an estimated 2,000 in the 12th and 13th centuries to 15–20,000 by 1450, when it became the capital of Scotland. Ruling noblemen were attracted to the city along with successful merchants and craftsmen, and by 1700 there had been a further increase to 25,000.

From around 1416 the Royal Burgh was governed by a council elected by the burgesses – those who owned property. These included a few noblemen but they were mainly merchants (who did very well as a result of various trade regulations passed by the council) and craft artisans. Indeed, until around the 1950s the councils were critically important in the overall governance of all towns and cities in Scotland, being responsible for safety, the overall structure and the common good of the town and its citizens. Although this included the health and well-being of the burgesses, until the early 19th century there was no concept of a 'duty' on civic authorities or the governing or employing classes to show responsibility towards the lower grades of society.

17th-century improvements

The original town of Edinburgh must have been very attractive. It was established a bow's distance from a fortification on the site of the present castle. Basically it comprised a single, wide street – or market-place – with 'enclosures' (or closes) along each side for which the burgesses paid rent to the council. Each holding had an eight-metre frontage and extended back for 150 metres – mostly down the steep slope from the crest of the hill to the Cowgate (where people accessed their cattle) in the south or to the valley to the north. Each 'enclosure' or 'land' had a dwelling to the front with gardens and orchards behind in which the inhabitants could compost their own waste. The gardens also provided access to fields beyond the Cowgate. A few public footpaths were left between some of the holdings and these were known as 'wynds'. A similar pattern of holdings was established around the Grassmarket (where grass was traded), thus making a total of around 350 dwellings within the city walls.

This arrangement was fine for a population of 2,000 but totally inadequate for the growing population. Three main techniques were used to extend the space:

- Firstly, the original houses were extended over the street; we can still see an example of this with John Knox's House on the High Street.

- Secondly, buildings were erected on the gardens and orchards until no green space was left, the homes to the back being accessed by a lane known as a 'close'.

- Finally, and this became a major public health problem, the 'tenements' (or holdings) were extended upwards with an amazing combination of wooden constructions – up to 14 stories at the back where the land sloped away.

The High Street was the main communication route through the town as well as an open market-place. Everyone – rich and poor alike – lived in the closes and wynds off this main public space. In one of his books Sir Walter Scott comments on the extreme height of the houses and the variety of gables, balconies and battlements: 'The population, close packed within the walls of the city ... absolutely swarmed like bees on the wide and stately street.'[2]

Outside the town walls there were flour mills at Dean Village, various agricultural villages all around the Borough Muir (an extensive area of forest and hunting grounds) and Borough Loch (now the Meadows) to the south. Also without the town itself – between the original King's Wall and the later Flodden Wall – were a number of ecclesiastical properties: Greyfriars, Blackfriars and Kirk o' Fields to the south and Trinity Hospital and Church to the north. These were important because they provided land for the later development of various schools and hospitals: the Tounis College (University of Edinburgh) on Kirk o' Fields (1583); a replacement High School and the original Royal Infirmary (1729) on Blackfriar's land; Heriot's Hospital (School) (1628) and the Merchant Maiden Hospital (now Mary Erskine School) (1694) on Greyfriars. While these endowed schools were for the children of the merchants, the council also provided 'vulgar' schools within the town, which gave a basic education to other children (boys and girls separately).

Water and sanitation

In 1681 water was brought into the town 'by a leaden pipe'[3] from Comiston to a reservoir at the top of Castle Hill, from where the water flowed to six wells in the High Street. By the 1780s the demand for water was so great that the wells could only be accessed during a three-hour period starting at midnight. Those with sufficient resources employed caddies to fetch their water; the rest had to queue. In 1819 a water company was established and supplies were increased. It was reported that there was more water coming into the burgh than people needed. Surplus supplies flushed down the street – and presumably helped to flush waste down the hills. In 1824 a new water supply was introduced which allowed water to be led into new buildings. This even enabled water closets to be introduced into the 'better parts of the city'[4] but it again led to a significant decrease in the availability of the public supply at the wells in the street, resulting in long waits to get to the single pipe where there had previously been two or three.

Overcrowding and increasingly insanitary conditions led, from 1492, to recurrent outbreaks of plague (or pest). These were greatly feared – for good reason – the last being in 1645 when 60% of the population of Leith are recorded to have died (Edinburgh data are not available). 'Control' of these epidemics was by removal and burial of the bodies, quarantine to wooden huts or 'hospital pavilions' built for the purpose on the Borough Muir (on the site of the Astley Ainslie Hospital), washing of the clothes of infected persons in the Borough Loch and fumigation of affected houses and burning of the contents.

Fear of further plague epidemics led the council, in 1721, to seek advice about prevention from the Royal College of Physicians. Their advice provides a clear indication that there was a good understanding of the need for effective waste management. They advised a range of public health actions but it was some years before the recommendations were implemented:

- draining of the North Loch, which functioned at the time as a cess pit

- formation of a canal with running water to remove the waste

- cleansing of the streets, closes and courts

- provision of public conveniences

- provision of dustcarts to allow servants to empty the 'fulzies' (refuse) from individual dwellings, in place of the existing system of throwing rubbish out of the window and shouting 'gardyloo'

- the removal of vagrants and beggars (who were assumed to be responsible for carrying the infection into the burgh).

The Scottish Enlightenment

In addition to attacks of the plague and, until 1745, intermittent attacks from the English, Edinburgh suffered from recurrent religious upheavals. In 1702 many of the merchants lost all their savings in the ill-fated Darien investment scheme in South America and, in 1707, the transfer of Parliament and most of the nobility to London changed the nature of the town.

Despite these setbacks the population was increasing, from 25,000 in 1700 to 50,000 by 1750, and conditions were getting worse and worse. In 1751 an old house collapsed and a survey showed much of the property to be in a similarly vulnerable condition.

By the mid-18th century change was imperative. It was the time of the Scottish Enlightenment – a philosophical movement characterised by a reliance on reason which sought to free religion and morals from tradition and prejudice – with some big thinkers ready to make far-reaching decisions. In 1752 substantive changes to the town were triggered by Lord Provost Sir Gilbert Elliot's statement: 'Let us boldly enlarge Edinburgh to the utmost.'[5] An enabling Act of Parliament followed, but it was not until 1767 that plans were agreed for the draining of the North Loch and the creation of a 'new town' to the north. Over the next 100 years the city was in a constant state of development and benefited greatly from a generation of outstanding architects. The 'new town' was created according to a series of overall plans, the first and best known being James Craig's design for the main block from St Andrew's Square in the east to Charlotte Square in the west, and from Princes Street to the south to Queen Street to the north. Within these plans, individuals and institutions commissioned their own buildings, which had to conform to a tight specification determined by the council. The earthen 'Mound', across the former North Loch, was created with the material excavated from the basements of the new buildings, and bridges were created to connect the 'old' and 'new' towns. On the south side of the town George Square was developed in 1766 as an additional new residential area. A new university was commenced in 1789.

Arrival of immigrant workers

With this expansion the more affluent burgesses moved out of the old town. Whilst this eased the overcrowding initially, the population continued to increase, doubling again to 100,000 by 1800. The next 50 years saw a further doubling of the population to 200,000 as immigrant workers – many escaping from the famines in Ireland – flocked into the city as labourers to contribute to the building of the Union Canal (1818–22), the railways (beginning with the Innocent Railway [1826] designed by Robert Stevenson to run between Dalkeith and Edinburgh), and the many fine new buildings in both the old and the new town. These workers also participated in the new industries that were developing as a result of steam power. While many of these workers crowded into the old town, others were accommodated in a ring of rather poor-quality accommodation which grew around the town at the various industrial sites.

This influx appears to have had a significant impact on the population. One contemporary writer observed that the Irish arrived:

> in such numbers as to drive the native labourer out of the market … they occupied the lowest description of houses never before considered habitable and every family kept a pig. … Native artisans and labourers were driven away, as they found it impossible to live in the midst of filth, vermin, quarrelling and fighting to which the immigrants were addicted in a remarkable degree. … Amongst this new class there was little attempt to furnish a home, their time and money being spent in taverns and public houses. … These Irish settlements marked an epoch in the history of the town when a definite deterioration began in manners, morals and health.[6]

This stereotype reminds us of the public health importance of attitudes that are based on humanity, equality, equity and justice. Heavy drinking was widespread and there was no control over the many taverns and shebeens.

A series of major fires occurred in the 1820s, and recurrent outbreaks of typhus and relapsing fever began in 1827 and increased in frequency until 1840. Cholera appeared for the first time in 1831/2 and, despite the introduction of some basic improvements, recurred in 1848/9 and 1853/4. While records of mortality had shown a steady improvement from 30 per 1,000 in the 1780s to 25 per 1,000 between 1810 and 1819, the rate worsened again to 30 per 1,000 by the 1830s. It was widely recognised that this was due to overcrowding, poverty and the filthy environment of the old town, which had remained basically unchanged despite the development of the new town and outer suburbs and a few grand buildings like the City Chambers (1811). The poverty, particularly amongst the immigrant families, was compounded by a commercial slump between 1825 and 1846, which put a break on the developments that had provided work for transient labourers. Work on the main-line railways provided a welcome respite.

A growing spirit of altruism

A general wave of public concern for the health of the poor was growing in the early years of the 19th century. While some of this was due to fear that the diseases so prevalent among the poor would spread to the 'better classes', there was also a growing spirit of altruism. Many of the leading physicians, surgeons and ministers of the day were prominent in this movement. In particular, Professor W. P. Alison gave lectures – initially as professor of medical jurisprudence and later as professor of medicine – in which he connected disease with the destitution he had observed ever since his appointment in 1815 as physician to one of the town's dispensaries for the poor. He and others were anxious for reform of the poor laws. Yet others, influenced by the French Revolution, had been seeking universal suffrage in 1792; there was a particularly heavy-handed government response and many were transported. However, this general concern for greater justice continued and there was widespread support for Earl Grey and the great Reform Act of 1832 – 10,000 people congregated in Edinburgh to hear the outcome of the vote when it arrived by mail coach from London.

In response to the cholera outbreak the Royal College of Physicians recommended the introduction of soil pipes, privies and WCs; paving; increasing the air, water and light in the closes; and general improvement to the old town. On this occasion the council were more responsive. Although earlier enactments had introduced scavengers with dustcarts to collect and sell waste collected from the streets and houses, this was clearly not effective in keeping the town clear of the waste still discarded by householders with the time-honoured cry of 'gardyloo'. Interestingly, the scavengers were almost self-financing – costing around £12,000 per annum but recouping £10,000 for the council by selling the manure to surrounding farmers.

A better solution was needed. In 1845 Dr James Stark, as registrar of mortality for Edinburgh and Leith, observed startling differences in death rates between different classes of the population. In 1847 he published his findings in a report on the sanitary state of Edinburgh.[7] For the first time, three sewers were completed – albeit they were unconnected to the dwellings. One ran along the north valley, one along the Cowgate and the third from George Square to the King's Park where they united to form the 'Foul Burn', which led out to irrigate the meadows of Craigentinny. The Water of Leith and other burns around the town were also effectively being used as sewers, resulting in the creation of pestilential swamps around the town. Initially, within the old town, much of the waste reached the sewers as a result of the excess water flowing from the public wells. However, in 1862 the council required landlords to install water in new properties. In practice, although the supplies of water had been increased, this requirement and the introduction of WCs into certain properties greatly reduced the availability of water in the public wells, and there was less water to flush waste into the sewers.

In 1856 the police commissioners, who had until then been responsible for implementing many of the activities that contributed to the public's health (such as scavenging, lighting and cleansing) merged with the council. More importantly, in 1861 another building collapsed, killing 35 people, and in 1864 a great fire destroyed much of the old town. The public outcry following the collapse of the building in Paisley Close led, in 1862, to the appointment of Henry (later Sir Henry) Littlejohn as the first medical officer of health, following a unanimous recommendation to the council from both the Royal College of Surgeons and the Royal College of Physicians.

In his report on the sanitary conditions of Edinburgh, Littlejohn proposed:

- paving and draining the closes

- house improvements – water, gas, repairs, cleansing

- reducing overcrowding, with a limit on the number of persons per room

- reducing the height of buildings

- removing ruinous buildings

- opening up the worst localities, e.g. Blackfriars Street and the Cowgate.

On receipt of this report Lord Provost Chambers ordered drainage and sanitary improvements, a major programme of demolition and the construction of new streets. These plans were formalised in the 1867 Improvement Act and were to be funded by an increase in the rates for 20 years. Although there was some opposition it is important to note that the public was generally supportive. There were impressive contributions to the overall improvements by the council and the various charities working together. Implementation of these plans opened up certain key routes into, and through, the old town, giving us, basically, the overall structure we see today, together with a more comprehensive sewage system.

Sir Henry Littlejohn was clearly an impressive public health leader. In 1879 he introduced the compulsory notification of infectious diseases, at a fee of 2s. 6d. (12.5p) – a significant sum in those days. This allowed preventive steps to be taken to reduce the spread of infectious diseases. Earlier, in 1875, the university initiated a BSc in Public Health on his recommendation. However, he was less than enthusiastic about the 'new' concept of WCs in the tenements because of their unreliability and tendency to pool sewage on the common stair:

> I cannot imagine a more disastrous condition of matters for the poorer districts of our city than the general introduction of water closets so long as the present system of housing prevails … my experience of the poor of this city has led me to the conclusion that they are not yet prepared to make a proper use of these conveniences … some have requested landlords to withhold the benefit of this so called boon … one dirty neighbour disgusts another and their houses were never intended for this sanitary improvement.[8]

Littlejohn's public health department was responsible for the fever hospital, for the public dispensaries and for the hospital care provided to the poor and destitute in workhouses such as Craigleith (now the Western General Hospital). His period in office saw the building of an impressive new fever hospital (the City Hospital) at Greenbank (1903) with specific pavilions designated to each of the most prevalent diseases – diphtheria, whooping cough, measles, enteric fevers, tuberculosis. In addition, the Royal Infirmary moved in 1879 from its previous location in High School Yards to its present site in Lauriston Place, and various new hospitals were endowed for the treatment of the sick.

The process of slum clearance and rebuilding continued in the 20th century. In the early years the worst of the old town slums were replaced with 'houses for the working classes … in the hope of achieving a permanent cure for the worst elements of this evil inheritance which has been handed down from the Middle Ages and has defied the efforts of a long succession of social reformers'. This was associated with a growing range of provision targeted at the poor by both the authorities and many charitable groups. A further period of slum clearance occurred in the 1950s and 1960s, but the housing was of poor quality and there was little in the way of social amenities. Current regeneration schemes in the north, west and south-east of the city are seeking to correct the mistakes of the past. I wonder how our successors will judge them.

Sickness and health in Edinburgh

Over the centuries a succession of serious epidemics of infection has afflicted the citizens of Edinburgh in addition to the 'traditional' endemic fevers of diphtheria, typhoid, measles and smallpox. As we have seen, there was:

- plague, 1492–1645

- cholera, 1831–54

- typhus, especially 1827–40.

In addition, the late 19th and the 20th century have seen:

- tuberculosis

- HIV/AIDS.

Tuberculosis increased in importance as a cause of early death as the epidemic fevers came under better control. Overcrowding and poor nutrition contributed to its spread, but the establishment in 1887 of a designated clinic and sanatorium by Sir Robert Philip and early 20th-century slum clearances contributed to some control of tuberculosis in the early 1900s. However, it continued to be a growing public health problem in Scotland after the Second World War, even though it was reducing everywhere else in Europe except Portugal. The introduction of streptomycin in 1948, followed by the innovative triple therapy regime developed in Edinburgh by Sir John Crofton in the 1950s, removed, for the first time, the 'death sentence' from those with advanced disease. The success of this programme led, in 1958, to a massive case-finding programme using mass miniature X-ray (MMR), to the screening of all 13–14-year-old schoolchildren and to the administration of BCG vaccine to those found to be susceptible.

In 1984–1985 Edinburgh was found to have far and away the highest rate of HIV infection in Europe – mainly among a young drug-using population on the periphery of the city who had suffered a few years earlier from an epidemic of hepatitis B. Although the rate is still higher than most other UK cities an extensive treatment and prevention programme has prevented a major epidemic and Edinburgh has long been overtaken by many other cities in the developed world – not to mention the tragedies caused by the spread of the disease in Africa and India.

The practice and teaching of medicine in Edinburgh

All recorded histories of illness in Edinburgh suggest a range of responses from complacency and resignation to devoted care. Distinctive surgical and medical care developed in the 16th century. Surgeons, initially as barber-surgeons, were recognised as a trade guild from 1505. The practice of physic by physicians developed rather later, with the initial practitioners learning their skills in Europe, mainly at the university of Leiden. In the 17th century Edinburgh's physicians started to meet regularly to promote improvements in practice and, like the surgeons, to distinguish themselves from the many quacks of the day by defining quality standards and training requirements. In 1681 they established the College of Physicians and were granted a Royal Charter by Charles II. In 1699 they published the first of 12 editions of the *Edinburgh Dispensatory*. For the following 250 years (until the establishment of the National Health Service) fellows of the college gave their services free of charge, often with the support of medical students, to the poor in the Royal Infirmary and in the various dispensaries around the town.

Medical teaching in Edinburgh was established around 1697 and based initially on the practice of anatomy, observation and the preparation of botanical remedies. Hospices and dispensaries were established for the poor, and fever hospitals protected the rest of the population from infection. Those with more resources were treated in their own homes.

In 1729 the first voluntary hospital in Scotland opened near the university and in 1736 became the Royal Infirmary of Edinburgh. In 1741 it moved to a larger site in the same area. Surgical extensions – known as the 'old' and 'new' surgical hospitals – followed in 1832 and 1853. The isolation hospital for fever patients was nearby. When he returned to Edinburgh as Regius professor of clinical surgery in 1869, Joseph Lister continued to develop his antiseptic techniques in the old surgical hospital.

In 1879 the Royal Infirmary moved to a new site in Lauriston Place as a combined medical and surgical hospital, and in 1884 the present medical school building was opened next door. In 1903 the fever hospital moved to Greenbank, as the City Hospital, with specifically designated wards for the major infectious diseases. The late 19th century also saw the building of a number of endowed general hospitals in Edinburgh, all of which transferred their services to the Royal Infirmary and Western General between 1985 and 2000.

The year 2003 saw a further move of the Royal Infirmary and much of the medical school to a new greenfield site at Little France near the southeast boundary of Edinburgh. The Infectious Diseases Unit, which – thanks to the effective introduction of immunisation and antibiotics – latterly required only a small proportion of the City Hospital, transferred to a modern unit at the Western General in the late 1990s and the City Hospital was closed.

Throughout the period of hospital development the provision of treatment and care in the community has remained vital. General practice, which developed from the early dispensaries, has remained the foundation for medical practice, with GPs and primary care teams now working in partnership with hospital-based specialists.

Notes

[1]   *Edinburgh, 1329–1929* (Edinburgh: Oliver and Boyd, 1929), p. 391.
[2]   C. Johnson (ed.), *The Abbot: Walter Scott* (Edinburgh: Edinburgh University Press, 2000), p. 181.
[3]   *Edinburgh*, 1329–1929, p. 402.
[4]   Ibid. 18.
[5]   Ibid. 404.
[6]   Ibid. 19.
[7]   J. Stark, *Inquiry into some points of the Sanitary State of Edinburgh* (Edinburgh: Stark and Co., 1847).
[8]   *Edinburgh, 1329–1929*, p. 27.

3. Edinburgh's contribution to public health

Raj Bhopal

> The further back you look, the further forward you can see.
> (WINSTON CHURCHILL)

We honour those who gave us cause for celebrating 100 uninterrupted years of service by an academic public health department. Following the appointment of Charles Hunter Stewart in 1898 as the first holder of the Alexander Bruce and John Usher Chair of Public Health, Sir John Usher of Norton joked that 'a chair without an institute is not much good'. (Figures 3.1 and 3.2). The University of Edinburgh made land available, Sir John provided the funds and by 11 June 1902 the John Usher Institute of Public Health was formally given to the university (Figure 3.3). The first students were admitted on 1 October 1902.

What has Edinburgh contributed to public health? A slight bias towards academic achievements is warranted but I intend to sketch the whole.

Figure 3.1   Charles Hunter Stewart (*left*)
Figure 3.2   Sir John Usher of Norton (*right*)

Figure 3.3 The John Usher Institute of Public Health, Edinburgh

Where is the monument marking Edinburgh's contribution to public health?

Francis Crew, the third professor of public health (Figure 3.4), said of Sir Henry Littlejohn (Figure 3.5), the first medical officer of health (MOH) of Edinburgh and Scotland, appointed in 1862, '*Si monumentum requiris, circumspice*' (if you seek a monument, look around). The monument to public health is modern Edinburgh and its vibrant people. In the 19th century Edinburgh was famed for its squalor, stink and degradation, as proclaimed by its nickname 'Auld Reekie' and the warning call 'gardyloo' as the household sewage was thrown at 10 p.m. each night from high windows on to the streets below.

The Regulations of St James Court 1786 stated: 'No person shall at any time throw out, from any window or door in the Court, any water, ashes, or nastiness of any kind, under the penalty of 2s. 6d., for the first offence, 5s. for the second.'[1] By and large they had modest effect.

In 1970 a letter to *The Scotsman* from staff at the Eastern General Hospital, about 55 million gallons of raw sewage going into the Firth of Forth at Seafield, said 'in recent years Edinburgh has indeed been powdering its nose but neglecting to wipe its bottom'.[2]

Figure 3.4 Brigadier Francis A. E. Crew (*left*)
Figure 3.5 Sir Henry Littlejohn (*right*)

In the late 19th and 20th centuries the city was transformed as one of the greatest cities and tourist attractions in the world. Savage and killing diseases such as smallpox, cholera, typhus, typhoid fever, scarlet fever and diphtheria were banished and tuberculosis was decimated. The pattern of morbidity, as for example in hospital admissions (Appendices 1 and 2) and life expectancy (Table 3.1) has changed to a dramatic and, surely, unpredictable extent. The Royal Infirmary of Edinburgh's general register of patients 100 years ago testifies to different outcomes, younger patients and longer durations of stay for problems that would now be managed outside hospital. It is noteworthy that outcome data were recorded then but not now. The estimated life expectancy in 1902 was under 50 for men and women; in 2002 it was well over 70 (Table 3.2). The life expectancy is still rising, and Edinburgh is faring well in comparison to the rest of Scotland.

Table 3.1. Life expectancy at birth in four time periods (in years)

Year	Male	Female
1891–1900	44.7	47.4
1910–1912	50.1	53.2
1997–1999	72.6	78.0
2001–2002	73.6 (projected)	78.7 (projected)

SOURCE: Rachel Wood, Information and Statistics Division, NHS Scotland.

Table 3.2. Life expectancy at birth: estimates for 1902 and 2002 (in years)

Year	Male	Female
1902	47.1	49.9
2002	73.8	78.9

SOURCE: Rachel Wood, Information and Statistics Division, NHS Scotland.

Establishing public health and the role of Edinburgh

Until the late 19th century there was little distinction or professional boundaries between public health and clinical care. One of the most prominent Edinburgh doctors who contributed to prevention and control of diseases – and hence public health – was James Lind. Lind was born in Edinburgh and graduated MD at Edinburgh University in 1748. He reported in 1753 that 'scurvy alone, during the last war, proved a more destructive enemy, and cut off more valuable lives, than the united efforts of the French and Spanish wars' and that scurvy 'raged with great violence in some journeys, not at all in others'. He generated many hypotheses – including the sea climate and particularly the moist air – but chose to investigate diet. Lind conducted his famous experiment aboard the *Salisbury* in 1747: he 'ordered' 12 patients, divided into pairs, who received cider, elixir of vitriol, vinegar, sea-water, an electuary, and oranges and lemons. He found that 'the most sudden and visible good effects were perceived from the use of the oranges and lemons.' Lind's experiment is described on a plaque put up in the medical school quadrangle in 1953 by the Sunkist citrus growers of California and Arizona. It proclaims him to be the Hippocrates of naval medicine and states: 'These works led to the conquest of scurvy, the development of modern social hygiene, and the growth of tropical medicine.'[3]

British public health as an institution took root in the 19th century, and Edinburgh was at the forefront in academic innovation and service leadership. Appendix 3 briefly summarises the history of public health, with an Edinburgh bias. Both service and academic public health grew out of medical jurisprudence at this university. The first seven professors of medical jurisprudence are listed in Appendix 4; the first, Andrew Duncan, delivered lectures on public health; this tradition was continued by his successors.

William Pulteney Alison, the second professor of medical jurisprudence in Edinburgh, prepared a report that was far-sighted in grasping the social basis of disease. He was unconvinced by the miasma theory as proclaimed by Edwin Chadwick, who conceived the role of the medical officer of health. Henry Littlejohn, who was later professor of jurisprudence in Edinburgh University and, in 1862, the first medical officer of health of Edinburgh (and the third in the UK), set up the BSc in Public Health in 1875, the first postgraduate course in the subject in the UK. This course was international from the beginning – of the first four graduates two were from England, one from Scotland and one from the Cape of Good Hope. Littlejohn also pioneered the UK's introduction of legally sanctioned compulsory notification of infectious diseases.

Clause 208 of the Edinburgh Municipal and Police Act 1879 stated: 'every medical practitioner practising within the burgh shall, within 24 hours … report to the MOH … cholera typhus … etc. … under a penalty not exceeding 40 shillings … if diagnosis was correct … shall be paid a sum of two shillings and six pence'.[4] This system was more just than capital punishment – hanging for men, drowning for women – for failing to report plague, as happened in the 16th century. Littlejohn's foresight meant that notification was achieved in Edinburgh 18 years before anywhere else. In 1907 compulsory notification of tuberculosis was another first for Edinburgh as part of the Edinburgh tuberculosis scheme. These actions illustrated Professor Crew's aphorism: 'The House of Commons is the pharmacy of Social Medicine.' The medical officers of health have, from the time of Henry Littlejohn, been deeply involved in public health education, innovation and research. They have made a huge contribution to the university (Appendix 5).

In 1884 Louis Pasteur attended the 300th anniversary celebrations of Edinburgh University. He enthused Alexander Bruce (Figure 3.6), who generated the impetus and funds for a new chair in public health. Sadly, Alexander Bruce died in 1893, at the age of 54, before his ambition was realised. The Younger firm of brewers and John Usher of Norton contributed to Bruce's legacy for the chair and in addition funded the Usher Institute, which opened in 1902. Charles Stewart, the first professor of public health, was Littlejohn's assistant in jurisprudence. John Usher expressed his wish that the new department make a major contribution to the city of Edinburgh, but he saw that the relationship between 'town and gown' was not easy: 'I thought that in a matter of this kind "town and gown" might work very well together for their mutual advantage – but that was not the opinion of all those who have the management of our current affairs.'[5] Files in the university archives testify to the tensions 'between town and gown', which came to the fore on the retiral of the first professor of public health and the appointment of Percy Lelean (Figure 3.7). The public health functions of the city transferred to the Lothian Health Board in 1974. The relationship between town and gown continues to be perceived as vital, although hard to achieve, as the inaugural lecture of Sir John Brotherston (Figure 3.8) testifies: 'We are in the process of trying to develop this partnership with the Lothian Health Board in relation to teaching, research and service.'[6]

Figure 3.6   Alexander Bruce (*left*)
Figure 3.7   Colonel Percy Lelean (*centre*)
Figure 3.8   Sir John Brotherston (*right*)

Appendix 6 lists all the professors who have held the Alexander Bruce and John Usher chair, including Stuart L. Morrison and Michael M. Garraway (Figures 3.9 and 3.10). The heads of department, in the interregna, were Donald Cameron, Una MacLean and Gerry Fowkes. Una Maclean has written a splendid history of the Usher Institute, upon which I have gratefully drawn.[7]

Health and public health: achieving this in Edinburgh

How did we achieve better health in Edinburgh? Healthy people are alive (literally and metaphorically); energetic; functioning in their home, workplace and community; free from pain, impairment and disease; and feel well and contented, if not happy. Public health, in its broadest compass, is the driver of the engine of health. Public health is simply all activity that is designed to

Figure 3.9 Stuart L. Morrison (*left*)
Figure 3.10 Michael M. Garraway (*right*)

improve health, or, in the words of the Acheson report: 'The science and art of preventing disease, prolonging life and promoting health through the organised efforts of society.'[8]

Many professions, disciplines and institutions contribute to public health, which has been known by several names including public health (medicine), medical police, state medicine, social medicine, community medicine, preventive medicine and many other variants. In earlier times medical jurisprudence and forensic medicine, sanitary engineering and other disciplines played a pivotal role. Public health medicine is the speciality that takes the lead responsibility for public health on behalf of the medical profession. The Edinburgh academic department has enjoyed most of these titles over the years and yet its fundamental goals have remained the same, as captured by Una MacLean: 'As has happened so frequently before in the history of public health, a change in the perceived functions of its proponents has necessitated a symbolic modification in nomenclature.'[9]

Improvements in health in Edinburgh did not occur by accident or luck. There is no inevitability about better health – witness the catastrophic declines in life expectancy in much of eastern Europe and sub-Saharan Africa. Equally, economic advancement alone is not a guarantee of good health, though health and wealth are intertwined and interdependent. Understanding the causes of health, disease and death is the key to action. At the time of Littlejohn's appointment in 1862, only 140 years ago, the five main causes of disease under debate were: (a) lack of religion; (b) lack of education; (c) drunkenness; (d) insanitary conditions (miasma theory); and (e) destitution.[10]

In his seminal report on the sanitary conditions of the city of Edinburgh in 1865 Littlejohn linked mortality to pauperism, insanitation, housing, destitution, malnutrition, intemperance and sickness. He understood the limitations of health education in the midst of poverty: 'to speak to the pauper poor of the necessity of cleanliness … when they have hardly enough support to keep soul and body together, is a mere waste of words.'[11] Littlejohn also knew the value of target setting, and his report aimed to reduce death rates to 25 per 1000 per year. (In Abbey it was 37.1, in the Grassmarket 33.) Littlejohn calculated that if this target could be achieved then 312 lives would be saved annually in Edinburgh.

Tips on how to stay healthy have been an integral part of public health endeavour, and historically there was heavy emphasis on housing and hygiene. It is difficult for us to imagine why in the 19th century the problem of insanitary living conditions was the top priority for public health, and as a result I believe we do not take enough pride in the public health history of this era. Modern public health too often trivialises these achievements, possibly to shake off the sanitary inspector image. As Michael Garraway, my predecessor, pointed out in his inaugural lecture, it was the control of environmental and infectious diseases that permitted the move from the population approach to the clinical one:

> The great infections which decimated the population in the earlier years of this century are now distant memories to the very elderly citizens of the country who lived through this era. They are history to the rest of us.[12]

The achievement in education, service and research founded on these events 100 to 150 years ago has been immense, and Edinburgh's influence has been worldwide. The full history is yet to be recorded, but the centenary of the department in 2002 provides the motivation and opportunity to begin to fill the gaps. Appendix 7 gives an overview of Edinburgh's contributions to public health: the City and its people; the pioneering urge; training and education for leadership; and innovative research that is applicable to the problems of the day.

A glimpse into the future of academic public health in Edinburgh

Understanding history is, as Winston Churchill said, a route to shaping the future. Academic public health in Edinburgh has a proud history on which to build. Public health teaching will remain important in both the undergraduate and postgraduate curricula, the latter continuing a 127-year tradition. As many important research questions derive from practical problems, we must ensure research and practice intertwine. I foresee a need to narrow the gap between theory and practice in research and education. New types of practice-based undergraduate, masters and PhD-level curricula offer a way forward.

We will increase the emphasis on research and expand our doctoral programmes. The impetus for research and evidence as the basis for national public health policy and practice gives us the ideal motive to narrow the gap between theory, empirical research and practice.

The academic public health community will continue to participate in the international research endeavour, yet the most important research questions may derive from practice. To produce research with international significance, therefore, we need to ensure that the multi-disciplinary public health workforce is research orientated. This requires that academics win the respect of this workforce by serving them and our communities well. We need to be able to straddle the service–academic divide following the excellent example of the pioneers we follow and honour.

The proposed creation of an Edinburgh University School of Public Health, Primary Care and Health Policy, possibly as a collaboration between the university colleges of medicine and humanities, provides a natural focus for service and academic exchange. The title of the Usher Institute has not been rescinded. The University of Edinburgh Centre for Public Health and Primary Care Research has been established. In 1990 Michael Garraway suggested that the Usher Institute title be used for a collaboration across the city departments, including nursing studies and many others, and he proposed an advisory council to oversee the education of those participating in the MSc in Public Health. Such a vision is close to what we have, independently, created.

The perennial problem of economic and health inequalities will hold centre stage in public health, as it has done for 200 years, and it will continue to be a preoccupation for us in Edinburgh. 'Health risks and inequalities' is one of the four core research themes identified for the newly created Centre for Public Health and Primary Care Research.

In many developing countries the traditional public health problems of inadequate sanitation, inadequate nutrition and communicable diseases combine with those of the post-industrial era. We are moving to a greater international orientation, both in teaching and research, to continue the directions set as early as 1875. We aim to boost international recruitment of students and promote exchange of staff.

We intend to underpin our research on vascular disease and cancer epidemiology (two of the four themes of the research centre) with social, epidemiological and genetic perspectives. Molecular science will deepen understanding of the inter-action between the environment, lifestyle and the gene, but the public health dividend will come from altering the pattern of risk factors in the whole population. This, in turn, requires an understanding of how to deliver messages and services that improve health – hence the fourth theme in our new research centre will be effectiveness in primary care and public health.

This university has recruited, educated and inspired leaders who have influenced public health on a global scale. It is our privilege and duty as public health scientists and practitioners to build upon our legacy.

Figure 3.11 Raj Bhopal

Acknowledgements

I thank my colleagues in the History of Public Health in Edinburgh Group for their ready assistance. The members of the group are: Raj Bhopal (Figure 3.11), Helen Zealley, Una McLean, Ian Milne, Mike Barfoot, Colin Fischbacher, Ginna Robertson, John Crofton and John Last. Mike Barfoot gave much advice and provided images and other information. The Information Services Division of the Common Services Agency supplied information on life expectancy and hospital admissions, as acknowledged in the tables. The University of Edinburgh's archivist, Arnott Wilson, provided advice, a photograph of Charles Hunter Stewart and access to archived files. Many members of staff in Public Health Sciences provided useful information and materials. Hazel King, as ever, gave wide-ranging secretarial assistance. Of the many sources of information I have consulted, the history of the Usher Institute by Una Maclean stands out, and I am indebted to her. I am fully responsible for all remaining errors and misunderstandings.

Notes

1   *Public Health in 19th-Century Edinburgh* (Edinburgh: Edinburgh Corporation, 1975).
2   Ibid.
3   J. Lind, 'A treatise of the scurvy in three parts, containing an inquiry into the nature, causes, and cure of the scurvy', reprinted in C. Buck, A. Llopis, E. Najera and M. Terris (eds), *The Challenge of Epidemiology. Issues and Selected Readings* (Washington DC: Pan American Health Organization, 1988), pp. 20–3.
4   H. P. Tait, *A Doctor and Two Policemen: the history of Edinburgh Health Department 1862–1974* (Edinburgh: Edinburgh Health Department, 1974).
5   U. Maclean, *The Usher Institute and the Evolution of Community Medicine in Edinburgh* (Edinburgh: Department of Community Medicine, 1975), p. 47.
6   J. Brotherston, *Community Medicine Revisited* (Berwick: The Tweeddale Press Group, 1979).
7   Maclean, *The Usher Institute*.
8   D. Acheson, *Public Health in England* (London: HMSO, 1988).
9   Maclean, *The Usher Institute*.
10 F. A. E. Crew, 'Centenary of appointment of the First Medical Officer of Health for the City of Edinburgh'. *Scottish Medical Journal* 8 (1963): 53–62.
11 Ibid.
12 M. Garraway, *The Medical Pendulum: Inaugural Lecture* (Edinburgh: The University of Edinburgh, 1984).

REFERENCES

Acheson, D. *Independent Inquiry into Inequalities in Health.* London: The Stationery Office, 1998

Warren, M. D. *A Chronology of State Medicine, Public Health, Welfare and Related Services in Britain 1066–1999.* London: Faculty of Public Health Medicine of the Royal Colleges of Physicians of the United Kingdom, 2000

APPENDIX 1
Admissions to Royal Infirmary on 1 November 1902

Age	Diagnosis	Duration of stay (days)	Outcome
26	Gastic ulcer	17	Cured
70	Noevus of face and lipomata	22	Cured
44	Haemorrhoids	24	Cured
25	Trauma	9	Cured
40	Aortic aneurism	9	No change
56	Scrotal dermatitis and oedema	16	Cured
41	Nephritis and cardiac weakness	21	Relieved
27	Pelvic cellulites	45	No change
12	Trauma	9	Cured
22	Influenza and colic (intestinal)	13	Cured
36	Osteomyelitis of right femur	37	Died – secondary haemorrhage
56	Phimosis	4	Cured/relieved
60	Cardiac weakness and chronic nephritis	17	Relieved
23	Aortic regurgitation and acute Bright's	35	Relieved
49	Cataract	16	Cured
70	Hydrocele of left tunica vaginalis	9	Cured
13	Hysterical fit	3	Cured
7	Diarrhoea	31	Cured
61	Polls fracture	33	Cured
59	Foot ankylosed in extended position due to paralysis (amputation)	62	Cured
39	Alcoholism – cut ear	1	Cured
55	Ulcer of rectum	23	Cured
26	Acute suppurative appendicitis	40	Cured
15	Impetigo contagiosa	16	Cured
44	Asthma	49	Relieved

SOURCE: Lothian Health Services archive LHB1/126 /69.

APPENDIX 2
Admissions to Royal Infirmary on one day in 2002

Sex	Age group	Main diagnosis
Male	70–74	Malignant neoplasm, liver cell carcinoma
Female	40–44	Malignant neoplasm of upper lobe, bronchus or lung
Male	75–79	Malignant neoplasm of lower lobe, bronchus or lung
Female	30–34	Benign neoplasm of ovary
Female	75–79	Cataract, unspecified
Female	85–89	Cataract, unspecified
Female	85–89	Cataract, unspecified
Female	70–74	Cataract, unspecified
Female	65–69	Atherosclerotic heart disease
Male	60–69	Pulmonary embolism without mention of acute cor pulmonale
Male	40–44	Dissection of aorta (any part)
Female	85–89	Pneumonia, unspecified
Female	65–69	Acute respiratory failure
Male	40–44	Other specified diseases of anus and rectum
Female	20–24	Other specified intervertebral disc disorders
Male	35–39	Enthesopathy, unspecified
Female	50–54	Osteomyelitis, unspecified
Female	30–34	Noninflammatory disorder ovary fallopian tube
Female	35–39	Endometrial glandular hyperplasia
Female	30–34	Tubal pregnancy
Female	25–29	Incomplete spontaneous abortion complicated by delay/excess haemorrhage
Female	70–74	Dysphagia
Female	80–84	Fracture of lower end of radius
Female	75–79	Fracture of lower end of radius
Male	10–14	Sprain and strain of finger(s)

SOURCE: Information Services Division, Common Services Agency (SMR01 Ref: ACIG/20021204).

The age groups are specified to maintain confidentiality.

APPENDIX 3
History of public health in particular relation to Edinburgh

1450–1475	**City walls built to protect city but cause congestion**
1584	**James Henryson appointed to advise Edinburgh Town Council on plague – capital punishment for failing to disclose cases**
1617	**Privy Council in Scotland order cleaning up of Edinburgh town ('filthy')**
1645	**Last plague outbreak in Edinburgh**
1662	John Graunt publishes *Natural and Political Observations*
1747	**James Lind conducts his experiment on scurvy on the** *Salisbury*
1779–1829	Johann Peter Frank publishes nine volumes on medical police
1783	**Public Dispensary – first in Scotland – set up by Andrew Duncan (beginnings of primary care)**
1796	Edward Jenner vaccinates James Phipps
1809	**John Robertson publishes** *Medical Police: or the causes of disease with the means of prevention*
1821	René Louis Villerme publishes *Statistical Researches on the City of Paris*
1830	**William Southwood Smith writes** *A Treatise of Fevers*
1832	**Cholera epidemic in Edinburgh – 1,065 deaths**
1836	Compulsory registration of births, deaths and marriages
1840	**Not convinced by miasmata theory of disease, William Pulteney Alison (professor of medical jurisprudence at Edinburgh University and known as the Scottish Chadwick) publishes** *Observations on the Management of the Poor in Scotland and its Effects upon the Health of the Great Towns*
1842	Edwin Chadwick's report on the sanitary conditions of the labouring population of Great Britain says unsanitary living leads to poverty and poor health; **a section on Edinburgh recommends medical police**

1847	**First MOH in Britain in Liverpool – William Henry Duncan, an Edinburgh graduate**
1847	Rudolph investigates typhus epidemic in Upper Silesia (Poland)
1847	Ignaz Semmelweis initiates the practice of washing hands with chlorine liquida
1848	Public Health Act creates General Board of Health – **Thomas Southwood Smith, an Edinburgh student, appointed as medical advisor**
1854	Board of Health discontinued – cholera hits Soho
1855	John Simon appointed as equivalent of chief medical officer (CMO)
1855	John Snow publishes *On the Mode of Communication of Cholera*
1861	**Collapse of building at Paisley's Close, High Street – 35 die**
1862	**First MOH in Edinburgh: Henry Littlejohn elected by 17 votes to 16**
1865	**Littlejohn's report on the sanitary condition of the city of Edinburgh is published**
1867	Public Health Act Scotland confirms office of Medical Officer of Health
1871	First diploma in state medicine, Dublin
1875	Public Health Act – key advocate was Lyon Playfair, professor of chemistry, Edinburgh University and MP for universities of Edinburgh and St Andrew's
1875	**First postgraduate BSc in public health in UK led by Sir Henry Littlejohn (in faculty of science)**
1878	Louis Pasteur argued the case for the germ theory of specific disease before the French Academy of Medicine
1879	**Pioneering introduction of the compulsory notification of infectious diseases in Edinburgh: Edinburgh Municipal and Police Act**
1881	**Edinburgh Health Society founded**
1882	Koch identifies tubercle bacillus
1884	**Pasteur attends 300th anniversary of Edinburgh University. He meets and enthuses Alexander Low Bruce who, in partnership with Younger Brewers and John Usher, funds first British chair in public health**

1887	**Robert Philip establishes Victoria Dispensary for consumption, paving the way for the Edinburgh Tuberculosis Scheme**
1888	Institute Pasteur founded
1891	British Institute for Preventive Medicine, later called Jenner Institute, then Lister Institute
1897	Public Health (Scotland) Act mandates sanitary departments
1898	**First university-based chair of public health at Edinburgh University: Charles Hunter Stewart**
1902	**Usher Institute of Public Health opens**
1904	**168 people affected by smallpox outbreak in Cowgate in Edinburgh**
1907	**Compulsory notification of tuberculosis in Edinburgh**
1909	Parliament rescinds compulsory vaccination
1917	**First chair in tuberculosis in Britain – Sir Robert Philip**
1919	**Diploma in Public Health (faculty of medicine)**
1946	First randomised controlled trial by Austin Bradford Hill and colleagues on streptomycin for tuberculosis
1948	**First general practice department in the UK (from Usher Institute)**
1948	Framingham study on coronary heart disease begins
1950	BCG vaccination to help control tuberculosis
1959	**Edinburgh University's nursing studies unit established, the first department of its kind; Francis Crew was a key proponent**
1963	**First chair of general practice in the UK – Richard Scott, from the Usher Institute of Public Health**
1964	**John Brotherston, professor of public health, appointed CMO, Scotland**
1974	**Faculty of Public Health Medicine established – Sir John Brotherston was a founding member and president, 1978–1981**
1974	**City health department closes – most functions transferred to Lothian Health Board**
1988	**Usher Institute moves to medical school quadrangle**

APPENDIX 4
Professors of medical jurisprudence

Name	Start date
Andrew Duncan	1807
William Pulteney Alison	1820
Robert Christison	1822
Thomas Stewart Traill	1832
Douglas Maclagan	1862
Henry Littlejohn	1897
Henry Harvey Littlejohn (son of Henry)	1906

APPENDIX 5
Medical officers of health and their successors

Name	Period of service	Length of service (years)
Henry Littlejohn	1862–1908	46
Alfred Maxwell Williamson	1908–1923	15
William Robertson	1923–1930	7
John Guy	1930–1938	8
William George Clark	1938–1953	15
Henry Edmund Seiler	1953–1964	11
James Leitch Gilloran	1964–1974	10
Ian D. Campbell	1974–1977	3
Colin Brough	1977–1988	11
Helen Zealley	1988–2000	12
Peter Donnelly	2000 to present	

APPENDIX 6
Bruce and John Usher Chair of Public Health at the University of Edinburgh

Name	Period of service
Charles H. Stewart	1898–1924
Brevet Colonel Percy S. Lelean	1925–1944
Brigadier Francis A. E. Crew	1944–1955
Sir John H. F. Brotherston	1955–1964
Sir John H. F. Brotherston	1977–1980
Stuart L. Morrison	1964–1975
William M. Garraway	1983–1997
Raj Bhopal	1999 to present

Sources include M. Warren and H. Francis (eds), *P197: Recalling the Medical Officer of Health* (London: King Edward's Hospital Fund for London, 1987).

APPENDIX 7

Overview of Edinburgh contributions to public health

- Building a great city
- A healthy population
- Pioneering policy, law, analysis, research and action, e.g.:
  - first MOH in Scotland
  - first postgraduate qualifications in public health in mainland UK
  - control of infections (smallpox and typhus conquered first)
  - demonstration that milk transmits TB
  - Edinburgh tuberculosis scheme
  - first Department of Public Health leading to creation of Medical Statistics Unit, and departments of General Practice and Nursing
  - modernisation of public health as community medicine (and back)
  - introduction of medical sociology to undergraduate curriculum (1958).
- Training distinguished and effective leaders, practitioners and academics for service overseas and at home, e.g.:
  - medical officers of health
  - CMOs and other influential government officers
  - professors and senior academics in medical jurisprudence and then public health
  - civil and academic honours.
- A distinguished record of research, e.g.:
  - infections
  - environment
  - vascular diseases
  - inequalities
  - cancer screening
  - health care evaluation
  - genetics and public health
  - methods in medical statistics.

4. Alcohol, the brewing and distilling industry, John Usher and public health

G. H. Palmer

The relationship between alcohol and public health tends to reflect old images such as Hogarth's depiction of 'gin drinkers' and the lax drinking laws of the late 19th and early 20th century, when even small children were allowed to buy alcohol. So common was the habit of excessive drinking that the public was warned through posters not to give soldiers 'drink' during the First World War. More recent images of alcohol and public health relate to drink driving, liver disease, domestic problems and possible (but not proven) links with a range of other diseases. Positive contributions of alcohol include 'uplifting' of social well-being through sensible drinking. Also, health benefits have been reported from the suppression of cholesterol by alcohol consumption. The damaging activities of the free radicals are also reported to be reduced by limited consumption of beer and red wine, which contain anti-oxidants. On all these aspects of alcohol more evidence is required.

Indirect links between alcohol and public health are less well known. The rapid development of the brewing and distilling industries, in post-industrial revolution Britain, increased the tax revenues of the government to levels not possible before, and today both the brewing and distilling industries contribute over £8 billion of tax revenues to the government – some of which is likely to be supporting various aspects of public health. These industries are large employers and users of water, grain, hops, yeast, packaging materials and transport. The industries associated with these raw materials benefit from their links with the brewing and distilling industries.

In order to maintain quality and secure public approval, the brewing and distilling industries have always had a strong research base. Brewing scientists have been involved in the breeding of barley, in initiating the concept of pure cell culture, in the development of universal methods for statistical studies (the student 't' test) and in the introduction of the Kjeldhal method for nitrogen (protein) determination. There was also the promotion of studies in refrigeration and the setting up of brewing schools in universities to study the composition of cereals and the biological mechanisms of the fermentation process. The contributions of Louis Pasteur (1822–1895) to the study of yeast fermentation were well received by brewers and the development of pasteurisation came from Pasteur's experiments with beer and wine. It is from this work that the concept of bacteria was developed. Pasteur even remarked that maybe the diseases of man are similar to those of beer and wine! Of course, the great man was correct as regards the damaging effects of bacteria. The brewing industry was one of the first industries to use James Watt's steam engine.

On a lighter note, the brewing industry is also responsible for protecting and developing the hop plant. Outside the alleged soporific effects of 'hop pillars', brewing is the only important commercial use of hops which imparts bittering factors to beer during its production. Although beer can be spoiled by lactic acid bacteria, pathogenic bacteria tend not to grow in beer, partly because of the hop boiling stage and partly because beer pH is normally acidic in nature. During past outbreaks of cholera in Britain, brewers who drank beer instead of water avoided the disease. In many parts of the world today, water is still less safe to drink than beer.

The link between Pasteur and public health in Edinburgh began when Pasteur visited Younger's Breweries in the city. He was attending the 300-year celebration (1884) of the life of the University of Edinburgh. He knew the Younger family and encouraged Alexander Bruce, the powerful company secretary and director, to set up a new chair of public health within Edinburgh University. This chair was established in 1898 from funding of £15,000 given by Bruce's family, the Younger's firm and Sir John Usher of Norton. Later, Sir John provided additional funding to erect a building for the teaching of public health. This building, in Warrender Park Road, was completed on 11 June 1902 and called The John Usher Institute of Public Health.

Who was John Usher? John Usher was born in 1828 and was one of the four sons of Andrew Usher, the great distiller of Scotch whisky. Andrew Usher was the exclusive agent of the famous Glenlivet whisky from 1840, but he is best remembered for his pioneering work on the blending of malt whisky with grain whisky to produce blended whiskies. This development in whisky production now dominates the Scotch whisky market, where 93% of the 70,000,000 cases of Scotch whisky sold annually are blends such as Chivas Regal, Johnnie Walker Red and Johnnie Walker Black, Ballantine's, J&B Rare, Grant's, Dewar's, Famous Grouse and Bell's. The funds invested in the Department of Public Health in Edinburgh University came from money earned by the brewing and distilling industries. The contributions made by these industries are unlikely to be seen again but they represent foresight and generosity at their very best. In Edinburgh, we also have the McEwan Hall and the Usher Hall (built by Sir John Usher's brother, Andrew), but the university's Department of Public Health Sciences is a living monument to the alcohol-producing industry that saw the necessity of supporting Pasteur's concept that science should be applied for the benefit of the public … and what is more important than the health of the public?

As we celebrate the 100th birthday of the Department of Public Health Sciences, we thank those men of great commitment who ensured that this concept was made viable. We all know the wonderful scientific achievements of this department in public health research and development and hope that it will be supported with the same vigour that produced its birth, to the next century and beyond.

5. History of the Usher Institute

Una Maclean

The opening of the Usher Institute in Edinburgh in 1902 was a fitting and necessary sequel to the establishment there of the first chair of public health in Britain four years previously. Both of these events around the turn of the century had been made financially possible by the philanthropy of two local brewers and distillers whose business had profited from the shrewd application of microbiological principles and whose generosity had been directed to find expression in a form which seemed well suited to the scientific needs and interests of their day. This impressive building, originally intended as a laboratory, was erected at a time of general university expansion. The event came towards the end of the most vigorous period of development in the field of public health, and the attainment of academic maturity was reached at the point when the major impact of the sanitary revolution in this country was already virtually over.

The geographical isolation of the Usher Institute, and its physical distance from its pre-clinical and clinical counterparts in the medical school, was not without a certain symbolic significance, the detachment of its position being in some ways peculiarly suited to a subject whose history reveals its distinction from most other academic disciplines. Successive professors each saw matters in a special perspective and applied their personal interpretation of the nature and importance of this elusive speciality to the health of their time and to the education of successive student cohorts.

The influence of public health upon the Edinburgh medical school had first made itself strongly felt in the work and lectures of William Pulteney Alison, professor of medicine in the middle years of the 19th century. In 1815, prior to any teaching appointment, Alison had become physician to the new town dispensary, which provided domiciliary care for the sick poor. There his daily clinical duties familiarised him with the infections, smallpox, typhus, cholera and relapsing fever, which were then so distressingly prevalent in the city and which he well described in the journals of the period. He soon became more concerned with the social environment in which these diseases were arising than with the clinical details of their manifestations.

Working amongst impoverished families who were living in slum conditions of desperate squalor and overcrowding, Alison was made acutely aware of his therapeutic impotence. The cholera epidemic of 1831–2, and the steady increase in fever cases admitted to the Royal Infirmary throughout the subsequent decade, reinforced his conviction that the palliation of individual patients was a totally inadequate response to the dangerous diseases which were then threatening entire communities. His views were ably put in his 1840 pamphlet, *Observations on the Management of the Poor in Scotland and its Effects upon the Health of the Great Towns*.[1]

Alison had become, in 1820, the second professor to hold the chair of medical jurisprudence. This subject, later called forensic medicine, was originally intimately linked with the emerging discipline of public health. The basis of their original connection lay in a common concern with the enactment and enforcement of legal measures for the promotion of the health of the public; in effect they covered relationships between the state and the medical profession. Before Scottish Poor Law had been reformed, Alison had been translated to the older and more prestigious professorship of medicine at Edinburgh. In his new position, which he took up in 1842, he persistently drew the attention of students to the social evils of the day, forcing them to contemplate the part which pauperism played in the (dissemination of) contemporary infections and urging their active promotion of planned social change.

Alison was involved in a number of contemporary academic controversies, some of which have an almost topical note. For instance, he challenged the currently prominent doctrine of Malthus, doubting whether there was sufficient evidence to support the view that poor relief would positively encourage irresponsible procreation. He was also partly at odds with the theories that underlay the practice of the great sanitary reformer Edwin Chadwick, considering that the widely held belief that epidemics were spread entirely by foul airs, or miasmata, was an incomplete explanation for a number of common fevers. Alison was unprepared to accept simplistic explanations for conditions which he perceived to have a complex background of inter-related causes.

Just after Alison's enforced retiral due to ill health in 1856, Sir Henry Littlejohn began his academic career in the extra-academical school of medicine and surgery at Edinburgh. At this period of the mid-nineteenth century, public health measures, supported by a fragile but growing administrative and legislative framework, could dramatically modify the health of town dwellers in Scotland. Littlejohn's appointment in 1862 as the first medical officer of health for Edinburgh allowed him to deal in no uncertain fashion with the unsanitary state of Edinburgh. His 1865 report on the city was soon followed by far-reaching housing improvements and public works. A gradual but perceptible improvement in the health of the community took place, as measured by a decline in the crude death rate and the disappearance of cholera and typhus from Edinburgh sooner than from any other large town in Britain.

Littlejohn's wide personal experience was allied to great oratorical gifts and his classes in Medical Jurisprudence were famous. Students packed his lectures, which were widely regarded as the most interesting in the entire field of medical education.

When Sir Henry Littlejohn's activities in the city of Edinburgh were well under way, medical officers of health had begun to be appointed up and down the country in increasing numbers, subsequent to the passage of the 1875 Public Health (England) Act.

Meanwhile, the science of public health was expanding at a tremendous rate. In 1864 Louis Pasteur invoked the germ theory to explain the results of his experiments of fermentation or souring, and by 1878 Koch had conclusively demonstrated the occurrence of specific micro-organisms in the bodies of patients with certain specified diseases. All of a sudden, previously unimagined possibilities of prevention were opened up, as bacteriology became allied to careful observation and the statistical enumeration of cases of disease or death. Lacking the means to destroy, in vivo, such infective agents as were identifiable, doctors and scientists nevertheless rapidly accumulated detailed knowledge regarding measures to reduce their dissemination.

The impetus that bacteriology gave to medicine at that time was exhilarating, prompting confidence in the ultimate defeat of disease. The sense of medical progress was pristine and undimmed, and evidence of the vital importance of public health and preventive medicine could be offered with confidence, not only to members of the profession but to intelligent laymen.

It was in a festival atmosphere of optimism and achievement that Edinburgh University celebrated its tercentenary in 1884. Among the guests was Louis Pasteur, who naturally took a keen interest in the breweries for which the capital city was renowned and which were all profitably applying the results of his own research. Pasteur stayed with Henry J. Younger who introduced him to Alexander Low Bruce, a partner in the Younger firm, who was already a keen admirer of the French scientist's work.

This meeting with Louis Pasteur fired Alexander Bruce with the ambition to found a new chair of public health at the venerable university of his hometown, but, unfortunately, he did not live to see his hopes realised. On his deathbed, however, he instructed his legal adviser, a certain Mr Crole, to ensure the proper use of his bequest for this purpose. Subsequently, donations were gradually collected from members of his family, the Younger firm and Sir John Usher of Norton. In this way a total of £15,000 was eventually offered to the university commissioners and, in 1898, an entirely new professorship in public health was established, totally separate from Medical Jurisprudence. The Bruce and John Usher Chair of Public Health was the first of its kind in Britain and set the final seal of academic respectability upon a subject, which the university had already been teaching at postgraduate level for over 20 years. Charles Hunter Stewart transferred from the Department of Medical Jurisprudence to become the first professor of public health.

Subsequently the principal was able to secure the tangible support of Sir John Usher for a further solid and worthy project, namely the building of the laboratories, which the medical school had so long required for the proper teaching of public health.

In his deed of gift Sir John Usher, the brewer, stated that he had always intended the chair of public health to be followed by the setting up of laboratories and classrooms for teaching purposes. This would depend upon the site of the proposed new building being provided by the university and it being called The John Usher Institute of Public Health. His wish that the new institute should be made useful to the public health administration of the city of Edinburgh was also made explicit.

The latter proviso was eminently reasonable, since the whole concept of public health was bound up with concern for active control of the local environment.

The developments, which had led to a degree in this speciality and its gradual divorce from forensic medicine, culminating in the establishment of a separate chair, were all manifestations of a highly significant movement in medicine away from the treatment and investigation of individual cases of disease towards the diagnosis and management of social ills. However, the desire of Sir John Usher for a union between city and university did not meet with universal approval.

From the early years of the 19th century there had been considerable tension between the university *Senatus* and the town council, specifically about the extent of control the city was entitled to exercise over courses in midwifery leading to graduation. Echoes of the conflict can be discerned in some of the words that Sir John Usher used when making the presentation of the completed building on 11 June 1902. After appropriate remarks about the university and the new professor, Sir John Usher joked about the fact that he had been informed that 'a chair without an institute is not much good'. When the building was being handed over to the university the students also made their views heard and presented an illuminated address regarding their appreciation of a gift which placed Edinburgh in the forefront of public health teaching.

After acceding to the chair, Professor Stewart and the architect had spent some time visiting scientific institutes on the Continent in order to ensure that the new building would accord with the best contemporary ideas of laboratory design. Terrazzo flooring in the entrance hall and porcelain tiles on the stairways contributed to an immediate impression of hygiene. The resultant clinical effect was partly offset by generous oak panelling. The stair windows were decorated in modish art nouveau style, supplemented with iron railings in the manner of Charles Rennie Mackintosh. Extensive laboratories occupied the upper two storeys, all provided with an elaborate system of under floor ventilation. At the west of the building was a very large amphitheatre, capable of seating over 200 students and extending to the height of two floors. Below the tiered seats was a long laboratory bench, fitted with the most up-to-date equipment, which the professor might require for demonstration purposes. Next door, after the characteristic fashion of a Scottish university, was the professor's retiring room, where he could divest himself of his gown and recover from his taxing public performances.

When it did double duty as a diagnostic laboratory for the city and a training ground for postgraduate students of applied science, the Usher Institute was functioning according to the intentions of its original designers. For the whole period of Professor Hunter Stewart's tenure of the public health chair the greater part of the building was given up to chemical and bacteriological work. There were also a number of research laboratories and a 'water analysis room' on the first floor. In the west wing, conveniently situated at ground level, were the 'town rooms' where specimens from all over the city were processed. The building also contained accommodation for experimental animals, an incubator room, and a large preparation room for the supply and maintenance of chemicals and equipment. A large proportion of the specimens regularly received were throat swabs and, when epidemics of diphtheria occurred in the child population, the pressure of work on the small staff was very great. To reduce the nuisance caused by carriages rattling up to the Usher, wooden planks were laid upon the cobbles in the street outside.

The atmosphere in these early days was one of intense and vital activity, with a keen sense of involvement in the day-to-day health of the Edinburgh community. Both undergraduates and qualified doctors were in no doubt of the importance of their practical studies to the society they were preparing to serve. While this impressive building was in the course of construction, Professor Stewart had already advertised 14 undergraduate lectures in public health in the 1900 university calendar. Such instruction had been offered separately from forensic medicine.

During the entire pre-war period – which saw the introduction of pioneering legislation relating to the medical inspection of schoolchildren, the development of schemes of infant welfare and the 1911 National Insurance Act – these important developments failed to receive specific notice in the advertised content of the applied science degree in Public Health. Bacteriology, meanwhile, had been elevated to the status of a new chair in the Edinburgh medical faculty in 1913. The four-year undergraduate medical course had been extended, in 1900, to five years. Public health lectures took place during the summer term of the fourth year. In a crowded timetable, after a half-hour lunch break and immediately before 'Insanity', the subject might seem to have been at some disadvantage. However, in those days systematic checks upon regular attendance were made by lecturers in the medical faculty.

Undergraduates had no opportunity to pursue practical exercises in the science of public health. The size of the undergraduate class during Professor Hunter Stewart's time reveals that, before the First World War, he must regularly have lectured to close on 200 students. The effect of the great post-war influx was seen in the graduate class of 1923, when the astonishing total of 351 was reached. Even when due allowance is made for the fact that a proportion of these students might be resitting, the number is impressive. An elderly technician, who began his long service in the Usher Institute during the First World War, recalled the days when students were seated all down the steps of the large lecture theatre.

After the First World War it became clear that a change in the two-year Doctorate of Science in Public Health was necessary. But, quite apart from its duration, the BSc in Public Health had by now become an elaborate anachronism, preaching the techniques and duties of Victorian sanitarians and hospital builders to the survivors of trench warfare.

The importance to the nation of close supervision of its children's welfare had been early recognised, following the discovery of serious malnutrition among Boer War recruits. In the early years of the century legislation had been passed on the medical inspection of schoolchildren, on school meals and in relation to midwives.

Tuberculosis had been treated in Edinburgh, at the Victoria Dispensary, Bank Street, since 1887. During the 1890s cases began to be visited at home so as to track down contacts. And a tuberculosis hospital (The Royal Victoria) was opened at Comely Bank. The first chair of tuberculosis anywhere in the British Empire was established during the war, in 1917, when Sir Robert Philip became the Edinburgh professor. Not long after, in 1922, the grading of milk was made obligatory, substantially reducing the incidence of tuberculosis in children.

After holding the chair for 26 years, the first professor died in 1924. In their special minute, the *Senatus* duly recorded their regret. They went on to add:

> Among the varied developments of Medicine in recent times no subject has advanced more than that of Public Health and, with the increase of knowledge, there has been a corresponding extension in the legislative control by the State of the conditions affecting public hygiene.

Unlike his predecessor, who had led a comparatively cloistered life within the Edinburgh academic community, Brevet Colonel Percy Samuel Lelean, who was appointed in December 1925, was a man of wide military experience. Born in Canada in 1871, he first acquired an FRCS and then a diploma in Public Health. In the Boer War he was a surgeon with the Royal Military Corps (RMC), serving thereafter in west Africa and, later, in India. During the Second World War he specialised in military hygiene and had been made professor of hygiene in the Royal Army Medical College. He had undertaken some of the earliest research work on anti-gas measures.

The arrival of Professor Lelean at the Usher Institute in February 1926 was the signal for marked change in the activities and disposition of all its inhabitants. No sooner had he taken up his post than the entire emphasis of the teaching changed: applied science gave way to studies that were broader in scope but more theoretical in content, and the close daily connection with the city's health was quickly severed. The colonel was impatient with the continued involvement with the city of an institute whose purpose he believed was no longer primarily bacteriological. So, with effect from 1928, the health department took their specimens elsewhere, to the medical buildings in Teviot Place. In addition, the new professor did not feel that he was either fitted or inclined to offer instruction on Sanitary Administration and the duties of medical officers of health.

Drawing upon his tropical experience, Professor Lelean stressed parasitology and entomology, arranging a roomful of exhibits to illustrate the life history of obnoxious insects and organisms that plagued the inhabitants of distant countries and far-flung outposts of the Empire. A further room was given up to models of different forms of heating and ventilation, and a special section of the museum housed plaster casts of all manner of nutritious diets.

Professor Lelean had a keen visual imagination and introduced a lengthy series of lantern slides into his lectures. These slides were painstakingly prepared in a darkroom on the premises by a faithful technician who was still working in the Usher long after his mentor had departed this life. Mr Bott was gratefully remembered by generations of students to whom he offered the invaluable extra-curricular facility of 'Bott's Swots' – for a modest sum he was prepared to show groups of undergraduates those of the professor's slides which he reckoned were most likely to feature in the final examination.

A further characteristic of the new regime and the new version of the discipline was Professor Lelean's personal enthusiasm for physical fitness. Refusing to regard health as the mere absence of disease he fostered the then highly popular physical culture movement, both among university students and a variety of boy's clubs.

By the time of Professor Lelean's retiral in 1944 the Second World War had broken out. According to the senate of that time (November 1944) he had been part of an enlargement of the whole idea of public health into what they termed 'the newer academic discipline of Social Medicine'.

Although he did take note of social and environmental factors in their impact upon physical and mental health, Professor Lelean does not appear to have been much interested in the halting steps that had been made towards an improvement in the actual delivery of health and welfare services. The inter-war period had been characterised by poverty and unemployment, and the consequent poor nutrition of many people had worsened their health prospects. But the main administrative change in the health services had been the opportunity given by the 1929 Local Government Act to local authorities to build and run their own hospitals. Limited provision had also been made for free 'panel' medical treatment for certain unemployed, insured workers. These administrative changes in the provision of medical care were on nothing like the scale of those which would presently be introduced, and their significance may have escaped a teacher whose ideas were formed in the twilight of Empire.

During the Second World War dissatisfaction with many aspects of social life in Britain at last found expression and were reflected in a determination to effect radical improvements. Just as the Boer War had revealed the miserable physical state of potential recruits at the beginning of the 20th century, so the evacuation of slum children from British cities in the 1940s brought their poor state of nutrition and hygiene to the horrified attention of the middle class. For the poor, food rationing was a positive blessing, bringing the assurance of fair shares in a balanced diet. Bombing had the effect of dramatically revealing the dreadful housing conditions in which thousands of families existed – and presented at the same time a challenge of environmental reconstruction. War permitted a more intimate examination of the physical body of the nation by the agents of government than had ever previously occurred in peacetime, and the resultant diagnosis of multiple ills was followed by all manner of prescriptions. The Beveridge Report, published in 1942, was a major cause for debate.[2] It envisaged a comprehensive system of social insurance, with the addition of 'health and rehabilitation services for the prevention and cure of disease and the restoration of capacity for work, available to all members of the community'. Its bold proposals would form the basis for the National Health Service Act 1948.

In Edinburgh, the retiral of Professor Lelean came at the precise juncture when a change in perspective was due. His successor, Brigadier Francis A. E. Crew had hitherto been a biologist but his experiences had well fitted him for expressing the modern view of his new discipline. Prior to the Second World War he had held the chair of animal genetics in Edinburgh; later, during his military service, he had reflected on 'the biology of war', its demographic and medical con-comitants. As he took up a chair which Edinburgh University had cautiously agreed to rename 'Public Health and Social Medicine', he began to write and lecture eloquently on the meaning of a professional role such as his in the post-war world:

> Social medicine is medical science in relation to groups of human beings. It is not circumscribed by what has come to be known as preventive medicine (since) it is not merely concerned with the prevention and elimination of sickness, but is concerned also and especially with the study of all social agencies which promote or impair the fullest realisation of biologically and socially valuable human capacities.

> Problems of social medicine are of two kinds, one concerned with the definition of the social environment in relation to the prevalence of morbidity and mortality, the other concerned with the social influences which are propitious to maximum health in the widest sense of the term.

Professor Crew was one of the first to introduce the idea of the 'science of human ecology'. Like his ex-army predecessor in Edinburgh, his military experience with fit troops led to a concern for the 'sociology of positive health'. He even envisaged social medicine as 'a new way of life', a notion not as preposterous as it sounds, since he was referring to the growing influence of the state in matters of health.

Professor Crew entered the Usher Institute at a time when most of the life had, literally, gone from Public Health. Formerly a place of vital activity and bacteriological and chemical analysis, the institute had long since lost its service role and its former chief functions were now undertaken by other specialised departments. The institute had become a cold museum of antiquities, demonstrating the dead agents of old pestilences and dutifully listing the legislative arrangements for protecting the public from specific infections whose power had been effectively sapped. Whilst there was still a need to train qualified doctors for posts in the existing public health service, the subject as it had previously been taught held little relevance for a new generation of undergraduates.

The first five sections of the new undergraduate course which he introduced – dealing with demography and social relations – carry the clear imprint of Professor Crew's personal vision. Later topics covered older facets of the discipline, in relation to sanitary engineering and the details of health service administration, but these were listed in a much more perfunctory manner and their teaching was relegated, in practice, to the city's medical officer of health. At the same time as the content of the undergraduate teaching was being enlarged and transformed there was also a change in methods of instruction. Now films and outside visits to places of interest were added to the main diet. Students who enjoyed Professor Crew's lectures in 1947 received the additional bonus of a complete, cyclostyled set of his lecture notes. The provision of duplicated notes of lectures has since become commonplace, but it was most unusual at that time and provides a unique contemporary commentary upon the state of Scotland's health. The bursting of such a powerful personality through the Usher Institute's revolving doors meant that the building itself, as well as the undergraduate course, soon had to undergo considerable alterations. Away went the slides, the paraphernalia of museums and the permanent demonstrations. In their place, a variety of livestock were installed. Professor Crew had bred generations of budgerigars on the roof of the War Office throughout the hostilities and now somewhere had to be found for his genetic experiments to continue. In addition, another of his earlier interests, the Pregnancy Diagnosis Laboratory, was transferred from its former breeding grounds among the suburban science departments of the King's Buildings. So small birds and spawning toads now enlivened a scene which had once been devoted to dangerous micro-organisms.

However, it was the enlargement of the library which constituted the most significant development from the academic standpoint. For this purpose a large room, which had once served for the preparation of chemical solutions, began to fill with books on a wide range of topics, indicating the extent and rapid extension of social medicine. Among these documents were the annual bound volumes of the Usher Institute papers, consisting of original contributions by members of the staff, from 1944 onwards. Professor Crew was a prolific writer and initially his own contributions comprised over half of the total content.

In the paper which he delivered to the Royal Sanitary Institute, dealing with the scope of public health after 1948, Crew declared:

> The most important function of the public health services of tomorrow will be in the field of education. Attached to the gifts of preventive medicine there is no emotional appeal and the acknowledgement of the reasonableness of a project in no way makes its execution more certain. The people and their political leaders have to be persuaded to jettison a multitude of false ideas and a number of frank falsehoods concerning health and disease.

> The steady, progressive extension of life expectancy resulting from the conquest of the killing disease of infancy is the greatest triumph of medical science in its application to human affairs. But, as its direct result, diseases which are characteristic of senescence have come to constitute the greatest problem in preventive medicine. Knowledge which would yield a significant retardation in the rate of depreciation of the ageing individual would be the greatest possible major advance in preventive medicine.

Professor Crew was convinced that his subject had an important place in the education of undergraduate medical students. He saw its value in terms of the broadening of clinical concepts, presenting the patient as a person and as a member of society. He was opposed to the idea that social medicine should strive for identity as a separate discipline, believing rather that it should contribute to students' complete understanding of their patients.

Professor Crew was not as free to influence the postgraduate course as much as he influenced his section of the undergraduate curriculum. Nevertheless, he was an inspiring teacher of all students and well deserved the lengthy accolade accorded by the faculty upon his retiral in 1955. He had given a total of 36 years of service to Edinburgh University and was one of the last of the old-style Scottish professors. With his charismatic personality and gifts of oratory he could present a clear and convincing image of his discipline. His successors inherited a subject which had expanded in many different directions, dealing, for example, with demography, epidemiology, health service organisation and the study of behaviour in relation to illness.

Professor Crew's leadership had been in tune with the optimism of the post-war era and he retired before the welfare state had come under serious fire. But by the late 1950s disillusionment with some aspects of the National Health Service had supervened upon the previous euphoria. The results of administrative divisions between the three sections of the service – public health, general practice and hospital medicine – were seen to be serious and harmful. It was also becoming clear that the general social welfare could not be ensured by the mere provision of curative medical services.

John Howie Flint Brotherston, who succeeded to the chair in 1955, had an unusual background, having taken an honours degree in History before becoming a doctor. His historical training prompted the choice of subject for his MD thesis – the early public health movement in Scotland. Later, he taught and carried out research at the London School of Hygiene and Tropical Medicine. After coming back to Edinburgh he was soon putting his interest in the social influence of medicine to wide-ranging practical effect, as dean of the faculty of medicine from 1958 to 1963.

During John Brotherston's first term of the chair a number of modifications took place in the content of social medicine as it was taught to undergraduates. The arrangements at various medical schools had lately been subjected to further scrutiny by the Royal College of Physicians, and their 1953 progress report revealed what they regarded as a gratifying state of affairs in most places. They had noted that:

In almost every school the curriculum in social medicine has been greatly expanded and former Public Health courses have been replaced by modernised courses in social and preventive medicine and the number of hours devoted to social medicine has been doubled.

Chairs of Social or Preventive Medicine have been created in almost every University where they were not already in existence. However, the consolidation of social medicine as a subject in the London curriculum lags behind the best provincial arrangements.[3]

In Edinburgh's 'provincial medical school' curricular changes had been responsible for extending the students' contact with public health and social medicine. The undergraduate degree course had been lengthened to six years. By the 1954–1955 session, in which Professor Brotherston took over, there was a significant addition. The first course in the pre-clinical part of the curriculum was described as 'forming an introduction to medical sociology'. Certain of the components of social medicine had been combined to constitute the part of the discipline mainly concerned with the historical and cultural aspects of behaviour in illness and with society's provision for medical care. As this was the first time that any course termed 'medical sociology' had been provided at Edinburgh University, its content at that early date is of some interest. The topics included:

Society, the state and the family; the history and purpose of the medical and welfare services; the meaning and methods of group, as opposed to individual medicine; measurements of public health; nature and nurture; the medico-social needs of sub-groups within the population.

Several innovations in teaching methods were introduced in 1955, the main one being provision for groups of about ten students to have tutorial tuition. This marked a break with the old tradition of formal lectures and gave much more room for flexibility, time being set aside for groups to undertake the study of chosen topics in some depth. Individual essay work was also set, and there were opportunities for outside visits and for attending evening discussion sessions or films. At about this time an effort was also made to incorporate social medicine teaching into hospital ward rounds.

In 1964 Dr Fred Martin of the Usher Institute perceived a valuable additional teaching opportunity in the first year of the Edinburgh undergraduate course.

Some students in this pre-medical year had time to spare from studying the basic science and were allowed to prepare for a BSc in Medical Sciences, taken concurrently with the MB ChB. A joint course on Psychology and Sociology in Relation to Medicine was devised by the Departments of Psychological Medicine and Social Medicine.[4] The inauguration of this course deserves mention as it predated, by four years, the recommendations of the Royal Commission on Medical Education regarding the incorporation of behavioural sciences in the early part of the curriculum of British medical schools. These observations by its originators convey the purposes they had in mind:

> There is a growing danger that the students may become so pre-occupied with the minutiae of the specialties and with the technology of the laboratory that they lose sight of the patient as a 'whole person', functioning in a social context.
>
> Differences in response to pain, illness, hospitalisation and other stresses; the influence of personality and social class on illness; communications and relations between patients, doctors and nurses; resistance to attitude and behaviour change in the context of preventive medicine – these are a few examples of everyday problems of medical decisions based on an understanding of human behaviour and institutions.[5]

By now the apparent conquest of most infectious diseases had left a legacy of chronic and degenerative conditions in which the behaviour of patients was an important factor, both in respect of prevention and the use of services.

Meanwhile Professor Brotherston was exercising an influence far beyond the confines of the academic department. He was a warm, dynamic, far-sighted individual, very skilled in committee work and tirelessly involved in the profound changes which were by then in process within the National Health Service.

In the university John Brotherston was preparing himself for his forthcoming central role in the reorganisation of the health services in Scotland. Meanwhile he had lectured on the history of Scottish medicine, presided over and encouraged numerous research projects and forged close links between the staff of the Usher Institute and the Scottish Home and Health Department. In 1963 he was offered the post of chief medical officer of health for Scotland and for this he 'relinquished' his chair in January 1964.

Stuart Love Morrison, who succeeded him, had been a senior lecturer in the department from 1962 to 1964, during which time he had also been honorary director of the Health Services Operational Research Unit at the Scottish Home and Health Department. Previously he was attached to the Social Medicine Research Unit at the London Hospital.

From the outset, Professor Morrison declared epidemiology to be the central, scientific core of his discipline, a point of view he put forcibly in his inaugural address:

> Clausewitz defined war as 'the continuation of policy by other means': social medicine can be described as 'the continuation of clinical medicine by other means'. Social medicine starts from the same point as clinical medicine, the sick person, but tries to contribute to the understanding of disease by difference means, by extending scientific enquiry to the circumstances under which disease occurs. The aim is the modification of behaviour or of the environment to prevent illness, and it works towards this aim by attempting to define the actions that control disease. Much of the work of academic social medicine is epidemiological; this includes the study of disease in the population, of the factors that influence its occurrence, of the effects of disease on the community and of the measures that can be adopted to prevent, control or limit disease.

He included in the concerns of social medicine a critical study of the working of health services, since he felt that it was only through these means that the findings of his subject could be put to practical effect. Systematic investigation into the effectiveness and efficiency of health services was only just beginning at the time when Professor Morrison came to Edinburgh; since then medical care studies have become a major preoccupation of policy makers.

Holding a conception of his subject which relieved it of its former trammels, Professor Morrison presently thought it appropriate to alter the name of his department. In the year he arrived, the Edinburgh medical faculty agreed to drop the old, revered term 'Public Health' and to use the simple title 'Social Medicine' for the long-established teaching department in the Usher Institute. A committee of the Royal College of Physicians had conceived of social medicine as an academic discipline which must now review what was valuable in the tradition of preventive medicine and public health as well as look forward to the future.

Being in the mainstream of contemporary practice, Professor Morrison went further than his predecessor in the introduction of the technology of medical statistics and computing into the Usher Institute. That portion of the building which had once been a quiet museum was soon humming with electronic sound and inhabited by the disciples of a new discipline. Banished forever were the last traces of the former Pregnancy Diagnosis Laboratory from the nether regions of the institute, leaving room for the secretarial and research services that such a large department required. In terms of permanent full-time established teaching posts, the Edinburgh Department of Social Medicine was now the largest in the British Isles, and it was responsible for an extensive programme of undergraduate and postgraduate instruction.

Dissatisfaction with the structure and functioning of the National Health Service on many counts had been vented repeatedly during the 1950s. In the late 1960s a series of plans for reorganisation were put forward in the form of Green Papers by successive ministers of health and were subjected to criticism by powerful pressure groups within the medical profession. The general theme of reorganisation assumed the desirability of integration between the existing three sections of the service, namely hospital medicine, general practice and the local authority public health services. But tentative suggestions that health should become a responsibility of local government, under council control, were vigorously opposed, both by general practitioners, who were determined to retain their status as independent contractors, and by hospital doctors, who had no desire to return to their brief experience of local authority control in the period after 1929.

In the event, the new legislation constituted an uneasy compromise in Scotland. Health boards, whose members were nominated by the secretary of state, were to be responsible for planning comprehensive health services in their own area. General practitioners, through family practitioner committees, succeeded in maintaining their independence. From the point of view of the subject of this brief history, the most remarkable feature of the reorganisation was the metamorphosis of the former medical officer of health. He was once a considerable power to be reckoned with, but local authority health departments, as they had previously existed, now disappeared from the scene. The majority of their functions that related to the maintenance of the public health were taken over by the new health boards or passed, in another form, to social work committees and to environmental health departments within local government.

In drawing up a document on community medicine in Scotland (1973), John Brotherston was joined by his immediate successor, Stuart Love Morrison. This paper is worth quoting, as it provided a considered statement of the view of two men who had to transmit the venerable tradition of public health teaching in Edinburgh. In discussing the new speciality in Scotland, the authors made reference to a previous paper from the Scottish Home and Health Department in 1971, in which the 'new' discipline had first been defined:

> Put at its simplest, community medicine is concerned with the study of health and disease in populations. The function of the specialist in community medicine is to investigate and assess the needs of the population so that priorities may be established for the promotion of health, the prevention of disease and the provision of medical care. The speciality is also concerned with co-ordinating medical expertise so that policies which are in accord with medical need can be presented to the central department, area health authorities, and those responsible for the management of services below area level. We consider that the speciality has a major contribution to make to the successful integration of medical work.[6]

Stuart Love Morrison had worked in the Social Medicine Research Unit of the London Hospital, before moving north to become honorary director of the Health Services Operational Research Unit at the Scottish Home and Health Department. When he came to the Usher Institute in 1964 he faced a major challenge. It was necessary to bring about a rapid metamorphosis, transforming people who had hitherto served contentedly enough under local authorities into specialists in an evolving clinical discipline within health boards. The prevailing uncertainty and sense of personal insecurity was intense as individuals lost their former jobs and had to apply for ill-defined new positions.

It was greatly to Stuart Morrison's credit that he managed to engineer a smooth transition through the development of a programme of crash retraining courses in the academic department. Simultaneously, by means of the year-long diploma, he proceeded to construct a sound academic foundation for cohorts of keen post-graduate recruits for what then seemed an exciting, fresh speciality. Professor Morrison never wavered in his own support for the new direction which public health was then taking, and he managed to convey his personal enthusiasm to numerous young doctors who would subsequently recall with affection his warmth and influence. Similarly, visitors from abroad enjoyed a generous welcome and picked up a sense of urgency and progress from the professor. Stuart Morrison was a retiring man who did not like the limelight. But his modesty hid great determination as well as unusual scholarly interests. He left Edinburgh, for health reasons, in 1975.

Following the departure of Stuart Morrison, Sir John Brotherston, who had recently come to the end of his period as Scotland's chief medical officer, was asked to resume the Edinburgh chair. In this, his second period in the role, he was able to continue the many developments he had initiated earlier. He had been behind the establishment in Edinburgh of the first university department of general practice in the UK; he started the Livingstone experiment, where general practitioners would use a new town health centre and also have hospital appointments; he paid special attention to the health needs of families in deprived areas and was concerned with the roles of community nurses; and he mounted the survey of medical education in the British Isles. All this time his enthusiasm for community medicine was boundless. He undoubtedly envisaged specialists in this new discipline as literally having a leading role in the new National Health Service. He himself became the third president of the Faculty of Community Medicine, and the university department in the Usher Institute was accordingly renamed yet again. He encouraged health education, or health promotion as it came to be called, and backed campaigns against smoking. His was a powerful presence in the old building and he inspired loyalty and admiration amongst staff and students.

After Sir John left in 1980 the university chose not to re-advertise the chair until 1983, when Michael Garraway became professor. His central discipline and concern had always been epidemiology; this he proceeded to emphasise at the expense of medical management and administration, which had thrived in the previous regimes. He attracted substantial research funds for cardiovascular disease, for stroke, for rugby injuries and for benign prostatic hypertrophy. The number and variety of postgraduate degrees multiplied. Professor Garraway wished to put a distance between general practice and the theory and practice of epidemiology, but he encouraged the development of a new research unit in health and behavioural change, which was presently brought within his ambit.

Shortly after becoming professor, Michael Garraway decided that the department should leave the old Usher Institute. Accordingly, in 1986, everyone moved across the Meadows to assorted rooms that had become vacant in the 'new' quadrangle. However, the name, if not the local habitation, was retained. This late move was ostensibly designed to bring Public Health Sciences (as the department was yet again re-designated) into closer physical proximity with clinical disciplines in the Royal Infirmary. The sense of identity and coherence that the old Usher Institute had managed to provide, in spite of repeated changes of name, became dispersed amongst a variety of rooms, on various levels, designed originally for other uses and other branches of medicine. Paradoxically, the Royal Infirmary of Edinburgh itself would shortly move away to a new location on the outskirts of the city.

Professor Garraway retired, due to ill health, in 1997. His successor and department head is now Raj Bhopal, one of several professors in a department which previously had but one. The story of public health and its teaching continues, under changing names and in changing circumstances.

Notes

[1]   W. P. Alison, *Observations on the Management of the Poor in Scotland, and its Effects on the Health of the Great Towns* (Edinburgh: W. Blackwood and Sons, 1840).

[2]   W. H. Beveridge, *Social Insurance and Allied Services: Report by Sir William Beveridge. Presented to Parliament, November, 1942* (Domestic Transactions, Royal Messages, Speeches from the Throne, etc.), III. Chronological Series, George VI [1936–1952] [Parliamentary Papers. Session 1942–3, vol. 6] (London, 1942).

[3]   Royal College of Physicians, *Progress Report on the Teaching of Social Preventive Medicine* (London, 1953), p. 14.

[4]   F. M. Martin, F. M. Macpherson and P. R. Mayo, 'A course in psychology and sociology for medical students'. *The Lancet* 2 (1967): 411.

[5]   *Report of the Royal Commission on Medical Education, 1965–68* [The Todd Report] (London: HMSO, 1968), pp. 26–7.

[6]   Scottish Home and Health Department (Joint Working Party on the Integration of Medical Work, Sub-group on Community Medicine), *Community Medicine in Scotland* (Edinburgh: HMSO, 1973).

REFERENCES

Annual Reports of Department of Public Health and Social Medicine, University of Edinburgh

Brotherston, J. H. F. *Observations on the Early Public Health Movement in Scotland*. London: H. K. Lewis and Co. Ltd, 1952

Brotherston, J. H. F. 'William Pulteney Alison: Scottish Pioneer of Social Medicine' (Chadwick Public Lecture, delivered in collaboration with the University of Edinburgh, October 1957). *The Medical Officer* 99 (1958): 331–6

Comrie, J. D. *History of Scottish Medicine, Vol. II* (published for the Wellcome Historical Medical Museum). London: Balliere, Tindall and Co., 1932

Crew, F. A. E. 'The changing emphasis in medicine: the growth of social medicine in Great Britain'. *Acta Medicinae Legalis et Socialis* I, 1948

Glaister, J. *A Text-book of Public Health*. Edinburgh: E. and S. Livingstone, 1910

History of the Usher Family in Scotland. Edinburgh, 1956

Logan Turner, A. *Sir William Turner: Professor of Anatomy and Principal and Vice-Chancellor of the University of Edinburgh*. Edinburgh and London: William Blackwood and Sons, 1919

Logan Turner, A. *History of the University of Edinburgh 1833–1933*. Edinburgh: Oliver and Boyd, 1933

Macleod, R. M. 'The anatomy of state medicine: concept and application, in medicine and science in the 1860s'. In F. N. L. Poynter (ed.), *Proceedings of the Sixth British Congress of the History of Medicine*. London: Wellcome Institute of the History of Medicine, 1968

The Medical Directory. London: J. and A. Churchill, 1875

'Medicine and society'. *British Medical Journal* 2 (1943): 648

Minutes of Senatus Academicus of Edinburgh University

National Health Service (Scotland) Act 1947. Edinburgh: HMSO, 1947

National Health Service (Scotland) Act 1972. London: HMSO, 1972

Pemberton, J. 'Possible developments in social medicine'. *British Medical Journal* 2 (1943): 754–5

Report on the teaching of Social Medicine in British Medical Schools (prepared by R. N. M. Macsween, Education Officer, British Medical Students' Association). Horsham (Sussex): Ciba Laboratories Ltd., 1958–9

Royal College of Physicians, London, Social and Preventive Medicine Committee, Interim Report, 1943

Royal College of Physicians, London, Report on Departments of Social and Preventive Medicine, 1966

Ryle, J. A. 'Social medicine, its meaning and its scope'. *British Medical Journal* 2 (1943): 633–4

Scottish Home and Health Department, *Doctors in an Integrated Health Service*. Edinburgh: HMSO, 1971

'Two reports from the RCP'. *British Medical Journal* 2 (1943): 553

University of Edinburgh Calendars

University of Edinburgh Journal, 1926

THE PRESENT

6. Healthy survival: public health in the world today

David M. Macfadyen

My son, an arts graduate of Edinburgh University, introduced me to the essays of Isaiah Berlin on Russian thinkers.[1] One of Sir Isaiah's essays begins with a fragment of a Greek poem. In the seventh century BC, Archilochus of Paros wrote:

> Many a trick the wise fox knows;
> But the hedgehog has one, worth a lot of those.[2]

Berlin states that these words mark one of the deepest differences between human beings. We are divided by a great chasm. On one side stand those who relate everything to a single central vision – the hedgehogs. On the other side are those who pursue many ends – the foxes. I stand with the hedgehogs – driven for half a century by a unitary, all-embracing principle based on the pursuit of healthy survival. As a first-year medical student, I was encouraged to read *The Origin of Species*. 'We may console ourselves', says Charles Darwin, 'with the full belief, that the war of nature is not incessant … and that the vigorous, the healthy, and the happy survive.'[3]

While I was working in east Africa, Jane Goodall was observing primate behaviour at Gombe Stream. An epidemic of poliomyelitis spread from the villagers of Kagoma to Goodall's chimpanzees. She was angry that disabled survivors received no help from their fellows. A clue as to how we should define humanity is provided by her reaction to this chimpanzee epidemic. The human primate was moved by the suffering of her fellow beings, unlike the chimpanzee, and administered polio vaccine to the primates under her observation.

An editorial of the proceedings of the Royal College of Physicians of Edinburgh reminds us of Goodall's altruism and the palaeolithic origins of such behaviour.[4] Sixty-five-thousand years ago, in Shanidar, Iraq, a diseased and injured human being appears to have survived through being cared for by companions. Here is a reflection on this find by Stuart Piggott, a former professor of prehistoric archaeology of this university, and his co-author:

> The fact that an individual so disabled from infancy should have been able to attain what must be regarded as old age argues for a degree of concern for the individual far transcending anything shown in animal societies. … The concern manifested for the cripple of Shanidar shows that love and compassion were especially necessary for men. … It was solidarity … that in the last resort made possible the future achievements of man.[5]

Altruism is the identifying behaviour of the human species, an idea that was first put forward at this university in the 1937 Gifford Lectures delivered by the Nobel laureate, Sir Charles Sherrington:

> Zest-to-live takes on new aspects. Thus, in our humankind, altruism extending to the family and beyond, to the tribe and beyond, knitting social ties of planet-wide comradeship and good will. Love of life extends beyond self … Altruism as passion; that would seem as yet Nature's noblest product; the greatest contribution made by man to Life … We have, because human, an unalienable prerogative of responsibility which we cannot devolve … We share it only with each other.[6]

Sherrington's landmark lectures were delivered at a time when it was not evident that compassion contributed to survival. Jane Haining – a Scottish presbyterian – was deported to Auschwitz from Hungary because she was seen weeping as she sewed the yellow stars of David on to the dresses of children. She was gassed on 16 August 1944 – No. 79467.

Within a decade, Sherrington's notion of planet-wide comradeship was embraced universally. For public health, the all-absorbing concerns for the survival of humankind on the planet were to reduce child mortality, control poverty-related diseases and help mothers achieve the birth spacing they desire.[7] But it was not until the decade of the 1970s that a planet-wide survival strategy was made explicit in the goal of health for all (HFA) by the year 2000. Halfdan Mahler, director-general of the World Health Organization (WHO) at the time, and a powerful advocate, said that the most important word in the slogan was 'all'.

The century of human survival

As the 20th century drew to a close, it was seen as a century of unprecedented human survival. Viewed globally, succeeding birth cohorts progressed through the life span with ever-decreasing deaths during childhood, adolescence and adulthood. The upward push of the world population survival curves observed between 1955 and 1995 is summarised as an increase in life expectancy at birth from 48 years to 65 years (Table 6.1).

Table 6.1. Life expectancy, world

Life expectancy in years	1955	1975	1995
Life expectancy at birth, male	47	57	63
Life expectancy at birth, female	49	60	67
Life expectancy at birth, both sexes	48	59	65

SOURCE: *World Health Report 1998* (Geneva: World Health Organization, 1998), Figure 1.

Despite the unequal rates of progress between geographic regions (not included in Table 6.1), the succeeding tiers of survival lines in Figure 6.1 depict a unique success for planet-wide survival.

A global transformation in human survival began to take effect in the century that the Usher Institute of Public Health and this department have existed. This is a marvel – a marvel that altruism towards the entire human species became entrenched in the policies of all nations and a marvel that we are able to measure the transformation.

The life table is an elegant way of measuring population survival. Life tables were first constructed during the latter part of the 17th century by Edmund Halley, drawing upon the ideas first enunciated by John Graunt.[8] They have been a basic tool of public health scientists for much longer than this department has existed. The summary survival statistic derived from the life table, expectation of life at birth, is widely understood by lay people. And advances in a population's health status are measured by monitoring life expectancy trends. The prime objective of the American nation, for example, is to help individuals of all ages increase life expectancy and improve their quality of life.[9]

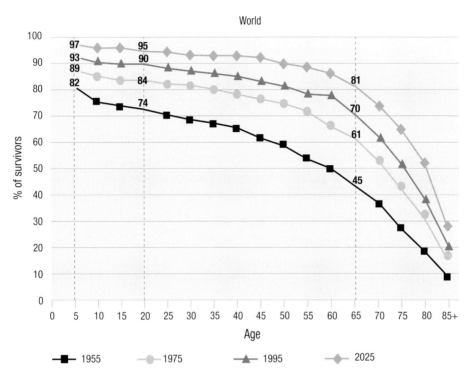

SOURCE: *WORLD HEALTH REPORT 1998* (GENEVA: WORLD HEALTH ORGANIZATION, 1998), FIGURE 2.

Figure 6.1   Survival curves, 1955–2025

What is observed globally is true of Scotland. The number of deaths registered in 2000 (57,799) was the lowest recorded since civil registration was introduced in 1855. Expectation of life at birth for the period 1998–2000 was 72.8 years for men and 78.2 years for women.[10] Over the era being celebrated, there have been huge gains in the life expectation of Scotsmen and Scotswomen. This was documented for the period 1900–1983 by Stanley Sklaroff of this department in a collation of essays in honour of the late Sir John Brotherston.[11]

The General Register Office for Scotland reports that between the periods 1891–1900 and 1950–1952 the span lengthened by 19.7 years for males and 21.3 for females. In the second half of the century, the corresponding values were 8.4 and 9.5 years.

Comparisons with life expectancy in other populations indicate that Scots should not be complacent about the survival they have achieved. The World

Health Organization computes annual life tables for its member states. The first ever compilation of life tables for all 191 member states accompanied the publication of the *World Health Report 2001*. Life expectancy at birth was 77.6 for males in Japan, almost 5 years greater than in Scotland.[12]

The life tables are one-dimensional. They measure exit from a hypothetical birth cohort of 100,000 by the force of mortality. In the early 1970s, during a period of graduate public health studies, I measured disability-free survival for 50 states by calculating separate and additive decrements due to mortality plus disability. Data were obtained from the 1970 United States census, 1968 vital statistics of the United States and a 1966 United States disability survey of a national population sample. The method and concept were derived from Daniel F. Sullivan's work in developing a single index of mortality and morbidity,[13] the latter component derived principally from annual national health interviews of samples of the US population.

Policy interest has recently been revived in summary measures of population health that integrate information on mortality and non-fatal health outcomes. In the United States, 'years of healthy life' is used for the healthy people initiative. The difference between life expectancy and years of healthy life reflects the average amount of time spent in less than optimal health because of chronic or acute limitations.

The World Health Organization's *World Health Report 2000* presented estimates of disability-adjusted life expectancy (DALE) for each of WHO's 191 member states. This measure was originally calculated for the global burden of disease study.[14] Disability weights reflect social preferences for seven severity levels of disability. Controversy surrounded the methods, particularly the weighting, on which the *World Health Report 2000* is based.[15]

Healthy life expectancy (HALE) was introduced in the *World Health Report 2001*. HALE is based on life expectancy but includes an adjustment for time spent in poor health. Healthy life expectancy is described by WHO as follows:

> Healthy life expectancy builds on the concept of life expectancy. Life expectancy is adjusted to allow for the fact that people live part of their lives in less than full health. These states are given weights between

0 and 1 to reflect their severity compared with full health (valued at 1). In rich countries, between 7 and 10 years are typically spent living in less than full health. ... In poor countries, people may spend over 20 years of their expected life span in poor health. Taking into account these weights, ill health and its consequences reduce healthy life expectancy by between 5 and 11 years across 191 countries.[16]

As with the life expectancy indicator, the top-ranking country for healthy life expectancy in men is Japan. Values for top-ranking states are given in Table 6.2.

Table 6.2. Healthy life expectancy (HALE) at birth, males

WHO member states	Estimates for 2000
Japan	73.8 years
Switzerland	72.1 years
Australia	71.5 years
Sweden	71.4 years
Italy	71.2 years
Iceland	71.2 years
Greece	71 years
New Zealand	70.8 years
France	70.7 years
Spain	70.6 years
Norway	70.5 years
Malta	70.4 years
Austria	70.3 years
Canada	70 years
United Kingdom	69.9 years

SOURCE: *World Health Report 2001* (Geneva: World Health Organization, 2001).

The World Health Organization is continuing its endeavours to develop a survey instrument for cross-country comparisons on health derived from the domains of WHO's international classification of functioning, disability and health (ICF). Details of the world health survey and related technical papers are available on the WHO website.[17]

WHO is applauded for beginning a new century with aspirations for measuring advances in health as well as reductions in mortality. However, the improved survival that the world achieved in the 20th century is fragile. In the last decades, reversal and interruptions were seen in upward survival trends in several African and East European countries.

Life expectancy in sub-Saharan Africa declined overall by three to five years in the 1990s. In Zimbabwe in 1999, male life expectancy at birth would have been 18.6 years higher if there had been no deaths due to HIV/AIDS.[18] For females, the largest impact in 1999 was in Botswana, where female life expectancy at birth would have been 23.2 years higher if there were no deaths due to HIV/AIDS.

The upward trend in survival was also interrupted in eastern Europe over the last two decades. While life expectancy in the European Union rose as a whole, over the last decade it fell in the newly independent states (NIS) of the former USSR. On average, people in the NIS die 10 years younger than those in western European countries.

Men die 11 years younger than women in the NIS. As to expectancy of years of healthy life, the average is only 56 years in the NIS, in contrast to 70 years in western countries. Describing the dramatic decline in life expectancy in the NIS during the past decade, the Report on Health in Europe says: 'There is practically no precedent for changes of this magnitude in peacetime.[19]

Having an all-embracing principle makes decision making consistent. In the following paragraphs examples are cited from the decades of the 1970s, 1980s and 1990s to show how public health action was guided by considerations of survival.

In the decade of the 1970s the World Health Organization's regions began to compile data on vital statistics and other indices that would help assess progress towards the organization's health-for-all goals. In the European region this has grown into the substantial HFA database,[20] which remains an invaluable tool for public health scientists. The HFA goals included, for all countries, the target of achieving an expectation of life at birth of more than 60 years. The region for the western Pacific began compiling time series data in the 1970s. On disaggregating total mortality experience, pneumonia emerged as a predominant cause of death in Papua New Guinea (PNG), the Philippines and, to a lesser extent, Fiji. Country-to-country variations in the mortality rate of toddlers aged 1–4 were respectively 93, 71 and 12 times higher in these countries than in Australia (see Table 6.3).

Table 6.3. Mortality rate from pneumonia/influenza per 100,000 children aged 1–4

Country (year)	Rate per 100,000	Ratio to Australian mortality
Australia (1974)	4	1
Tari, PNG (1970/71)	380	93
Philippines (1974)	291	71
Fiji (1975)	49	12

SOURCE: R. M. Douglas, *Assignment Report, 8 December 1977 to 20 January 1978* (Manila: World Health Organization, 1978), Tables 1, 2 and 8.

Simple effective technologies were assembled to establish a WHO programme for the control of acute respiratory infections (ARI), which was based on timely and effective intervention. The ARI programme was set in action in 88 countries initially, with the aim of improving child survival and reducing inequalities. The programme emerged and continues to develop because WHO is responsive to the imaginative ideas of microbiologists, care providers and public health scientists. The achievements of the programme from 1980 to 1995 have been recently reviewed,[21] and evolution of the programme continues. Control of respiratory diseases is now part of a wider WHO programme for the management of childhood illness. ARI control is now integrated with other measures of improving child survival, namely the control of malnutrition, measles and malaria as well as diarrhoeal diseases.

My contact with Edinburgh University's Department of Public Health Sciences began in the decade of the 1980s, when I began to manage WHO's global programme on aging. Professor Michael Garraway contributed to a WHO scientific group report on the 'Uses of epidemiology in the study of aging'.[22]

The approach of partitioning survival into disability-free life expectancy and disabled life expectancy was gaining strength at that time. Table 6.4 shows comparisons across country, gender and time for life expectancy at age 65. This is derived from life tables plus active life expectancy, which is derived from surveys of functional status.

Table 6.4. Life expectancy and active life expectancy at age 65 and percentage time spent in an active state

	Life expectation (years)	Active life expectancy (years)	Percentage spent in active state
Canada			
Men, 1978	14.4	8.2	57
Men, 1986	14.9	8.1	54
Women, 1978	18.7	9.9	53
Women, 1986	19.2	9.4	49
England and Wales			
Men, 1976	12.5	6.9	55
Men, 1985	13.4	7.7	57
Women, 1976	16.6	8.2	49
Women, 1985	17.5	8.9	51

SOURCE: J. Grimley Evans and T. Franklin Williams (eds), *Oxford Textbook of Geriatric Medicine* (Oxford: Oxford University Press, 1992), Table 3, p. 7.

It appeared that 65-year-old women in Canada were surviving longer than those of England and Wales; that survival at this age lengthened over the period of a decade in both nations; and that substantial gender differences in survival continue beyond 65. Epidemiologists are wary of comparisons of active life expectancy because of the inconsistencies of functional measurement. Nonetheless, in both countries it appears that the benefit of the greater longevity of women may be offset by their spending more years in a disabled state.

The policy debate for the embryonic WHO programme was focused on a polemic concerning the upper end of the life table. With the upward push of the survival curve, was morbidity being compressed into a narrow time interval, just before death? The focus on the survival curve led the programme in the direction of seeking and advocating interventions to reduce the frequency of disability in the face of rising life expectancy. This continues to be the focus of WHO's 'healthy aging' programme.

Thomas McKeown animated a debate in the 1970s on the reasons for gains in survival. In a Nuffield Foundation symposium he called for a historical 'examination of the conditions under which man developed and of the major influences which affected health at different stages of his evolution'.[23] The controversies surrounding McKeown's scepticism on the achievements of health services need to be revisited by analysing current survival at higher ages. Such an analysis would address the major policy question of how improvements in health care of the elderly are contributing to population survival and healthy survival at age 65. Indeed, McKeown himself felt 'the possibility should be considered that specific measures for preventing and treating disease are relatively more important in populations with long expectation of life.[24]

The title of this presentation derives from a consideration of the World Health Organization's role in humanitarian assistance. The issue was settled in the 1990s by simply focusing on survival. Survival is threatened by conflicts that displace populations. A survey in the eastern Democratic Republic of Congo found that the fighting there resulted in at least 1.7 million excess deaths between January 1999 and May 2000.[25] Most deaths were the result of a combination of violence, lack of services, extreme vulnerability and common diseases. In one case in eight the direct mechanism of death was a weapon.

Impact on survival may be calculated in many ways. The simplest is to compare monthly crude mortality rates (CMRs) with baseline rates. Rates for internally displaced persons were significantly higher than the baseline rates for various conflicts of the 1990s. In the most extreme case, Somalia, CMRs for internally displaced persons were 50 times the baseline. In contrast, excess mortality rose slightly against the baseline in Bosnia (see Table 6.5).

Table 6.5. Mortality rates* relative to baseline: internally displaced persons

Liberia, 1990	7
Iraq, 1991	13
Somalia (Baidoa), 1992	51
Sudan (Ayod), 1992/93	23
Bosnia (Sarajevo), 1993	3

*Crude Monthly Mortality Rates: deaths per thousand per month

SOURCE: E. Noji, *Public Health Consequences of Disasters* (New York: Oxford University Press, 1997).

In the early 1990s, experience showed that deaths in situations where populations were displaced were readily preventable or treatable. Major threats to survival can be lessened by proven, low-cost public health interventions. For example the major causes of death in refugee children under 5 in Malawi in 1990 are shown in Table 6.6.

Table 6.6. Major causes of death in refugee children in Malawi, 1990

Malaria	26%
Malnutrition	23%
Diarrhoea	11%
Measles	10%
Pneumonia	8%
Other	22%

SOURCE: A. Moren, D. Bitar, I. Navarre, M. G. Etchegorry, A. Brodel, G. Lungu and P. Hakewill, 'Epidemiological surveillance among Mozambican refugees in Malawi, 1987–89'. *Disasters* 15.4 (1990): 363–72.

WHO's humanitarian intervention in Bosnia was public health led. From the outset, Sir Donald Acheson, who served in 1991–1992 as the special representative of the WHO director-general, kept WHO focused on public health technologies. These are progressively being developed and are described in explicit guidelines and manuals.[26] Sir Donald's collective term for applying the technology of humanitarian action was 'the public health of survival', a title I have borrowed for this presentation.

There is no longer debate over WHO's role in humanitarian assistance. Gro Harlem Brundtland, the former director-general, in a recent address to WHO's governing body, the World Health Assembly, stressed the importance of 'staying to the end and to come in early'.[27] WHO's obligation in humanitarian assistance is consistent with its single central vision. It is to help people everywhere, under any conditions, whenever it can, to prevent any deterioration of the health of populations caused by external or internal events.

Conclusion

Public health science during the past century has been directed to one main purpose – evaluating the determinants of healthy survival. During the 1930s the idea was put forward, in this university, that we survive and thrive as a species because of altruism – compassion for our fellow human beings.

Those who apply public health sciences are divided. On one side stand those who relate everything to a single central vision – the hedgehogs. On the other side are those who pursue many ends – the foxes. International public health has been led, since the 1970s, by those with a single central vision – healthy survival for the whole stock of humankind.

A transformation in global survival occurred in the 20th century. However, reversal and interruptions in upward survival trends occurred in countries where economic conditions precipitously declined. The role of public health and health services in extending healthy survival at higher ages is a question with huge policy implications. The overall purpose of public health science widened at the onset of the present century. It is now time to evaluate the influences upon which healthy survival depends and is maintained.

A challenging task for today's public health sciences is to establish the base for measuring health advances in the 21st century, as the upper limits of survival are approached.

Notes

1   I. Berlin, *Russian Thinkers* (Harmondsworth: Penguin, 1979).
2   F. L. Lucas (trans.), *Greek Poetry for Everyman* (London: Dent and Sons, 1951).
3   C. Darwin, *On the Origin of Species* [chapter 3: 'Struggle for Existence'] (London: Routledge, 2003).
4   'On altruism' [editorial], *Proceedings of the Royal College of Physicians of Edinburgh* 19 (July 1989): 261–2.
5   G. Clark and S. Piggott, *Prehistoric Societies* (Harmondsworth: Penguin, 1965).
6   C. S. Sherrington, *Altruism in Man on his Nature* (New York: Doubleday, 1953), pp. 262–98.
7   M. A. McCarthy, 'A brief history of the World Health Organization'. *The Lancet* 360 (2002): 1111.
8   J. Graunt, *Natural and Political Observations Mentioned in a Following Index and Made Upon the Bills of Mortality with Reference to the Government, Religion, Trade, Growth, Air, Diseases and the Several Changes in the Said City* (London: John Martyn, 1662).
9   *Healthy People 2010, Voume. 1* (Washington, DC: Department of Health and Human Services, 2000) (online at http://www.health.gov/healthypeople).
10   General Register Office for Scotland, 2002.
11   S. Sklaroff, 'The population and vital statistics of Scotland, 1900–1983', in G. McLachlan (ed.), *Improving the Common Weal: aspects of the Scottish Health Services 1900–1984* (Edinburgh: Edinburgh University Press, 1987).
12   *World Health Report 2001* (Geneva: World Health Organization, 2001) (online at http://www.lifetable.de/data/MPIDR/SCO_1951.pdf).
13   D. F. Sullivan, 'A single index of mortality and morbidity'. *HSMA Health Reports* 86 (1971): 347–54.
14   C. J. L. Murray and A. D. Lopez, *The Global Burden of Disease: a comprehensive assessment of mortality and disability from diseases, injuries and risk factors in 1990 and projected to 2020* (Cambridge, Mass.: Harvard University Press on behalf of the World Health Organization and the World Bank, 1996).
15   T. Ameson and E. Nord, 'The value of DALY life: problems with ethics and validity of disability adjusted life years'. *British Medical Journal* 319 (1999): 1423–5.
16   D. B. Evans, A. Tandon, C. J. L. Murray and J. A. Lauer, 'Comparative efficiency of national health systems: cross national econometric analysis'. *British Medical Journal* 323 (2001): 307–10.
17   Online at http://www3.who.int/whs
18   A. D. Lopez, J. Salomon, O. Ahmad, C. J. L. Murray and D. Mafat, *World Health Organization GPE Discussion Paper Series* 9 (EIP/GPE/EBD), p. 23.
19   *Health in Europe, 2002* (Copenhagen: World Health Organization, 2002).
20   Online at http://www.WHO.dk/hfad
21   'Evolution of diarrhoeal and acute respiratory diseases control at WHO: achievements 1980–1995 in research, development and implementation'. WHO/CHS/CAH/99.2.
22   'Use of epidemiology in the study of aging'. *Technical Report Series* 706 (Geneva: World Health Organization, 1984).
23   T. McKeown, 'A historical appraisal of the medical task', in T. McKeown and G. MacLachlan (eds), *Medical History and Medical Care: A Symposium on Perspectives* (Oxford: Oxford University Press, 1971), pp. 27–55.
24   Ibid. 40.
25   International Rescue Committee, *Mortality in Eastern Democratic Republic of Congo: results from five mortality studies* (New York: IRC Health Unit, 2000) (online at http://www.thierc.org/index.cfm?section+what&wwwID441&topicID=86&ppID=441).

26   General guidelines and manuals: http://www.who.int/eha/disasters; (drug donations)
http://www.who.int/eha/ftp/16836.html; (standard health kits)
http://www.who.int/eha/disasters/tghealthkits.html
27   Address by the Director-General to the 53rd World Health Assembly, 2000, Document A53, p. 9.

7. The next epidemiological transition in the Asia Pacific

Anthony J. Hedley

The founder of Hong Kong is regarded by many as Dr William Jardine. He graduated in medicine from Edinburgh in 1802 and that year became a ship's surgeon's mate aboard a ship of the East India Company. He apparently found his medical qualification something of a social and financial handicap and so became a trader on his own account, mainly dealing in opium, and with his partner Matheson, a fellow Scot, became very wealthy. The stigma of the opium trade is still a sensitive issue today, and whilst the Jardine Matheson company is now registered in Bermuda it remains a household name and the second biggest employer in Hong Kong.

Hong Kong is a tiny blip on the Asia Pacific rim around which there are huge gradients in both wealth and health, for example between the so-called Asian 'tigers' (Japan, Taiwan, Hong Kong, Singapore) and those countries constantly afflicted by the horsemen of the apocalypse – war, famine, pestilence and death (Laos, Cambodia, Burma, Vietnam, parts of Indonesia and the Philippines).

The Hong Kong Special Administrative Region (HKSAR) is an archipelago of 270 islands with a usable land area of only about 1000 square kilometres. It is a land of contrasts which includes an 'open zoo' with rich fauna and flora (the eating of wild species is prohibited) and rural landscapes with population densities of 500–600 people per square kilometre adjacent to dense urban areas with 50,000–60,000 people per square kilometre, and going up to 160,000 in some sub-districts. Average living areas in public housing are about 65 square metres. If we mapped Hong Kong on to central Scotland, with Alloa roughly at its centre, it would extend to Aberfeldy and Forfar in the north, Strathaven and Peebles in the south and a line joining Crianlarich and Paisley in the east; the west border would be formed by St Andrews and a point about halfway between Edinburgh and Dunbar on the A2 going east (Figure 7.1). In 2003, in little more than about 30% of this space, there were 6.8 million people living in Hong Kong, and the population is set to increase to 8.6 million by 2020.

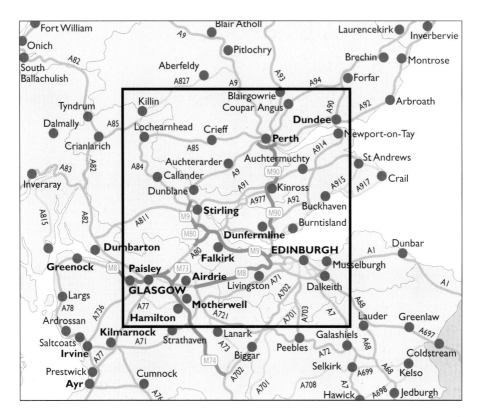

Figure 7.1 Area of Hong Kong superimposed on central Scotland

Unlike our near neighbours, such as the Philippines, where there is still a more or less conical population pyramid, Hong Kong looks boxy or oblongate like Scotland, albeit with a large spare tyre of young middle-aged (Figure 7.2). This is a rapidly ageing community. In Scotland the old-old have increased by 50% in 25 years, in Hong Kong by 300%. Around the Asia Pacific rim many of the middle-aged in countries like Japan are being socially and financially crippled by the problem of caring for their elderly. China's turn will come next.

Hong Kong newspapers in 1902 found space to report that Sir Robert Bannatyne was elected rector of Edinburgh University. The Scottish papers of that year were often dominated by two themes: the death of William McGonagall and Hibernian Football Club's triumph in the Scottish Cup – both somewhat novel events and possibly never to be repeated.

One hundred years ago, in 1902, health related news items in the *China Mail* and *Hong Kong Telegraph* included concerns about problems with the water supply.

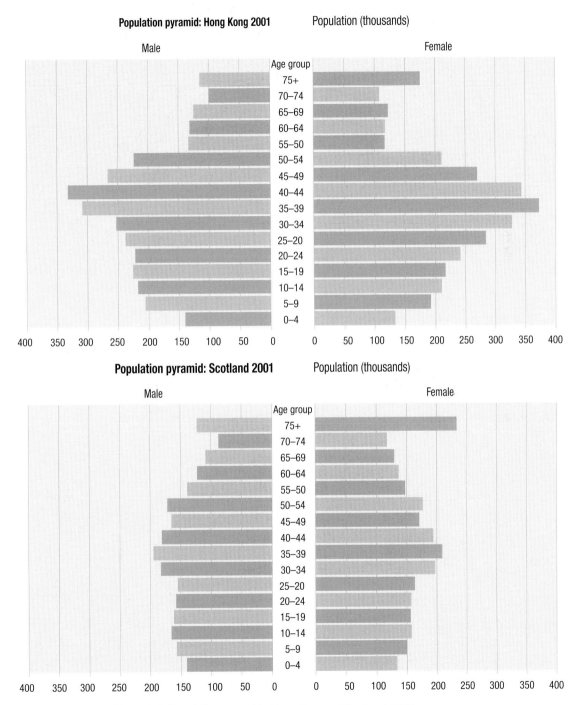

Figure 7.2 Population pyramids: Hong Kong and Scotland, 2001

This is still a topical issue today with Hong Kong being heavily dependent on drawing water from rivers across the border with the mainland, in Guangdong Province – rivers that are increasingly polluted by effluent from industrial and domestic sources.

Outbreaks of scarlet fever in Shanghai and cholera in the Philippines were typical of the almost daily reports on communicable disease risks in the region at the turn of the century. Bubonic plague was endemic in Hong Kong and southern China at that time. The great epidemic of the 1890s smouldered on into the early 1900s. A total of about 24,000 cases were recorded in Hong Kong between 1894 and 1929. Dr J. A. Lowson, a native of Forfar, was superintendent of the infectious diseases hospital in Hong Kong. He reported that in the first year of the epidemic there were 2,679 cases with 2,485 (93%) deaths. At that time the average age at death was probably about 25 for those living in rural areas.

Scottish medical graduates have made very substantive contributions to the development of medicine and health care in Hong Kong over more than a century. However, in 1902, in contrast to the mature seat of learning in Edinburgh, medical education in Hong Kong was in its infancy. The Hong Kong College of Medicine for Chinese was founded in 1888 by four Aberdeen graduates: three from medicine, Patrick Manson, Kai Ho Kai and James Cantlie; and a fourth, Frederick Stewart, a classics graduate, prominent educationist and the college's first rector. Manson, Ho Kai and Cantlie were later knighted for their various contributions to medicine, research, education and public service in Hong Kong and Britain. Manson and Cantlie became best known for (respectively) founding the London School of Hygiene and Tropical Medicine and developing ambulance services, especially in battlefields. Together they later rescued Sun Yat Sen from imprisonment in the Chinese Legation in Portland Street, London, by applying for a writ of habeas corpus. They saved him from certain death and thus determined the course of history in China.

Poverty and mortality

Wealth is health in the Asia Pacific and there is nothing so toxic as poverty. The gross domestic product (GDP) per capita of the wealthy Asian countries is less than that of Switzerland and the USA but more than that of the countries of the European Community. Burma, Laos and Cambodia are stuck in absolute poverty, with life expectancy 25 years below their neighbours.

Infant mortality is one kind of litmus test for the social and economic status of a community. The Scottish infant mortality rate (IMR) in the early 1900s was about 110, falling to 77 by 1938. In the post-war 1940s IMR in Hong Kong was about 100 but today is 2.9 per 1,000 live births – lower than that in Scotland, well below Thailand's rate and on a par with Japan and Singapore. Elsewhere in the region, IMRs in countries such as Myanmar, Cambodia and Laos probably still hover around the 100 mark although registration and records systems preclude accurate estimates.

Lifestyle and health

In 1995 a cartoon on the front cover of *The Economist* satirised the differences between the health-risk related lifestyles of westerners and our leaner Asian counterparts (Figure 7.3).

The westerner is portrayed as both tall and obese, unable to contain his abdomen with his trouser belt and yet relishing the taste of a burger while smoking. The Asian is wielding chopsticks to scoop up the remnants of a frugal meal, probably

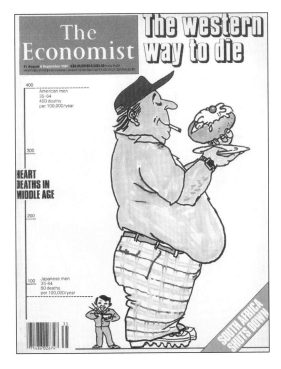

Figure 7.3 *The Economist,*
31 August 1995

rich in protective nutrients, from his rice bowl. For this image to truly represent Chinese, Japanese or Vietnamese males it should also feature a cigarette in the mouth of the Asian male. Nevertheless, when scaled against their deaths from heart disease in middle age (between 35 and 64) these caricatures reflect a five-fold difference in mortality risk. Hong Kong has much lower age-specific mortality rates for many common health problems than comparable post-industrial societies in the West.

Circulatory diseases are the most common registered causes of death in both Hong Kong[1] and Scotland.[2] The age standardised mortality rates for cardiovascular disease in males for Scotland and Hong Kong suggest that for all circulatory diseases, following a marked decline in deaths, Scotland is now where Hong Kong was 25 years ago (Figure 7.4). The magnitude of the differences and the recent trends, indicated by the international classification of diseases rubric for ischaemic heart disease, do not seem to suggest that the two regions are involved in a common epidemic. However, Hong Kong has experienced a significant downturn in mortality in the 1990s. Unfortunately we do not have good incidence data because a previous director of health declined the opportunity to participate in the MONICA (monitoring trends and determinants in cardio-vascular disease) project.

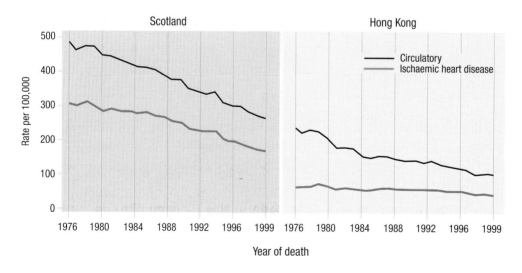

Figure 7.4 Age standardised mortality rates for circulatory diseases and ischaemic heart disease (male), 1976–1999

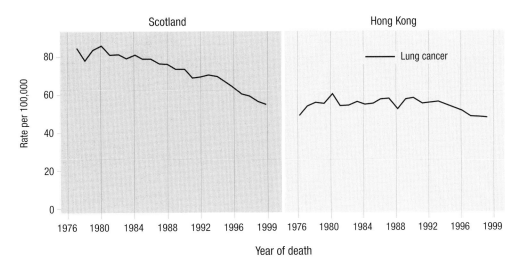

Figure 7.5 Age standardised mortality rates for lung cancer (male), 1976–1999

Mortality rates for lung cancer suggest that Hong Kong is at a different stage of the tobacco epidemic than Scotland, although it remains the most common tumour in men (Figure 7.5). The marked decline in Scotland reflects the effectiveness of tobacco control and health promotion over three decades. The increasing rates in Hong Kong during the post-war years have similarly been reversed since the introduction of a vigorous smoking prevention campaign in the 1980s, an important part of which was initiated by Dr Judith Mackay MB (Edin.), FRCPE. These measures may also be relevant to the trends for chronic obstructive pulmonary disease (COPD) for which the rates have been higher in Hong Kong, but the recent slope of the decline is apparently greater than in Scotland (Figure 7.6).

The influence and importance of environmental factors in health risks, and in some instances their interaction with genetic status, is dramatically demonstrated by the magnitude of the differences in mortality rates for hepatocellular cancer (HCC) and nasopharyngeal cancer (NPC) (Figure 7.7). The upward trend for HCC in Scotland has been associated with a high population prevalence of positivity for hepatitis B antigen (about 13%) and is likely to reflect exposure to both alcohol and hepatitis B and C infection from needle sharing and sexual contact. The rarity of NPC in Scotland contrasts with one of the highest rates worldwide observed in Hong Kong. This is now attributed to exposure to Epstein Barr virus and, possibly, other facilitating factors such as preserved foods with a high

Figure 7.6   Age standardised mortality rates for COPD (male), 1976–1999

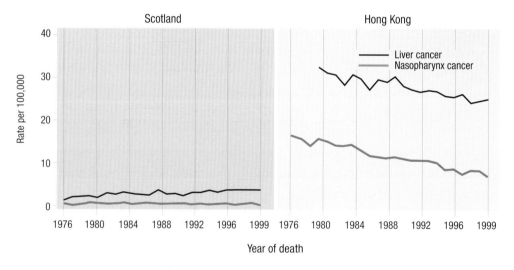

Figure 7.7   Age standardised mortality rates for liver and nasopharynx cancers (male),
1976–1999

nitrosamine content in a genetically susceptible southern Chinese population.
The decline in mortality from these two tumours reflects awareness of risks,
changes in some traditional dietary preferences, protection by hepatitis B vaccine
(which is now given to all neonates) and improved treatment, especially for NPC.

Screening

The patterns of mortality for breast and cervical cancer (Figure 7.8) prompt us to look at health care provision for secondary prevention. In Hong Kong cervical cancer deaths have been higher than in Scotland, and declining more slowly, for more than 25 years. Scotland's health service has at least provided opportunities for comprehensive screening coverage of the population at risk. Today in Hong Kong less than half of the women eligible for a pap smear have ever had one.[3]

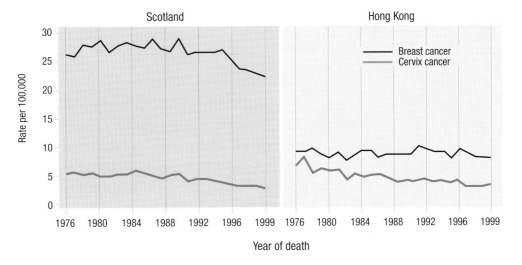

Figure 7.8   Age standardised mortality rates for breast and cervix cancers, 1976–1999

Those who have had a pap smear are now being over-screened. The government has finally established a committee to review cancer screening but it will inevitably be years before this problem is adequately addressed. Questions will remain about the impact of screening in this health care setting. One major problem in the promotion of preventive health care measures is that there is no system for primary medical care. Access to primary care procedures, such as cervical screening, in this very mixed medical economy is distributed across private practitioners, including those practising as general practitioners with or without specialist qualifications, specialists in gynaecology, government-run family health clinics and non-governmental organisations such as the Family Planning Association. On that basis, the concept of targeting defined populations at risk and evaluating the performance of the health care system is difficult to apply in Hong Kong at present.

Breast cancer presents a different kind of problem. Along with lung and colon cancers it is one of the most common tumours in women. However, the incidence and mortality rates in Edinburgh are two-and-a-half times higher than the rates in Hong Kong. This is a typical contrast between Asian and Western rates, even though Hong Kong probably has the highest incidence rates in Asia.[4] However, the observed increase in incidence is occurring in women under the age of 50 who have not been shown to benefit, by any criteria, from screening in the West. Both public and private health services in Hong Kong have in recent years been aggressively promoting breast screening by mammography, with the implied (or even explicit) promise that it leads to benefit. Mammography of the smaller, more fibrous Asian breast leads to problems of interpretation of test results. New technology may lead increasingly to improved images and their interpretation, but the lower prevalence of tumours at screening also means that the chance of a positive screen being a false positive is much higher. In the USA there is a greater than 50% chance of a false positive in women participating in a 10-year screening programme;[5] in Hong Kong the risk is predictably much higher. This compelling decision analysis issue in breast screening is rarely acknowledged and usually ignored by many clinicians and, indeed, public health specialists. It is a complex problem and in many ways represents a true dilemma. However, the public health viewpoint must prevail if we are to avoid doing more harm than good. Presenting a balanced view of what breast screening can and cannot achieve is going to be difficult in Asia. For example the message put out, in good faith, by a non-governmental organisation for cancer prevention reads: 'So you have time for dim sum but no time to have your breasts screened.' Coercive statements targeted at the population at risk are not new in breast screening. The American Cancer Society trumpeted: 'If you are forty and haven't had a mammogram then you need more than your breasts examining.'

Well-population mammography is a clear case where the potential harms and benefits of screening should be made absolutely explicit as a basis for women to make a real choice. That is now an imperative for health care providers in Asia.

Tuberculosis

Despite Hong Kong's generally healthy profile and age-specific death rates that are much lower than in the West, tuberculosis presents a sharply contrasting picture. The last 50 years have witnessed a progressively downward trend in both incidence and mortality.[6] Despite the dominance of private practice in primary care, the government services for chest diseases, including tuberculosis, provide continuous walk-in facilities free of charge to all users. The treatment approach is based on directly observed therapy, and Hong Kong was the setting for pioneering randomised trials of short-course therapy by the UK Medical Research Council in the 1970s. Nevertheless, the annual average incidence in the 1990s was about 100 per 100,000 people and has now risen to 120 per 100,000, reflecting a global upturn in the spread of tuberculosis (Figure 7.9). The principal reason for this appears to be demographic change, with high rates in elderly males and the rapidly increasing numbers of this age group. An important contributing factor is probably the relatively high prevalence of smoking in Chinese males. Reported rates of tuberculosis are uniformly lower in other Asia Pacific countries, but this almost certainly reflects the greater efficiency of Hong Kong's notification system. We recently estimated under-reporting to be only 3% in community-wide chest clinics.[7]

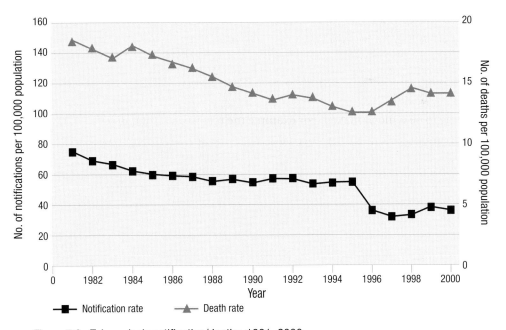

Figure 7.9   Tuberculosis notification/deaths, 1981–2000

HIV/AIDS and risk behaviour

Tuberculosis is a defining feature of HIV/AIDS, and the prospect of a combined epidemic of the two diseases is truly daunting. Both David Ho, the Chinese-American HIV researcher, and recently Kofi Annan have warned the People's Republic of China of impending disaster from the spread of HIV. The mainland government's response to AIDS activists and whistle-blowers on issues such as contaminated blood products has been to commit some of them to prison.

Increasing mobility and the migration of workers around the Asia Pacific is an important vector for HIV. Messages on prevention are often muted, and forthright statements in the vernacular on the hazards of unprotected sexual intercourse are often disallowed. Commercial sexual services are highly developed in many Asia Pacific countries. Many people travel for sex and many others have sex when travelling. In interviews with 4,000 single travellers at the Hong Kong international airport we identified 383 who had travelled as singletons within the previous 12 months. Of these, 44% had had sex with strangers on their last trip and 37% stated they did not use condoms regularly. The majority of those in this category were young, but we did identify an older group, apparently in stable relationships, who were exposed and who did not usually use condoms.[8]

The new epidemic of overweight

The headlines in the *British Medical Journal* of 5 October 2002 ('Obesity: an epidemic without treatment') and in no less authority than the *Daily Mail* ('Parents may soon outlive obese children', 10 September 2002) are now as relevant in the East as they are in the West. As a result of a dramatic change of lifestyle *The Economist's* previous dichotomy between the two hemispheres is well and truly out of date for all but the poorest Asian countries.

We need to understand better the reasons for these rapid trends. Some factors from population surveys seem to be obvious. In Hong Kong there is considerable and increasing aversion to exercise in young people, and even if they do exercise it is of poor quality.[9] The changing urban landscape in the Asia Pacific has included increasing numbers of escalators and moving pavements, car ownership and the ubiquitous franchises for McDonalds, Kentucky Fried Chicken, Pizza Hut and Dunkin' Donuts, which have changed young Asians' preferences and diets forever. In Hong Kong, McDonalds outlets have had some of the highest turnovers worldwide for more than a decade.

Studies by several groups now suggest that 40% of Hong Kong Chinese are overweight including one in four children. Cardiovascular risk factors rise sharply in those with a body mass index (BMI) of more than 21, rather than the Caucasian norm of 25. The Asian thrifty phenotype is under assault; it remains to be seen what the impact will be on morbidity and mortality. In the meantime the prevalence of diabetes and the glycaemic syndrome are rising sharply.[10] Maturity-onset type diabetes is now a common feature of morbidity in adolescents and young people. There can be few similar examples of such a rapid epidemiological transition in a community with a well-established healthy profile.

Pollution-related disease

Pollution has been a feature of human settlement since prehistoric times. The increasing consumption of the 'tiger' economies includes fossil fuels and this has resulted in some of the worst air pollution in the world in Asian cities. In 1988 we were asked to help develop an evidence base on the health effects of air pollution in children. We approached this by studying primary schoolchildren in the most- and the least-polluted districts of Hong Kong.

In 1988, from the window of a primary school in a mixed residential and industrial district, at 8 a.m. I could see plumes from factory chimneys drifting towards nearby apartment blocks and slow-moving diesel traffic near the school. This is typical of the environments in which many children live and study in Asia. Over a four-year period we interviewed and tested about 20,000 primary schoolchildren and their parents. We found substantial gradients in respiratory health between the districts. At the two-year point of this study something quite unusual happened. The government introduced restrictions on the sulphur content of fuels. The switch to new fuels occurred on Sunday, 1 July 1990. This was a defining moment because within days it led to a dramatic fall in sulphur dioxide levels in most districts, with the resulting mean level approaching that of the least polluted. There was no change in the concentrations of the other criteria pollutants – respirable suspended particulates (RSP), nitrogen dioxide or ozone.

Over the next two years we found a significant reduction in the between-district differences in health outcomes: first in bronchitic symptoms such as cough, phlegm and wheeze; and second in bronchial hyper-responsiveness estimated by histamine challenge tests.[11]

More recently we have analysed the impact of sulphur restriction on mortality over this period.[12] We found two things: first, a marked but transient change in the annual seasonal mortality cycle (increase in deaths from warm to cool season); and second, a longer-term downturn in mortality – both specifically for cardiopulmonary causes and particularly in the elderly. The seasonal deaths mortality change is particularly interesting. One supposition has been that pollution episodes take out the frail and susceptible who would have died anyway, say within a day or two – the so-called 'harvesting' of deaths. Figure 7.10 shows death counts for respiratory causes by months in each of five years, 1990/1–1994/5. The bold line is the expected pattern of seasonal mortality modelled from data in the period 1985–1989, five years before the intervention, and the broken line shows the trend in seasonal mortality in the period 1990/1–1994/5. In the first cool season (roughly October to March) after the sulphur restriction, the expected increase in deaths, especially cardiopulmonary causes, was much reduced. In the second and third years the cool season death counts were higher than expected and then gradually returned to the expected pattern in years four and five. The example shown is for the 65+ age group, but the findings were similar for all ages.

The longer-term impact of sulphur restriction on mortality is demonstrated by Figure 7.11. We estimated the average annual proportional increase in deaths (attributable to an ageing and expanding population) and estimated the trend following the fuel restriction. The reduction of 2.2% in the annual proportional increase indicates that there were 600 deaths avoided per year. The biggest reductions were seen in the elderly and for cardiopulmonary causes.

The results provide the best evidence so far that so-called harvesting not only involves the very frail but also those who would otherwise have survived for several years. It also shows that not only RSP but also the gaseous pollutants are likely to play a key role in morbidity and mortality from air pollution. Apart from Hong Kong's success in reducing sulphur pollutants, suffice to say that I am very pessimistic about further major air quality improvements in the region. The

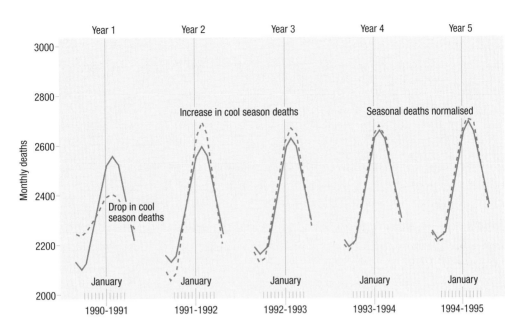

Figure 7.10   Seasonal mortality following reduction of sulphur in fuels, 1990/1–1994/5

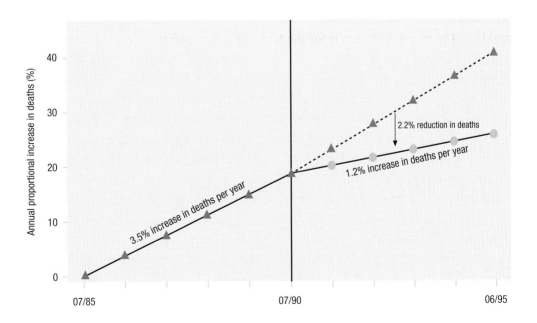

Figure 7.11   Effects of sulphur restriction: long-term trends in deaths, 1985–1995

inexorable trends in infrastructure development, expanding populations and heavy emphasis on road vehicular transport and power generation all indicate that south China and the rest of Asia will be shrouded by a 'brown cloud' for years to come.

The tobacco epidemic

No discussion on an epidemiological transition would be complete without documenting tobacco as an agent for chronic disease in the Asia Pacific.[13]

In Hong Kong we have just emerged from a period of intensive marketing of cigarettes to youth and women. In the 1990s Hong Kong Chinese-speaking primary schoolchildren recognised the cryptic Marlboro chevron and the Salem logo more accurately and reliably than the names and logos of McDonalds, Coca-Cola, well-known toothpaste brands and a local bakery.[14] In 1997, through new tobacco control legislation (greatly supported by published public health research on local avoidable morbidity and mortality), we gained much stronger environmental control of tobacco promotion, and hoardings, bill boards and light boxes have gone from our skyline. After intense lobbying by the tobacco industry 'point of sale' advertisements were still permitted and faulty law drafting led to abuse by the tobacco industry, with giant hoardings towering over tiny hawker stalls.

As part of its disinformation programmes the tobacco industry has long argued that smoking does not kill Asians like westerners. In 1998 we captured information on tobacco consumption on 28,000 deaths (directly from relatives or other informants registering the deceased at death registries) and on an appropriate living control group.[15] The findings show that for cardiovascular deaths and lung disease in Hong Kong Chinese there is a clear dose–response relationship with duration of smoking history. Hong Kong Chinese who smoke like westerners do in fact die like westerners (especially from cardiopulmonary disease) at the rate of 6,000 per year, amounting to about 20% of all deaths in Hong Kong. The association with tuberculosis mortality is very strong and particularly important for control of the disease in China (Table 7.1).

Of course, in terms of scale, if not severity, the harm from second-hand smoke exposure is as great as it is from active smoking. We have now examined passive

Table 7.1. Mortality and smoking: adjusted risk ratios for cardiorespiratory causes (males 35–69)

Causes	Years smoking		
	1–14	**15–24**	**25+**
Stroke	1.58	1.79	**2.20**
IHD	1.55	1.32	**2.53**
COPD/PHD	2.65	3.93	**8.62**
Respiratory TB	(1.02)	2.93	**6.62**
Excess risks (%)	55–165	32–293	**120–762**

SOURCE: T. H. Lam, S. Y. Ho, A. J. Hedley, K. H. Mak and R. Peto, 'Mortality and smoking in Hong Kong: case-control study of all adult deaths in 1998'. *British Medical Journal* 323 (2001): 361.

smoking risks in many groups of workers in Hong Kong, including 5,500 non-smoking police officers.[16] Their excess risks for respiratory problems is about 130% compared with those not exposed, and passive smoking is also associated with increased doctor consultations, sickness absence, use of over-the-counter medicines and higher health care costs to workers, employers and the government.[17]

One of the most vulnerable groups exposed to harm from passive smoking is that of workers in the catering industry, and this is where the new battle lines are being drawn in the next round of public health legislation. We recently analysed urinary cotinine in 170 non-smoking workers. The distribution of cotinine levels compared with our low-risk controls (public health physicians, nurses, other health professionals) indicated hugely increased risks for cancer and heart disease. If the only acceptable level of cotinine in body fluids is zero, then most of us are exposed and at risk from second-hand smoke exposure.

When I arrived at Edinburgh Airport for this meeting I heard the announcer say that they had a 'smoking policy' in the airport. Unfortunately this is true: the air quality in the Turnhouse terminal building is extremely poor and the primitive system of allowing open smoking in the communal air space offers no protection whatsoever to either workers or travellers. Let us do something about that before the bicentenary.

Second-hand smoke is a critical issue for the tobacco industry in the Asia Pacific. In 1978 the US Tobacco Institute's lawyers anticipated the problems to come and made the prophetic statement: 'This is the most important challenge we face.' In 1989, at a Philip Morris executive meeting in New York, it was recorded that:

> It is essential that we defeat or substantially water down the Council on Smoking and Health proposal in Hong Kong to ensure that it is not used as a precedent for the region.[18]

The Asia Pacific is vitally important to the tobacco industry. Every single issue of the industry's journal *Tobacco Reporter* focuses on some aspect of Asia Pacific markets, especially in countries such as Vietnam and China.

We need much more emphasis, not just on the victims of tobacco but also on the vectors for tobacco disease. Their containment and the neutralisation of their aggressive marketing of tobacco to youth is a question of political will on the part of governments and the provision of adequate resources in the public health sector. We need to be able constantly to redefine the unacceptable and destroy the social acceptability of the recruitment of children to nicotine addiction. As I indicated earlier, peer-reviewed research has made a considerable impact on attitudes and actions of legislators when they come to consider tobacco control measures in Hong Kong.

The new emergent public health threats

The health sciences are becoming dominated by the genome. In my own medical school as elsewhere there is a headlong flight to molecular biology and genomics. This involves the appropriation of most of the revenue which should be shared between different disciplines. I probably sound like a Luddite but I am concerned that in undergraduate education and research funding, social, environmental and behavioural research is being displaced by the aura of the genome.

Having said that, we all recognise that the use of molecular genetic tools is nowhere more prominent and important than in the area of emergent infectious diseases. In 1969 the US Surgeon General pronounced confidently that 'the book of infectious disease was closed … the war against microbes had been won'.[19] All regions of the world have had reason to fault this extraordinary piece of false optimism during the last 30 years, and that process is continuing. For example, the first outbreak of dengue fever in modern times occurred in Hong Kong in 2002. The emergence of indigenous dengue as a major health problem in more southern parts, for example in the modern urban environments of Singapore and Malaysia, is now a well-established fact of life. In Hong Kong the aedes albopictus mosquito is an inefficient carrier of the disease; nevertheless fuelled by imported cases, it may have established a new endemic pattern.

In 2003 the Hong Kong people and their health care system were completely overwhelmed by the emergent epidemic of severe acute respiratory syndrome (SARS). The cause of the epidemic, a new coronavirus not previously found in either human or animals, was isolated by Professor Malik Peiris in the University of Hong Kong in late March.[20] It is likely to have jumped species from animal reservoirs, and the Himalayan palm civet is the prime suspect. The palm civet is considered to be a delicacy, and a chef in Foshan, Guangdong Province, who specialised in exotic meats, has been identified as the first known case, diagnosed on 16 November 2002.

Also in November 2002 a 46-year-old male senior official, in a village near Foshan in Guangdong Province, became ill with a fever and headache. Three days later he and his wife drove to a hospital in Shiwan, where he was put on an intravenous drip. His condition deteriorated and his family took him to Foshan hospital where he developed diarrhoea and difficulty in breathing and was treated in intensive care. He eventually recovered but then his wife had a similar illness; she also recovered. On 17 December a similar case was treated in Heyuan hospital. This time eight medical staff and eleven other contacts fell ill. On 31 January 2003 a patient from Guangzhou with similar symptoms visited Zhongshan and was admitted to the Second Affiliate Hospital where 30 staff fell ill. He was transferred to the Third Affiliate Hospital where 26 staff were infected along with 19 family members. On 8 February he was transferred to Guangzhou Infectious Diseases Hospital (GIFD). In early February the Guangdong authorities apparently initiated surveillance of the new respiratory disease in the province.

On 15 February a professor of medicine from GIFD developed symptoms and on 21 February he travelled to Hong Kong. He stayed on the ninth floor of the Metropole Hotel. He was unwell with fever and a cough but socialised with his brother-in-law and went shopping. On 22 February he was admitted to hospital and died the next day. Several guests on the ninth floor of the Metropole, whose contact with the professor was apparently confined to congregating in the lift lobby, fell ill. A Chinese-American businessman passing through Hong Kong stayed at the Metropole and later became ill in Hanoi. The outbreak in Vietnam killed many health professionals, including the infectious disease expert who raised the alarm, Dr Carlo Urbani. People infected in the Metropole were admitted to the Prince of Wales Hospital where an explosive outbreak occurred among staff.

On 10 March the epidemic was formally recognised; by 30 April the cumulative total had reached 1,450, including 350 health care staff, and there had been 138 deaths. The calculation of the case fatality rate in the ongoing epidemic (an 'open cohort') led to debate among health authorities and rife speculation in the media.

The lack of disclosure of the true magnitude of the epidemic in mainland China led to a major political adjustment in the sacking of the health minister and mayor of Beijing. By 30 April the counts were in excess of 150 a day. There were a total of 3,300 cases and over 10,000 were in quarantine. A huge building programme was implemented to house quarantined subjects and cases, and the streets of Beijing emptied of the 13 million residents. A massive exodus to the provinces raised concern about the spread of SARS nationwide.

On 29 April, the premier Wen Jiabao, in a remarkably frank exposition at a meeting of ASEAN countries in Bangkok, declared 'China is in a time of difficulty'. The impact on the economy of the Asia Pacific rim was disastrous. The impact on the year's GDP was considerable. The prospect of further mutations and the persistence of an RNA virus, with development of effective vaccines possibly elusive, has caused deep concern.

By April analysis of the transmission dynamics of the epidemic suggested it had receded in Hong Kong to the point where the reproductive rate, an index of its potential to be self-sustaining, had dropped below unity. But uncertainty remained and it was too early to tell if it was aborted, especially as there were thousands of new cases accruing in the mainland, many with inadequate diagnostic, isolation and treatment facilities. It was clear at that time that Hong Kong may have had difficulty in protecting itself.

During the outbreak all teaching in the university stopped and in our department we abandoned all other work and devoted ourselves to working on SARS to support the various health authorities' management plans. In particular, we developed an integrated database from several sources, established a collaborative link with the Department of Infectious Disease at Imperial College (Professor Roy Anderson) and worked to produce useful epidemiological measures of the evolution of the epidemic and its response to various interventions.[21] Most of us knew someone with SARS, some gravely ill on a ventilator several weeks after admission. It became clear that there were to be many late deaths.

It seems likely that SARS will become endemic in this region if not globally. SARS along with the West Nile, hanta and nipa viruses will all lead to a new focus, from undergraduate education to everyday practice. The level of mobility and interconnectedness of Asian countries means that infection will cross borders much more readily than did the bubonic plague in the late 19th and the early 20th century. The border between Hong Kong and Guangdong Province has about 36 million transits each year.

There are many reviews and post-mortems on this event. They include a review of the ecology of the region, where we have high-density farming of pigs, ducks and chickens embedded in high-density human populations. It has been suspected that, as a zoonosis, modern influenza epidemics have developed from the mixing of human and avian species of influenza viruses in pigs. The possibility of other viruses jumping species in this environment will determine what kind of epidemiological transition we experience in the Pearl River delta.

The SARS virus is spread by heavy droplets and contagion of surfaces. The word fomites is now in everyone's vocabulary in all languages. Hong Kong has possibly never been cleaner than it is today. The current frenzy of cleaning signals a sea change in attitudes towards personal and public hygiene. What is also needed is a new investment in public health, including people, training and operational resources. This must include integrated networks of information systems including clinical settings and laboratories, with real time reviews of unusual events and trends.

Someone said 'cities are the graveyards of humankind', but I end by quoting the New York City Board of Health (1915):

> The city can have as much reduction of preventable disease as it wishes to pay for: health is purchasable … and a city can determine its own death rate.

This could surely be true for Edinburgh and Hong Kong in 2003 and in the coming century.

Notes

[1]   Director of Health, Department of Health 1999/2000, 2000/2001 and 2001/2002 Annual Reports (Hong Kong Special Administrative Region Government Printing Department) (online at http://www.info.gov.hk/dh).

[2]   Demography and Dissemination Branch, General Register Office for Scotland (Ladywell House, Edinburgh) (online at http://www.gro-scotland.gov.uk).

[3]   P. Adab, S. M. McGhee, J. Yanova, C. M. Wong and A. J. Hedley, 'Effectiveness and efficiency of opportunistic cervical cancer screening: comparison with organized screening'. *Medical Care* (2004) (forthcoming).

[4]   G. M. Leung, T. Q. Thach, T. H. Lam, A. J. Hedley, W. Foo, R. Fielding, P. S. F. Yip, E. M. C. Lau and C. M. Wong, 'Trends in breast cancer incidence in Hong Kong between 1973 and 1999: an age–period–cohort analysis'. *British Journal of Cancer* 87 (2002): 982–8.

[5]   E. J. G. Elmore, M. B. Barton, V. M. Moceri, S. Polk, P. J. Arena and S. W. Fletcher, 'Ten-year risk of false positive screening mammograms and clinical breast examinations'. *New England Journal of Medicine* 338 (1998):1089–96.

[6]   Director of Health, *Department of Health 1999/2001 Annual Report* (Hong Kong Special Administrative Region Government Printing Department, 2002) (online at http://www.info.gov.hk/dh).

[7]   A. J. Hedley, S. M. McGhee and R. Hardie, *Services for the treatment of patients with tuberculosis in Hong Kong: an audit of information obtained from the medical records of a cohort of patients and its use to support the future planning and evaluation of services* (Hong Kong: Health Services Research Group, Department of Community Medicine, 2000).

[8]   A. S. M. Abdullah, A. J. Hedley and R. Fielding, 'Sexual behaviour in travellers'. The Lancet 353 (1999): 595; A. S. M. Abdullah, R. Fielding and A. J. Hedley, 'Travel, sexual behaviour, and the risk of contracting sexually transmitted diseases'. *Hong Kong Medical Journal* 4 (1998): 137–44.

[9]   http://www.hksdb.org.hk/hksdb/html/pdf/research/200308c.pdf (Hong Kong Sports Institute Research Department, 25 Yuen Wo Road, Shatin, New Territories, Hong Kong).

[10]   J. C. N. Chan and C. S. Cockram, 'Diabetes in the Chinese population and its implications for health care'. *Diabetes Care* 20 (1997): 1785–90.

[11]   J. Peters, A. J. Hedley, C. M. Wong, T. H. Lam, S. G. Ong, J. Liu and D. J. Spiegelhalter, 'Effects of an ambient air pollution intervention and environmental tobacco smoke on children's respiratory health in Hong Kong'. *International Journal of Epidemiology* 25 (1996): 821–8; C. M. Wong, T. H. Lam, J. Peters, A. J. Hedley, S. G. Ong, A. Y. Tam, J. Liu and D. J. Spiegelhalter, 'Comparison between two districts of the effects of an air pollution intervention on bronchial responsiveness in primary school children in Hong Kong'. *Journal of Epidemiology and Community Health* 52 (1998): 571–8.

[12] A. J. Hedley, C. M. Wong, T. Q. Thach, Z. Ma, T. H. La and H. R. Anderson, 'Cardiorespiratory and all-cause mortality after restrictions on sulphur content of fuel in Hong Kong: an intervention study'. *The Lancet* 360 (2002): 1646–52.

[13] Details appear in J. MacKay and M. Eriksen, *Tobacco Atlas* (Geneva: World Health Organization, 2002).

[14] J. Peters, C. L. Betson, A. J. Hedley, T. H. Lam, S. G. Ong, C. M. Wong and R. Fielding, 'Recognition of cigarette brand names and logos by young children in Hong Kong'. *Tobacco Control* 42 (1995): 150–5.

[15] T. H. Lam, S. Y. Ho, A. J. Hedley, K. H. Mak and R. Peto, 'Mortality and smoking in Hong Kong: case-control study of all adult deaths in 1998'. *British Medical Journal* 323 (2001): 361.

[16] T. H. Lam, L. M. Ho, A. J. Hedley, P. Adab, R. Fielding, S. M. McGhee and L. Aharonson-Daniel, 'Environmental tobacco smoke exposure among police officers in Hong Kong'. *Journal of American Medical Association* 284 (2000): 756–63.

[17] S. M. McGhee, P. Adab, A. J. Hedley, T. H. Lam, L. M. Ho, R. Fielding and C. M. Wong, 'Passive smoking at work: the short-term cost'. *Journal of Epidemiology and Community Health* 54 (2000): 673–76.

[18] Philip Morris USA Inc., Document no. 2500101311/1323 (online at http://www.pmdocs.com).

[19] R. Porter, *Blood and Guts: a short history of medicine* (Harmondsworth: Penguin/London: Allen Lane, 2002).

[20] J. S. Peiris, S. T. Lai, L. L. Poon, Y. Guan, L. Y. Yam, W. Lim, J. Nicholls, W. K. Yee, W. W. Yan, M. T. Cheung, V. C. Cheng, K. H. Chan, D. N. Tsang, R. W. Yung, T. K. Ng and K. Y. Yuen (SARS study group), 'Coronavirus as a possible cause of severe acute respiratory syndrome'. *The Lancet* 361 (2003): 1319–25.

[21] C. A. Donnelly, A. C. Ghani, G. M. Leung, A. J. Hedley, C. Fraser, S. Riley, L. J. Abu-Raddad, L. M. Ho, T. Q. Thach, P. Chau, K. P. Chan, T. H. Lam, L. Y. Tse, T. Tsang, S. H. Liu, J. H. Kong, E. M. Lau, N. M. Ferguson and R. M. Anderson, 'Epidemiological determinants of spread of causal agent of severe acute respiratory syndrome in Hong Kong'. *The Lancet* 361 (2003): 1761–6; S. Riley, C. Fraser, C. A. Donnelly, A. C. Ghani, L. J. Abu-Raddad, A. J. Hedley, G. M. Leung, L. M. Ho, T. H. Lam, T. Q. Thach, P. Chau, K. P. Chan, S. V. Lo, P. Y. Leung, T. Tsang, W. Ho, K. H. Lee, E. M. Lau, N. M. Ferguson and R. M. Anderson, 'Transmission dynamics of the etiological agent of SARS in Hong Kong: impact of public health interventions'. *Science* 300 (2003): 1961–6.

8. Ushering in new epidemiology

Gerry Fowkes

Epidemiology is at the core of public health. Since its origins the methods and applications of epidemiology have been evolving in keeping with advances in science and changes in society. I shall briefly describe some history of epidemiology in relation to Edinburgh and the Usher Institute; describe some new applications of epidemiology; and finally mention the future for epidemiology in Edinburgh.

Historical perspective

The University of Edinburgh medical school was at one time one of the few centres of medical excellence in the civilised world. It might be tempting to believe that much of epidemiology began in Edinburgh but the origins occurred well before the formation of the university. Hippocrates, in 400 BC, took an epidemiological perspective in attempting to understand the origins of disease. In his treatise *On Airs, Waters and Places* he stated: 'Stagnant water from marshes … in winter will be cold and muddied by melting snow and ice … this makes it productive of phlegm and hoarseness.'[1] Hippocrates was making an epidemiological observation that there was an association between the frequency of stagnant water and the frequency of phlegm and hoarseness. However, he made the classic epidemiological faux pas of assuming that this association was indicative of a cause and effect relationship.

John Last and Raj Bhopal have described the great pathfinders in public health such as Graunt, Lind, Jenner and Snow. The contribution of Lind, who had a close association with the University of Edinburgh, has been noted. He carried out the first clinical trial, demonstrating that provision of limes to sailors in the British navy prevented the onset of scurvy on long sea voyages. James Lind was a naval surgeon whereas, almost a century later, Sir Henry Littlejohn, who was the first medical officer of health in the city of Edinburgh,[2] was very much a public health doctor. Littlejohn made many important contributions to public health but the most significant of these, from an epidemiological perspective, was that he was the first medical officer of health to carry out an epidemiological survey within a city in the UK. His report on the sanitary conditions of the city of Edinburgh was widely acclaimed and contained many tables describing the frequency of various diseases in the city. For example, he observed that 'diseases of the heart' occurred in 20% of individuals living in the upper New Town compared to only 6% of those living in the lower New Town. Such observations led to various theories and hypotheses about the causes of disease but also to targeted efforts to improve the environmental and sanitary conditions within the city.

Sir Henry Littlejohn, of course, carried out his great work prior to the formation of the Usher Institute in 1902. It was not until the Usher Institute had been in existence for almost half a century that epidemiological work on the investigation of chronic diseases began. Following the Second World War, James Douglas established the first national cohort study of childhood growth and development. This study is still continuing today and is one of the longest-running cohort studies that has been conducted anywhere in the world. In the early 1960s the importance of epidemiology to the evidence base of public health became more widely recognised. Indeed, in 1964, in his inaugural lecture as professor of public health, Professor Stuart Morrison stated:

> Much of the work of academic social medicine is epidemiological; this includes the study of disease in the population or the factors that influence the effect of disease in the community and the measures that can be adopted to prevent, control or limit disease.[3]

Epidemiology began to play a more important part in the activities of the Usher Institute, and in the ensuing years there were two individuals who did much to promote high-quality epidemiological investigation of chronic disease. Mary Fulton conducted studies on coronary heart disease and subsequently lead poisoning in children; Michael Garraway studied the epidemiology of stroke and prostate disease and conducted early randomised controlled trials of day care surgery and the effectiveness of stroke units, using methods that have become commonplace in current health services research. These studies were characterised by rigorous attention to detail and limitation of bias. This approach was undoubtedly influenced by the fact that Mary Fulton, Michael Garraway and others in the Usher Institute had 'learnt their trade' from Professor Jerry Morris – a founding father of modern epidemiology in the UK – at the London School of Hygiene and Tropical Medicine. At the same time, others closely associated with the Usher Institute were carrying out high-quality innovative epidemiology. Rosamund Gruer was almost unique in conducting major studies of high academic calibre in a health service setting, while Michael Heasman and Vera Carstairs were doing much to promote and utilise the national systems of data collection that had been established in Scotland. However, within the Usher Institute itself, the tradition has been primarily not to carry out 'armchair epidemiology' using data collected elsewhere, but rather to conduct 'shoe leather epidemiology' in which the conduct of the survey is itself a major aspect of the work.

New epidemiologies

During the last 20–30 years some new approaches to epidemiology have emerged. Some of these I shall illustrate with reference to work conducted in the Wolfson Unit for Prevention of Peripheral Vascular Diseases in the Usher Institute (today called Public Health Sciences). Although some aspects of epidemiology may be considered 'new', in reality most research develops slowly, building incrementally on previous work. In the Wolfson Unit two of our major studies, the Edinburgh Artery Study[4] and the Edinburgh Vein Study,[5] developed naturally from previous work conducted in Edinburgh. Mary Fulton, Rudolph Riemiersma and Michael Oliver were involved in major studies of coronary heart disease: the Edinburgh Study of Acute Coronary Disease; the Edinburgh Stockholm Study; the Edinburgh Fife Study. Vaughan Ruckley in the Department of Surgery carried out a major investigation of venous disease: the Lothian and Forth Valley Leg Ulcer Study. Our research in Edinburgh has also been built on the epidemiological expertise in peripheral vascular diseases developed elsewhere. Leo Widmer of the University of Basle conducted, in the 1960s and 1970s, the first epidemiological study of peripheral vascular disease – on workers in the pharmaceutical industry.[6]

Turning now to the new epidemiologies, many studies are now employing 'iceberg epidemiology'. The iceberg phenomenon, described in 1963 by John Last,[7] in a simple and illustrative way highlights the fact that much disease is hidden beneath the surface and that in clinical practice we tend to see only a small proportion of the disease burden. In a similar way many epidemiological studies in the past have tended to simply measure clinically overt disease, but advances in technology now permit us to study asymptomatic disease. For example, surveys of peripheral vascular disease formerly employed only questionnaires of intermittent claudication, but more recent surveys have also measured the ankle brachial pressure index (ratio of systolic pressure at the ankle to that at the arm) using Doppler ultrasound. This index has been used by specialist vascular clinicians for many years to indicate the severity of atherosclerosis. Also the advent of duplex scanning has permitted direct non-invasive visualisation of underlying arteries and veins and the assessment of blood flow in these vessels. Such advances mean that in assessing the prevalence of arterial disease in the general population, it has now been possible not only to identify the prevalence of intermittent claudication, but also to demonstrate that there is an even larger proportion of the population with significant asymptomatic disease. We have shown in Edinburgh that these individuals with asymptomatic disease have a greatly increased risk of future major cardiovascular events.[8]

Much epidemiological work over the years has involved the investigation of lifestyle and environmental risk factors. Smoking has been studied intensively in relation to many diseases. Smoking is known to be an important risk factor for peripheral arterial disease and in the Edinburgh Artery Study we demonstrated that a history of smoking occurred more frequently in individuals the greater the severity of disease.[9] In recent years, however, there has been much interest in what might be termed 'multi-level epidemiology' in which, as well as studying environmental risk factors, attention is being paid to intermediary factors and the underlying pathogenesis of disease. For example, it has been suggested that the effects of smoking might be mediated via the coagulation and fibrinolytic system in the blood. Fibrinogen is related to the propensity to clot formation and may be involved in the development of the atheromatus plaque. In the Edinburgh Artery Study individuals who had intermittent claudication or major asymptomatic disease had significantly higher levels of fibrinogen than those with minor asymptomatic or no disease.[10] Also, the plasma fibrinogen level was strongly related to the amount of smoking. So the hypothesis might be that cigarette smoking raises plasma fibrinogen, which in turn leads to an increased development of peripheral arterial disease. However, on conducting multivariate analysis of smoking, fibrinogen and disease it was noted that, at the same levels of plasma fibrinogen, smokers still had a higher frequency of disease than non-smokers.[11] The implication then was that smoking might not only lead to an elevation of plasma fibrinogen but might also enhance any effect of fibrinogen on the risk of disease (Figures 8.1, 8.2 and 8.3).

Genetic epidemiology is the new branch of epidemiology which is creating more excitement than any other recent developments, but it remains to be seen the extent to which this new approach will have a major impact on the public health. In relation to fibrinogen and peripheral arterial disease, it is known that genes affecting the form and production of fibrinogen are located on chromosome 4. We investigated the extent to which an allele at the b fibrinogen locus might affect the risk of developing peripheral arterial disease and might influence plasma fibrinogen levels. Interestingly, we found that genotype was related to peripheral arterial disease; however, any influence was not mediated simply by way of increased fibrinogen concentrations but could be due to a structurally variant fibrinogen or close association with a neighbouring gene.[12]

In keeping with developments in genetic epidemiology there is also greater interest in 'inter-generational epidemiology'. Many well-established epidemiological studies, particularly in the cardiovascular field, are now proceeding to study the offspring of the original cohort. It is well known that environmental factors and lifestyle behaviours such as cigarette smoking are often transmitted from one generation to the next. However, we do not know the extent to which the risk of disease is related to genotype and the mother's nutritional and other status affecting the programming of future disease of the foetus in the womb. This interest is partly a belated recognition on the part of epidemiologists that

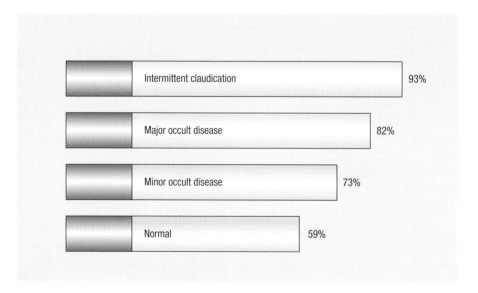

Figure 8.1 Smoking and peripheral arterial disease

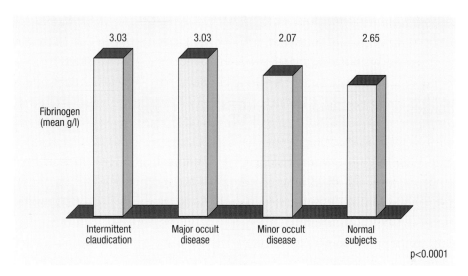

Figure 8.2 Fibrinogen and peripheral arterial disease

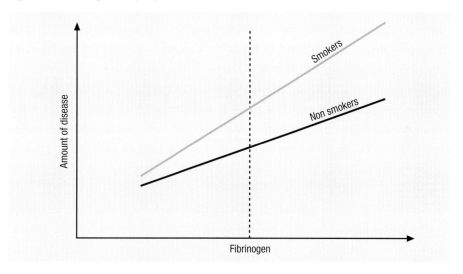

Figure 8.3 Smoking, fibrinogen and peripheral arterial disease

chronic diseases do not simply begin at one point in time but often develop during an individual's lifetime – so-called 'life course epidemiology'. This is well illustrated in relation to the development of atheroma. The earliest observable lesion, the fatty streak, is often observed in children in the early teenage years and from this fatty streak more severe atheroma develops over the years and leads to a wide range of clinical syndromes. Although measuring risk factors at one point in time during an individual's lifetime does provide useful information on their importance, it is only a part of the picture in relation to the development of disease.

The final new epidemiology which I would like to mention is 'big trial epidemiology'. Traditionally in clinical practice many trials have been conducted on small numbers of patients, usually fewer than 100, but to acquire results that are robust and provide reasonable precision on the size of the benefit, much larger numbers are often required. For example, in the Wolfson Unit we have collaborated with Charing Cross Hospital in conducting the UK Small Aneurysm Trial. The dilemma which had been facing vascular surgeons was that if a small asymptomatic abdominal aortic aneurysm was identified, is immediate surgery to repair the aneurysm or routine ultrasound surveillance of the aneurysm the best approach? Surgery would provide an immediate long-lasting solution but unfortunately operative mortality is not insignificant, at around 5%. Surveillance on the other hand would permit surgery only to be carried out if the aneurysm became larger and was at considerably increased risk of rupturing and causing death. On the other hand, surgery carried out later might entail greater risks for the patient and an aneurysm might rupture between surveillance examinations. We therefore carried out a randomised controlled trial of these two approaches and found that there was indeed, after five years of follow up, no statistically significant difference in survival for individuals having major surgery or ultra sound surveillance.[13] On the other hand, those having surgery had an immediate mortality suggesting that the best approach overall was to recommend routine surveillance. The large size of the trial provided robust findings and produced a result which has been clinically convincing to surgeons and has led to changes in vascular practice in the UK and elsewhere.

Thus during the last two decades or so we have seen the emergence of several new epidemiologies: iceberg epidemiology, multi-level epidemiology, genetic epidemiology, inter-generational epidemiology, life-course epidemiology, and big trial epidemiology (Figure 8.4). There may well be others but certainly in recent years in the Usher Institute these new approaches have been utilised – not only in the Wolfson Unit investigating vascular disease, but also by others such as Freda Alexander and Harry Campbell in their research on cancer.

Epidemiology in Edinburgh: the future

During the last few years, major reorganisation and restructuring within the faculty of medicine and the University of Edinburgh has taken place so that this provides an opportunity to plan the future of epidemiological and other aspects of research in the Usher Institute. Epidemiological investigations are becoming

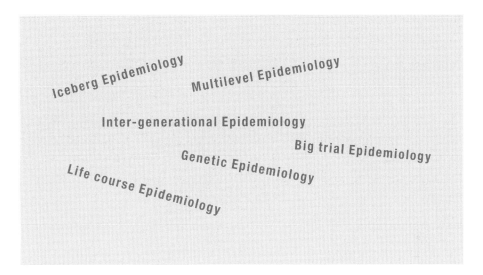

Figure 8.4 'New epidemiology'

more complex and, with the opportunity of encompassing the new epidemiologies, it is not possible to have the wide-ranging portfolio that might have been possible in the past. Our intention is to focus our efforts primarily on cancer and cardio-vascular disease – in which we already have some strength – and to develop the current interest of Pam Warner in reproductive health.

The university is committed to concentrating its research efforts in a series of new research centres. A new Centre for Public Health and Primary Care Research has just been established. This will act as the focus for our epidemiological endeavours, although at the same time we will be working very closely with other very important centres in the university such as the Centre for Cardiovascular Science, Centre for Cancer, Centre for Reproductive Science and Centre for Neuro-science Research. Within the Centre for Public Health and Primary Care Research the approach will be very much multi-disciplinary, encompassing epidemiology, the social sciences, primary care and statistics. This multi-disciplinary approach will, I believe, provide added value and greater insights into the cause, management and prevention of disease. This should ensure that epidemiology in the Usher Institute continues to have a bright and productive future.

Notes

[1]   J. Chadwick and W. N. Mann (trans), *The Medical Works of Hippocrates* (Springfield, Ill.: C. C. Thomas, 1950).

[2]   H. D. Littlejohn, *Report on the Sanitary Condition of the City of Edinburgh* (Edinburgh: Edinburgh City Council, 1865).

[3]   U. Maclean, *The Usher Institute and the Evolution of Community Medicine in Edinburgh* (Edinburgh: Department of Community Medicine, 1975), pp. 1–47.

[4]   F. G. R. Fowkes, E Housley, E. H. H. Cawood , C. C. A. Macintyre, C. V. Ruckley and R. J. Prescott, 'Edinburgh Artery Study: prevalence of asymptomatic and symptomatic peripheral arterial disease in the general population'. *International Journal of Epidemiology* 20 (1991): 384–92.

[5]   J. Evans, F. G. R. Fowkes, C. V. Ruckley and A. J. Lee, 'Prevalence of varicose veins and chronic venous insufficiency in men and women in the general population: Edinburgh Vein Study'. *Journal of Epidemiology and Community Health* 53 (1999): 149–53.

[6]   L. K. Widmer, H. B. Stahelin, C. Nissen and A. da Silva, *Venen-, Arterien- Krankheiten, Koronare Herzkrankheit bei Berufstätigen* (Bern: Hans Huber, 1981).

[7]   J. M. Last, 'The iceberg: completing the clinical picture in general practice'. *The Lancet* 2 (1963): 28–31.

[8]   G. C. Leng, A. J. Lee, F. G. R. Fowkes, M. Whiteman, J. Dunbar, E. Housley and C. V. Ruckley, 'Incidence, natural history and cardiovascular events in symptomatic and asymptomatic peripheral arterial disease in the general population'. *International Journal of Epidemiology* 25 (1996): 1172–81.

[9] F. G. R. Fowkes, E. Housley, R. A. Riemersma, C. C. A. Macintyre, E. H. H. Cawood, R. J. Prescott and C. V. Ruckley, 'Smoking, lipids, glucose intolerance, and blood pressure as risk factors for peripheral atherosclerosis compared to ischaemic heart disease in the Edinburgh Artery Study'. *American Journal of Epidemiology* 135 (1992): 331–40.

[10]   G. D. O. Lowe, F. G. R. Fowkes, J. Dawes, P. T. Donnan, S. E. Lennie and E. Housley, 'Blood viscosity, fibrinogen and activation of coagulation and leucocytes in peripheral arterial disease and the normal population in the Edinburgh Artery Study'. *Circulation* 87 (1993): 1915–20.

[11]   Ibid.

[12]   F. G. R. Fowkes, J. M. Connor, F. B. Smith, J. Wood, P. T. Donnan and G. D. O. Lowe, 'Fibrinogen genotype and risk of peripheral atherosclerosis'. *The Lancet* 339 (1992): 693–6.

[13]   UK Small Aneurysm Trial Participants, 'Mortality results for randomised controlled trial of early elective surgery or ultrasound surveillance for small abdominal aortic aneurysms'. *The Lancet* 352 (1998): 1649–55.

9. Social sciences and public health: facing the challenges

Sarah Cunningham-Burley

The place of public health in the medical school at the University of Edinburgh has changed over the past 100 years, physically and conceptually, as have the roles of public health, as discipline and practice, in influencing the health of the public within Scotland and elsewhere.

These have also been 100 years of enormous social change, perhaps increasing in scope in the postmodern era. As Giddens has said, 'we live today in an era of stunning social change, marked by transformations radically discrepant from those of previous periods.'[1] The upheavals of the industrial revolution invigorated public health and sociology alike, but old certainties have come to be questioned – diseases have not been eradicated, family life has changed markedly, work patterns have been transformed as a result of de-industrialisation, and old ways of knowing and explaining the world around us seem inadequate. Nonetheless, some old values and structures continue despite such change, and they may continue to underpin some of our approaches to understanding and improving public health. Social science, as one of the core disciplines in public health, seeks to understand social change and the social processes underlying it and to examine relationships at the societal and cultural level.

Despite a long history of association, the relationship between social science and public health is necessarily and creatively one of tension and ambivalence. Social science leads us to question even those values we might hold most dear. Health is one such 'taken-for-granted' value and therefore needs our sociological attention. It constructs much of our everyday experience: being healthy, it seems, is something that we should all aspire to by controlling our own bodies and ourselves. Yet, of course, social science has already told us that we do not really do that – at least not all the time. Many studies show how individuals stray from the strictures of individual health surveillance promoted by institutions concerned about the health of the public; how they have their own perceptions of risk; and how behaviour is embedded in a social context. For example, when interviewing North Americans Crawford found that a discourse of personal control was countered by one of release.[2] Backett, interviewing middle-class Scottish people, found that they justified their health-related behaviours in terms of balance and moderation along with age-related risk taking.[3]

It seems that, just as we reach a point in health gain where we can be more assured of our own health and longevity, increasing focus is being placed on health maintenance. Health is experienced as precarious or problematic – and potentially always at risk. Whole industries and 'technologies of the self'[4] have been built up to sustain such a view of health. Relatedly, just as we come to question, increasingly, the results of modern medicine, evident through increased scepticism and distrust of scientific institutions, we are also ever more reliant on high-technology medicine and pharmaceuticals. Such ambivalence is characteristic of a 'risk society',[5] where risk creation and management dominate our institutions and our lives.

Social science must always make us uncomfortable – conducting research at the margins, turning upside down what we take for granted. We do not want, as Beck has caricatured, 'a sociology so specialised in the status quo that it becomes the status quo'.[6] We need always to be asking questions, such as why health, whose health, which publics and in whose interests?

I shall highlight both general and specific elements of the contribution of social science to public health, using illustrative examples from work conducted at the University of Edinburgh over the last 20 years or so. The future, as I shall conclude, is one of challenges and promise.

Social science and public health: educational embeddedness

Public health at the University of Edinburgh seems to have always been multidisciplinary – professors came from a variety of backgrounds. At first, the 'social' side was trusted to the broad vision and minds of successive professors, whether public health was linked to sanitary science or bacteriology. Keen to understand the human condition, they also wanted to inculcate an appropriate sense of citizenship and the 'whole person' into the minds of undergraduates and postgraduates alike. Public health has long recognised the need to understand the relationship between the individual and his or her environment.[7] But, from the late 1950s onwards, social science became an institutionalised part of the teaching of medicine and public health – part of the status quo, though doubtless always somewhat marginal.

Comparing the curriculum from the days of Dr Fred Martin in the 1960s to that of now, it is perhaps not so very different – there was an emphasis on the whole person, on the social context, on understanding human behaviour and social institutions. Concepts such as social class and social stratification, the mainstay of sociological understandings of society at the time, were being taught, as was the understanding of families. Promoting social critique and sensitising students to wider social issues were aims then as they are now.

Our reach today is, I hope, further and deeper and our teaching methods are more diverse, including more self-directed learning. Undergraduates have the opportunity in their first year for first-hand experience of the 'real world' through 'talking to families', which is run by Mike Porter from the General Practice as part of Health and Society course, itself a core component of the new under-graduate curriculum.

From the 1960s onwards social sciences in general were developing across universities, building a stronger theoretical and empirical base. Trends in sociology, especially the rise in social constructionism and the adoption of approaches stemming from phenomenology, influenced the practice of medical sociology. The specialty gradually changed from being something of a branch of social medicine to a sub-discipline of sociology, with the essential position of critique that implies. Exploring and understanding lay people's own views and experiences of health and illness, as well as examining issues of social structure and its influence on health, are core elements to this critique.

Researching for the new public health

The new public health and the rise of health promotion from the 1970s onwards reinvigorated an emphasis on social conditions and their influence on health.

One of the most significant contributions of social sciences and social epidemiology in the 1980s and 1990s was to keep inequalities in health on the research agenda and, wherever possible, in the public and political sphere. This was, of course, against the political grain at a time when most emphasis was placed on individual behavioural factors. This emphasis was in deliberate opposition to the recommendations of the Black Report.[8] The Research Unit in Health and Behavioural Change (RUHBC), when it was set up in the 1980s, was conceptually, if not administratively, linked to public health and health promotion. RUHBC published a book which helped to define the field and set an agenda for social science research, highlighting the ways in which social science contributes to public health while at the same time shaping it.[9] The challenge of the new public health is that it must take inequalities seriously, listen to lay perspectives, understand behaviour in its social context and broaden its focus from disease to health. I will focus on four themes which, although by no means exhaustive, help illustrate the contribution social science has made to the academic discipline of public health at the University of Edinburgh: inequalities in health; lay perspectives; involving communities and evaluating interventions; and the new genetics.

Inequalities in health

The health effects of massive social upheaval are now strongly evident in eastern Europe. There are more subtle effects here – we see it in the rise of mental health problems in young men, smoking amongst young women and Scotland's continued poor health record compared with much of the rest of western Europe. Concern about housing and health persists today, just as it was present 100 years ago.

Platt, Martin, Hunt and Lewis conducted a survey of housing conditions and health in 1988 in Edinburgh, Glasgow and London. Identifying the need for such work came from a local community, and their involvement continued throughout the project and its dissemination – something very innovative at the time. The study was well designed and analysis took into account confounding factors. They found that only 30.8% of the public housing surveyed was dry; the rest was either damp (23.3%) or mouldy (45.9%). Adult respondents (mostly female) in damp or mouldy dwellings were likely to report more symptoms overall. Most worrying of all was the finding that children living in damp and mouldy dwellings had a greater prevalence of respiratory symptoms (wheeze, sore throat, runny nose), headaches and fever compared with those living in dry dwellings.[10] Findings were taken back to the community as well as published in academic journals and there was a direct influence on policy and practice in some areas. The study also showed the value of working across disciplines, with microbiologists, to understand the factors influencing the public's health. The new Research Centre on Public Health and Primary Care will continue to focus on issues relating to inequalities in health as one of the key problems of and for public health.

Lay perspectives

Another area where social science makes a significant contribution is in the examination of lay perspectives. How people understand issues relating to health, illness and risk is essential for public health. People's own interpretations and ways of making sense of the world must be considered valuable and insightful of the constraints and contexts in which they operate.

The research profile of social sciences in public health began to develop within the changing context of academic public health (increasingly defined as a research-based discipline) and research on lay understandings was produced. Una Maclean had conducted seminal work in west Africa, exploring people's reactions to misfortune and their use of local healers; and she demonstrated how Western medicine could only be effective if it worked with rather than against local culture.[11] This 'meaning-centred' approach was then used in a more local context, in a project that examined mothers' perceptions of their children's illnesses. Very little work at that time had taken the views of women seriously, or moved away from a focus on medically defined symptoms and disease. Irvine and Cunningham-Burley found that mothers' perceptions of normality underpinned their negotiation of illness; however, the concept of normality was dynamic – it changed over time but was related to common-sense knowledge about what was normal and acceptable in a child of a particular age.[12] More specifically, it was found that a process of monitoring and evaluating behavioural change was used by mothers to interpret what was going on with their children. These findings are very relevant for primary care, as what is important for mothers is not the same as what is important for general practitioners in making a medical diagnosis. Relatedly, Cunningham-Burley and Maclean found that far from 'bothering the doctor with trivia' the women studied were most likely to use proprietary medicines and home remedies/nursing.[13] At the time little was known about patients' behaviour before consultation, although the 'symptom iceberg' had been identified.[14] This led the researchers to conclude that the first question a general practitioner should ask a parent bringing in a child is: 'What have you done so far?'[15] This work places the mother as an expert in interpreting her own child's health and health-related symptoms.

Concern with young children and family health has been part of public health from the early 20th century onwards. Social science is making an important contribution to understanding children's perspectives. The need to listen to young people and children about issues affecting their lives lies at the heart of government policy and is enshrined in European, UK and Scottish legislation.

Considerable work on young people and health is being conducted within Public Health at the University of Edinburgh, particularly looking at the social context of health behaviours. One recent contribution, funded under the Economic and Social Research Council's 'Children 5–16' programme, focuses on younger children aged 9–12 and adds a lived-experience dimension to debates about health inequalities – all the more important given that understanding children's lives must be a precursor to improving them.

In this study in-depth interviews using child-appropriate techniques were conducted with 35 girls and boys from contrasting areas of the city along with 30 of their parents.[16] Children and parents described starkly contrasting lives and opportunities, which regularly involved material differences. However, children appeared to locate inequalities as much in relationships and social life as in material concerns. They spoke of the importance of control over their life-world, of friendship and acceptance. The effects of material inequalities seemed to be downplayed, demonstrating resilience on the part of children and their families. Children seemed to moderate their demands, and families seemed to moderate the effects of material inequality – the more affluent by 'not spoiling' and the less affluent through putting their children first, or through the use of resources outwith the nuclear family. Parents and children seemed openly to embrace a discourse of 'no difference' while still noticing and dealing with difference in material and social status.

Involving communities and evaluating interventions

Involving communities also lies at the heart of much government policy, in an attempt to improve health and tackle social exclusion and poverty. However, health, morality and the maintenance of social order are now linked in more subtle guises than they were in the late 19th century.

Smoking is a major cause of inequalities in health among women in Scotland. It is the single most important preventable cause of ill health and premature death among women in Scotland. Graham has pointed out that smoking is now associated with social and material disadvantage, whereas once it was associated with affluence. Smoking is one way of dealing with the pressures of gender and class disadvantage, and thus also a way of containing them.[17] Amos and colleagues have been involved in developing community-based approaches to smoking reduction which are sensitive to women's needs and day-to-day lives.[18] Exploratory research directly influenced subsequent policy emphasising community-level approaches to smoking reduction. However, the extent to which involving local communities in matters of health and health inequalities is likely to result in positive health outcomes, or even meet the expectations of communities, remains to be thoroughly explored.

Lewis, Saulnier and Renaud argue that 'the evidence for health-oriented social policy is epistemologically less solid than the evidence arising from controlled clinical trials at the heart – in theory – of contemporary medicine.'[19] Medical methods are not always suitable ways to investigate or evaluate the non-medical problems of public health.[20]

The Healthy Living Centre (HLC) programme of the Scottish Executive's New Opportunities Fund aims to improve quality of life, health and well-being among the most disadvantaged in society and to reduce health inequalities. RUHBC is involved in evaluating Healthy Living Centres, and the aim of the study, involving six diverse HLCs, is to explore pathways between activities, processes, contexts and outcomes. Multiple qualitative techniques – individual face-to-face interviews, telephone and group interviews, observation of participants and activities, and documentary analysis – are being used. In this way, the team is extending the reach of evaluation research through methodological pluralism and thus extending the evidence base of public health policy.

Lay and professional expertise – the challenge of the new genetics

The new genetics poses particular challenges for social scientists as well as for public health. Concerns about geneticisation of disease and society have been raised, as well as concerns about the concept of informed or individual choice around issues such as genetic testing.[21] Much debate is centred on professionals' constructions and the management of genetic and eugenic risks. What counts as a social concern is often conceptualised as relating to the application of knowledge rather than to the production of knowledge itself.

Work conducted in Edinburgh by Kerr, Cunningham-Burley and Amos highlighted the existence of lay expertise relating to genetics and explored the use of focus groups in enabling such expertise to be displayed.[22] Ambivalence was expressed about a range of issues, suggesting the need for more inclusive public debate and involvement.

Kerr and Cunningham-Burley have argued that sociological analyses of the new genetics are crucial in order to generate open discussion of contemporary practices. This should include working with those directly engaged in the production and application of the new technologies in order to create better regulation and a more thorough consideration of the responsibilities and interests of professionals, users and the broader communities of interest in which these technologies develop and operate. 'By combining detailed empirical and theoretical insights into the new human genetics, we must continue to provoke and challenge, not relieve and mollify, policy-makers and experts.'[23]

Social science and public health: facing the challenges of the future

In their introduction to *The Handbook of Social Studies in Health and Medicine*, three prominent social scientists – Gary Albrecht, professor of public health at the University of Illinois at Chicago, Ray Fitzpatrick, professor of public health and primary care, University of Oxford, and Susan Scrimshaw, professor of community health sciences and anthropology at the University of Illinois at Chicago – identify a number of challenges for social scientists involved in health. These are highly relevant to any conclusion about the relationship between social science and public health specifically and social science and medicine more generally:

> a ... challenge to our ability to contribute to understanding that is immediately sensed by anyone involved in the social sciences and health is the limited resource invested in the social compared with the

biomedical sciences. Despite occasional and growing institutional scepticism about the capacity of biomedical sciences alone to deliver all that is promised, the allure to public and private funding sources of supporting the biomedical sciences is enormous.

Despite growing recognition of the need to complement biomedical with social scientific understanding of the nature of health and illness, the social sciences will always struggle to attract the scale of funding of their biomedical colleagues. With funds come glamour, attention, impact, and a voice to shape policy. The social sciences will continue to work with more modest resources and a limited voice.[24]

Another challenge, they say, is the two seemingly contradictory roles of social sciences. They are:

established disciplines with their own body of knowledge, thinking and commentary of the social world but are also part of the problem solving system that seeks to explain, prevent, cure or manage disease – whether it's government, health care professionals, medical or other scientists, or publics and providers that seek our help.[25]

This echoes the earlier distinction, made originally by Strauss in 1957 and repeated in most text books on medical sociology and no doubt in many an introductory lecture – namely a sociology 'in' and 'of' medicine.[26] The former involves working in an applied context, the latter analysing from without.

In Public Health Sciences at the University of Edinburgh I think we are uniquely placed to meet these challenges. Social scientists are many now, not few, and the Division of Community Health Sciences incorporates not only those working in public health, but also in general practice and in the associated research centres – RUHBC, the Centre for Research on Families and Relationships and the Research Centre for Public Health and Primary Care. Those working outside the College of Medicine and Veterinary Medicine are linked through the Inter-disciplinary Research Group: Social Processes, Society and Health.

Social science within Public Health at Edinburgh is interdisciplinary and pluralistic in its approach – with a broad commitment to a range of social science perspectives, both theoretical and methodological. It aims to be collaborative, not only within the diverse social science disciplines, but also with a range of clinical, biomedical and epidemiological subjects. Collaborations extend to those outside academia interested in research and dissemination, thus helping to build bridges between research, policy and practice. The social scientists working in public health at the University of Edinburgh embrace the multi-disciplinary environment of public health in the 21st century, yet retain a strong link to our parent disciplines, thus bridging the 'in and of' divide, and making creative use of the tensions this brings.

We are directly involved in research and research training, gaining funds from a variety of sources (Economic and Social Research Council, Medical Research Council, the Scottish Executive, research charities), thus ensuring a future for public health research and practice. The vibrancy of our postgraduate community is testament to this – social scientists, for example, are studying for PhDs in a range of topics relevant for academic public health and public health practice, whether this be working with epidemiologists to develop cross-culturally sensitive instruments appropriate for the lay population of multi-ethnic Britain, or examining participants' perspectives relating to randomised controlled trials for preventive medication. They are exploring young people's knowledge and behaviour relating to tobacco and cannabis use, examining the process of developing smoking reduction projects at local level and exploring contested values of partnership working for inequalities in health, to highlight but a few.

We are committed to improving the health of the public as well as shaping the future of public health as a broad-based multi-disciplinary endeavour that must never lose sight of its civic role. Public health faces its own challenges at a time of rapid change in our knowledge at a molecular level – echoing perhaps the biological transformations at the turn of the last century. This area – perhaps more than any other – evokes partnership between social science, genetics and public health.

Being critical and reflexive is essential in social science, and it must become second nature to all those who seek to understand and influence the factors that promote health and well-being and those that cause disease and ill health.

Notes

1   A. Giddens, *Modernity and Self-Identity* (Oxford: Blackwell, 1991), p. xv.

2   R. Crawford, 'A cultural account of "health": control, release, and the social body', in J. McKinlay (ed.), *Issues in the Political Economy of Health Care* (London: Tavistock, 1984).

3   K. Backett, 'Taboos and excesses: lay health moralities in middle class families'. *Sociology of Health and Illness* 14 (1992): 255–74.

4   Giddens, *Modernity and Self-Identity*.

5   U. Beck, *Risk Society: towards a new modernity* (London: Sage, 1992).

6   U. Beck, *The Reinvention of Politics: rethinking modernity in the global social order* (Cambridge: Polity Press, 1997), p. 18.

7   U. Maclean, *The Usher Institute and the Evolution of Community Medicine in Edinburgh*, (Edinburgh: Department of Community Medicine, 1975), pp. 1–47.

8   P. Townsend and N. Davidson, *Inequalities in Health* [the Black Report] (Harmondsworth: Penguin, 1982).

9   Research Unit in Health and Behavioural Change, *Changing the Public Health* (Chichester: John Wiley and Sons, 1989).

10   D. S. Platt, C. Martin, S. Hunt and C. Lewis, 'Damp housing, mould growth, and symptomatic health state'. *British Medical Journal* 298 (1989): 1673–8.

11   U. Maclean, *Magical Medicine* (London: Allen Lane, 1971).

12   S. Irvine and S. Cunningham-Burley, 'Mothers' concepts of normality, behavioural change and illness in their children'. *British Journal of General Practice* 41 (1991): 371–4.

13   S. Cunningham-Burley and C. M. U. Maclean, 'The role of the chemist in primary health care for children with minor complaints'. *Social Science and Medicine* 24 (1987): 371–7.

14   D. Hannay, *The Symptom Iceberg: a study of community health* (London: Routledge and Kegan Paul, 1979).

15   S. Cunningham-Burley and S. Irvine, '"And have you done anything so far?" An examination of lay treatment of children's symptoms'. *British Medical Journal* 295 (1987): 700–2.

16   K. Milburn, S. Cunningham-Burley and J. Davis, 'Contrasting lives, contrasting views? Understandings of health inequalities from children in differing social circumstances'. *Social Science and Medicine* 57 (2003): 613–23.

17   H. Graham, 'Women's smoking and family health'. *Social Science and Medicine* 1 (1983): 47–56.

18   For example, E. Crossan and A. Amos, *Under a Cloud: women, low income and smoking* (Edinburgh: HMSO, 1994).

19   S. Lewis, M. Saulnier and M. Renaud, 'Reconfiguring health policy: simple truths, complex solutions', in G. L. Albrecht, R. Fitzpatrick and S. C. Scrimshaw (eds), *The Handbook of Social Studies in Health and Medicine* (London: Sage, 2000), pp. 509–24, 513.

20   J. Gabbay, 'The socially constructed dilemmas of academic public health', in S. Griffiths and D. J. Hunter (eds), *Perspectives in Public Health* (Oxford: Radcliffe Medical Press, 1999), pp. 261–8.

21   A. Lippman, 'Prenatal genetic testing and screening: constructing needs and reinforcing inequities'. *Amercian Journal of Law and Medicine* 17 (1992): 15–30; T. Marteau and M. Richards (eds), *The Troubled Helix: social and psychological implications of the new human genetics* (Cambridge: Cambridge University Press, 1996).

22   A. Kerr, S. Cunningham-Burley and A. Amos, 'Drawing the line: an analysis of lay people's discussions about the new genetics'. *Public Understanding of Science* 7 (1998): 113–33.

23   A. Kerr and S. Cunningham-Burley, 'On ambivalence and risk: reflexive modernity and the new human genetics'. *Sociology* 43.2 (2000): 283–304, 298.

24   Albrecht, Fitzpatrick and Scrimshaw, *The Handbook of Social Studies in Health and Medicine*, p. 2.

25   Ibid. 3.

26   A. Strauss, 'The nature and status of medical sociology'. *American Sociological Review* 22 (1957): 200–4.

10. Communicable disease conquered?

Colin N. Ramsay

In 1969, the US Surgeon General W. H. Stewart stated: 'It is time to close the book on infectious diseases.' He and many others at the time felt that communicable disease, as a significant cause of human morbidity and mortality, was a spent force that could be safely consigned to history.

Yet, by 1982, the US Congress was holding hearings on infectious disease in response to the emerging threat from AIDS and HIV infection, and asking the question: 'why do we have so many new infectious diseases?' Dr Richard Krause of the US National Institutes of Health responded by saying: 'Nothing new has happened, plagues are as certain as death and taxes.'

Rather than being seen as an historical aberration, a mere transient phase in human experience, the phenomenon of communicable disease and its impact on mankind might be better looked upon as an ongoing saga, a saga in the truest sense. Traditional Scandinavian sagas were historical accounts describing family lineages and heroic achievements. The saga of communicable disease can be viewed as a historical narrative of the entire human family, featuring heroic endeavours, notable setbacks and celebrated victories.

The late-20th-century cinematic saga *Star Wars* also has a familiar story line of triumphs and setbacks, chronicled in episodes entitled 'A New Hope', 'The Empire Strikes Back', 'Attack of the Clones' and with, at the time of writing, an as yet incomplete and untitled final chapter. These titles have a convenient resonance with the tale of mankind and communicable disease, and will be borrowed (with acknowledgements to George Lucas and colleagues) to chart the episodes of what could be so aptly called 'Bug Wars'.

Prologue

To start as all good sagas start. A long time ago in a place far, far away, the enslavement of mankind to communicable disease began. Man became the unwitting victim of his impatient desire for progress, his evolution from hunter-gatherer to a more settled agrarian society. Early humans lived as isolated tribal groupings or as nomadic travellers, spending very little time in large groups, relying on wild animals and the native flora for food. This changed in some of the first recognisable civilisations in the land between the Tigris and Euphrates, in historical Mesopotamia, modern Iraq.

As social evolution continued, previously isolated cultures made contact through war, conquest, trade and commerce. History became a chronicle of devastated populations, each succumbing to diseases carried by infected visitors. The course of human history, the rise and fall of empires and the gradual predominance of western culture were shaped by the spread of epidemic infections such as measles, smallpox, plague and tuberculosis.

By the mid-1800s, infectious disease was still the major cause of death and illness on a global scale. Edinburgh, capital of Scotland, was typical of cities of that era in having a tally of infection-related death and disease as illustrated by contemporary data (Table 10.1). In 1863 deaths due to diseases such as measles, scarlet fever and diphtheria were relatively common (zymotic disease), as was fatal tuberculosis (phthisis). These diseases predominated due to poor hygiene standards and over-crowding, as illustrated by the population density – four times that of modern Edinburgh.

Episode 1: 'A new hope' – the public health era

In a few enlightened and important cities such as Edinburgh, the first glimmerings of 'a new hope' were seen. Pioneering figures such as John Snow began to lay the foundations of modern day infectious disease epidemiology by mapping the cholera epidemics in London. Edwin Chadwick did much to uncover the plight of the poor and common people. The first medical officers of health were appointed with a specific remit to improve the health of their communities, just as Dr Henry Duncan Littlejohn set out to do in Edinburgh. The focus of their efforts was communicable disease.

The role of environmental factors such as contaminated drinking water in spreading disease became apparent, providing the stimulus to develop clean and safe municipal drinking water supplies. The relationship between the incidence of

Table 10.1. City of Edinburgh: infectious disease statistics, 1863–1972

Year	Population	Birth rate	Death rate	Infant mortality rate	Phthisis death rate	Zymotic diseases death rate	Area of city (acres)	Density of population (persons per acre)
1863	170,444	34.2	25.9	145	2.5	6.2	–	49.0
1908	350,761	20.8	14.2	114	1.1	0.7	11,416	30.7
1923	425,298	20.4	13.8	82	0.9	0.9	32,526	13.1
1930	425,951	18.8	14.2	82	0.8	0.7	32,525	13.1
1938	469,448	16.1	12.7	61	0.3	0.3	32,526	14.4
1953	470,847	15.4	12.3	24	0.2	0.1	33,183	14.2
1963	476,228	17.9	13.1	23	0.03	0.1	34,781	13.7
1972	449,632	12.9	12.9	15	0.04	0.1	34,781	12.9

SOURCE: H. P. Tait, *A Doctor and Two Policemen: the history of Edinburgh Health Department 1862–1974* (Edinburgh: Edinburgh Health Department, 1974).

infection and other factors such as nutrition, overcrowding, unsanitary conditions, poverty and population density became better understood.

Concepts such as the surveillance of disease were introduced in the form of a system of notifiable diseases, based on the compulsory reporting of clinical cases. Systematic recording of data was the first step in assessing the scale of the problem and the first element needed to develop disease control strategies. Isolation of infected cases, their removal to publicly funded infectious diseases hospitals and the quarantine of contacts became familiar routines.

Towards the end of the Victorian era, the early reliance of public health control measures on the identification of clinically ill cases was augmented by the increasing contribution of the new science of microbiology, exemplified by the work of Pasteur, Koch and others. This was the point where public health in Edinburgh took shape in the Usher Institute, mirroring similar developments across Europe. Theories relating to the role of the environment in the spread of infection were vindicated by the work of the early microbiologists, including Koch confirming the discovery of the cholera vibrio.

The first counter-strike in the 'Bug Wars' had begun. The first significant steps to reduce the impact of pathogens on population health were taken. Gradually, the killer epidemics were controlled and their causal factors managed through preventive strategies. The universal provision of safe supplies of water for drinking, washing and sanitation helped to control diseases such as cholera, typhoid and dysentery. Techniques of food preservation and food hygiene helped reduce further the toll associated with gastro-intestinal infections. The invention of pasteurisation alone helped to reduce the burden of disease associated with contaminated milk, including diseases such as salmonella, brucellosis, Q-fever, bovine strain tuberculosis and staphylococcal food poisoning. Improvements in nutrition and in housing standards, the reduction of overcrowding and reduced population densities contributed to the progressive decline in the burden of diseases such as respiratory tuberculosis, as shown by the data from Edinburgh between 1863 and 1972 (see Table 10.1).

The advent of vaccination against smallpox in 1798, and later of various other forms of active and passive immunisation, further reduced the already declining impact of infections such as diphtheria, tetanus, polio, pertussis, tuberculosis and measles in Edinburgh, within the UK and in the rest of the developed world. From the 1940s onwards, the successful development of antibiotics for treating infections reduced the burden of mortality and morbidity even further.

Hence, by the 1970s, the situation in Edinburgh, as elsewhere, had improved beyond all recognition and gave rise to the optimistic but, with hindsight, complacent perception typified by the US Surgeon General's comment. The 'bugs' seemed to be in full retreat. More and more opportunities for primary prevention arose with vaccines for mumps, rubella, haemophilus influenzae type b, hepatitis A and B, meningococcus and influenza.

The first complete victory against a virus was with smallpox. In 1958 smallpox was endemic in 33 countries and killed approximately 2 million people world-wide. The World Health Organization (WHO) declared a worldwide vaccination campaign to eradicate the disease. After a mammoth effort of organisation and global cooperation, the last natural case of Variola Major (classical smallpox) was recorded in Somalia in 1977. Tragically, the last human case in 1978 was not due to natural infection but to the escape of the virus from a research laboratory in Birmingham, UK. In 1980, WHO declared the global eradication of the smallpox, the first disease in human history to be eradicated by human efforts. Stocks of the virus were, however, retained by the USA and the USSR for 'research' purposes and have since been acquired by a few other nations.

The successful eradication of smallpox remains the only complete victory against the pathogens to date. The campaign succeeded thanks largely to the effective organisation of disease surveillance, as well as the planning of vaccination by WHO. Smallpox was a good candidate for eradication. The disease was spread from person to person. There were no other potentially problematic animal or other environmental vectors to control. The disease had a relatively short incubation period and was readily diagnosed by clinical observation alone, allowing the rapid identification of individual cases. The prompt control of outbreaks was made possible by vaccinating known contacts of the cases – the containment strategy. Few other diseases have such accommodating characteristics, hence the slow progress in eradicating other serious global threats to health.

The next WHO target for eradication, polio, is gradually being beaten into submission, with only a few remaining pockets of resistance in Africa and Asia. Hopes are high that eradication will be achieved in the next few years.

Vaccination then and now has proved to be one of the most useful weapons of the 'new hope' era. Even where eradication has not occurred there have been significant reductions, even in recent years, in the incidence of diseases such as measles, mumps and rubella thanks to the use of combined vaccines (Figure 10.1). Most recently the incidence of meningococcal infection due to meningococcus C strains has fallen in the UK in association with the introduction of universal vaccination.

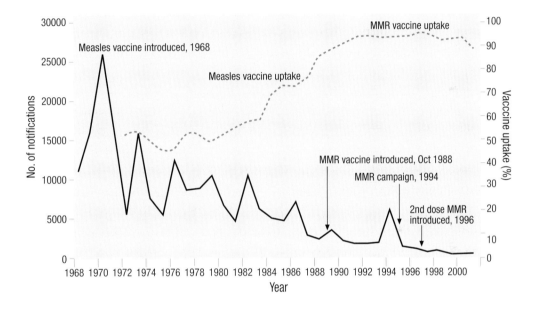

Figure 10.1 Measles notifications in Scotland, 1968–2001

Vaccination as a strategy is not without its problems. In 1968 a global epidemic (a pandemic) of Hong Kong influenza A occurred, with massive global morbidity and significant mortality. In 1976 an outbreak of 'swine' influenza occurred at Fort Dix, USA, causing the death of a fit young serviceman. This prompted immediate concern that this was the harbinger of the next pandemic. The US government took a rapid but controversial decision to mount a national influenza vaccination programme. Sadly, it backfired. A number of deaths of fit people and cases of paralytic Guillain-Barré syndrome were attributed to the vaccination. As a direct result, the US public lost confidence in the programme, which then collapsed. Billy Carter, brother of President Jimmy Carter, was quoted at the time as saying he would 'rather get stoned to death with booze than have a swine flu shot'.

Subsequent investigation proved interesting, however. Despite the apparently virulent swine influenza being given a relatively free run by the poor uptake of the vaccine, a large-scale outbreak did not occur. Coincidentally, another influenza strain, influenza 'A' Victoria, was circulating in the population at the same time. This strain was more infectious but less virulent, i.e. it caused less severe morbidity. The swine flu strain may not have spread in part because of competition from its more successful but benign relative.

Successful efforts at communicable disease control focused not just on the organisms and the hosts but also on the intervening vectors which played a prominent part in spreading deadly diseases such as malaria. In the US, before 1947, the focus of malaria control was mainly on the drainage of swamps acting as breeding grounds and the use of quinine to treat cases. Between 1947 and 1952, efforts were redirected at eradicating malaria-carrying mosquitoes by the extensive use of DDT. By the end of 1952, malaria was effectively eradicated from the USA.

This success led the US government to believe that similar efforts could be repeated on a global scale. Vast sums of money were directed at malaria eradication programmes, funded mainly by the USA. Between 1958 and 1963, US$ 430 million was spent on mosquito eradication worldwide (equivalent to US$ 1.9 billion in 1991 terms). Examples of early successes included Sri Lanka, where, in 1955, one million cases of malaria occurred. By 1963, following DDT control programmes, malaria cases were down to 18. However, in 1963 the US Congress decided to halt the funding of international mosquito eradication efforts. After 1963 cases gradually increased again due to the increasing spread of DDT resistance among mosquitoes. Resistance to the most widely used treatment, chloroquine, also appeared. By 1975 global malaria incidence was 2.5 times that of 1961 and in India alone there were six million cases compared to the one million in 1961. Malaria had therefore become an example of a re-emergent disease, and the true potential of micro-organisms to survive man's efforts to eliminate them began to be revealed. The era of 'new hope' was drawing to a close and the next episode in the 'Bug Wars' saga was beginning.

Episode 2: 'The empire (of the bugs) strikes back'

Retaliation by the micro-organisms has taken two forms: first through the re-emergence of diseases thought to be under control (as with malaria); and second via new or 'emerging' infections. This second category includes new diseases not previously seen due to the evolutionary adaptation of new organisms to human hosts. However, the term 'emerging infections' is misleading as it implies a new phenomenon. In fact, as noted by Joshua Lederberg, 'infections have been "emerging" since the first microbe tried to climb the food chain ladder, by preying on the proto-algae.'[1]

Disease emergence and re-emergence can be traced to several factors. The first infectious disease epidemics were recorded in Mesopotamia in 2000 BC. This was when pastoralism and the habit of living in close proximity to domesticated animals enabled the zoonotic spread of diseases from animals to man. These diseases then adapted to human hosts, resulting in the person-to-person spread of new diseases such as measles. Farming and a stable food supply enabled population growth, which reached the critical threshold levels needed to allow the circulation of infections. Mathematical modelling suggests that measles requires a population of approximately 500,000 people to be sustained as endemic. Urbanisation resulted in overcrowding, poor hygiene and inadequate sanitation, and all of this encouraged disease amplification. Population movement associated with war, invasion, colonisation, trade and peaceful migration all ensured the free movement of harmful micro-organisms. Human behaviour, both cultural and sexual, often facilitates the spread of infections.

Newly identified causes of long-known diseases continue to be found and constitute another group of the emerging diseases. These have included causes of pneumonia such as *Legionella*, causes of gastro-enteritis such as campylobacter and crypto-sporidium, and causes of hepatitis including hepatitis C and E viruses. Newly identified causes of viral haemorrhagic disease such as the Lassa, Ebola and Marburg viruses, and causes of hard-to-diagnose diseases such as meningo-polyneuritis due to Lyme borrieliosis, have all been identified.

Truly novel diseases have also continued to appear, presenting new challenges for control. Examples include E. coli 0157, causing haemorrhagic colitis and haemolytic uraemic syndrome; hantavirus, causing pulmonary disease; and new variant Creutzfeldt–Jakob disease (vCJD), causing spongiform encephalopathy. The most devastating new disease to emerge in the later part of the 20th century was undoubtedly HIV, causing AIDS. By 2001, 40 million adults were thought to be living with HIV infection worldwide. The tally of emerging infections identified since 1973 – the scope of the 'strike back' – is truly impressive (Table 10.2).

Table 10.2 Emerging infections: major pathogens identified since 1973

1973	Rotavirus	1985	Chlamydia pneumoniae
1975	Parvovirus B19	1986	Clycospora
1976	Cryptosporidium	1988	Human herpes virus
1977	Ebola virus	1989	Hepatitis C virus
1977	*Legionella* sp.	1989	Ehrlichia chaffensis
1977	Hantavirus	1990	Hepatitis E virus
1997	Campylobactor	1991	Guanarito virus
1980	HTLVI	1992	Vibrio cholerae 0139
1981	Staphylococcus aureus toxic shock)	1992	Bartonella henselae
		1993	Sin nombre virus
1982	Escherichia coli 0157:H7	1994	Sabiavirus
1982	HTLV II virus	1995	Human herpes virus type 8
1982	Borrelia burgdorferi	1996	Andes virus
1983	HIV-I	2002	Metapneumovirus
1983	Helicobacter pylori		

SOURCE: World Health Organization, 1995.

Re-emerging infections have also been encouraged by the increased use of air travel for business and leisure, which has helped the spread of many infections including resistant malaria strains. International commerce has also assisted the spread of disease, for example, used tyres containing water infested with *Aedes albopictus* – the 'Asian tiger' mosquitoes imported to the USA in 1985 from the Philippines – enabled the spread of dengue fever to Texas and within two years to 17 US states.

In the UK, food-borne infection re-emerged when infection of hens' eggs led to an explosion of salmonella food poisoning cases (and the political demise of the cabinet minister, Edwina Currie, who admitted the truth in public). When asked a direct question about salmonella in 1988, she replied: 'We do warn people that most of the egg production of this country, sadly, is now infected with salmonella.'

Re-emerging infection has appeared where public health infrastructures have deteriorated, as in the former USSR countries, where epidemic diphtheria returned. Tuberculosis re-emerged as a significant problem on the back of HIV/AIDS in New York and London in the 1990s, and soon spread worldwide in the wake of the spreading global pandemic of HIV/AIDS.

Loss of public confidence in the UK and concern about possible brain damage associated with the use of a whole cell vaccine dented the successes of vaccination in recent years and led to the re-emergence of pertussis in the 1970s and 1980s. More recently, measles has returned in the UK due to the falling uptake of measles vaccine and the lingering controversy over the MMR (measles, mumps and rubella) vaccine. The public are more sceptical about the benefits of vaccine programmes and much more likely to question the advice being offered by health professionals.

The optimism of the 'new era' has, therefore, given way to a new realism in the understanding of the interplay between mankind and the microbes and an appreciation that, if anything, evolution favours the 'bugs'. The increasingly important role that genetics will play in the final outcome of the 'Bug Wars' leads us to the next definable episode.

Episode 3: 'Attack of the clones'

This episode charts the spread of new variants of organisms with genetically acquired resistance to anti-microbial chemicals and drugs.

In 1944 penicillin was introduced as the 'miracle drug'. In 1952 Joshua and Esther Lederberg of the University of Wisconsin identified genetic characteristics conferring penicillin resistance in certain bacteria. They believed that inherent genetic resistance due to bacterial evolution predated the discovery and use by humans of antibiotics. Resistance had, therefore, existed for aeons, due to the existence in nature of the *Penicillium* mould itself. The scope for transfer of this inherent genetic capability already existed.

The significance of this finding became apparent soon enough. In 1977, five hospitalised children in Durban, South Africa, developed infections with Strepto-coccus pneumoniae type 19A, a new strain found to be resistant to penicillin and

12 other common antibiotics. By 1978, in Johannesburg 50% of all Strepto-coccus pneumoniae infections were due to type 19A. This novel strain was eventually traced to a single genetic clone first identified in New Guinea in 1967. The power of genetic adaptation had been demonstrated and was set to become an increasingly potent force. The increasingly indiscriminate and widespread global use of antimicrobials, in both the human and animal populations, created conditions which selectively favoured either a pre-existing resistant clone, or the creation of a niche for a new resistant spontaneous mutation. Transfer of resis-tance capability, by exchange of genetic material involving plasmids and other mechanisms, has ensured that resistance in one species can readily migrate to other pathogens.

Clones with drug resistance have been identified with mycobacterium tuberculosis (multi-drug resistant MDR–TB), for staphylococcus aureus (MRSA) and vancomycin resistance in enterococci (VRE) – as well as antibiotic resistant strains of typhoid, shigella and gonococcus. Drug-resistant malaria is a significant and growing global problem induced partly by the excessive and inappropriate use of drug therapies. Anti-viral resistance is a growing threat in the control of HIV.

Looking at the tally of casualties in the 'Bug Wars' to date, then, shows that human-kind has so far eradicated one disease – smallpox. On the microbes' side, WHO estimates in 1995 put the figure for deaths due to infections at approximately 17 million per year. This compared to 15 million deaths per year attributed to cardiovascular disease and six million deaths due to cancers. Allowing for the potential limits to the accuracy of global health statistics, it is clear that human-kind has a long way to go before claiming a decisive victory against the bugs.

Data collated by WHO also reveal the types of infection and modes of transmission responsible for this toll of death and disease (Table 10.3).

This leads us to the final chapter in our saga. But what will be the title of the last episode?

Table 10.3. Global mortality from infection

Mode of transmission	Deaths
Person to person	11.2 million
Food- and water-borne	3.7 million
Insect-borne	2.3 million
Animal-borne	0.006 million

Disease group	
Lower respiratory tract	4.4 million
Gastro-intestinal infection	3.1 million
Tuberculosis	3.1 million
Malaria	2.1 million
Hepatitis B	1.1 million
HIV/AIDS	1.0 million
Measles	1.0 million

SOURCE: World Health Organization, 1995.

'The phantom menace', perhaps

The phantom of biological warfare has become a prominent concern of the early 21st century. Events after 11 September 2001 included attacks on US citizens with weaponised strains of anthrax. In the USA, UK and elsewhere there has been an increased effort to set up surveillance systems capable of identifying clusters of unusual or suspicious illnesses. Vaccination against smallpox has been re-introduced, having been abandoned in the late 1970s, and health care staff in the UK are being asked to volunteer for diagnostic teams ready to move rapidly to identify and confirm any suspect cases. The shadow of a once-conquered disease has returned to menace a new generation.

Alternatively, might the theme of the latest episode be different? Might the 'force' of evolution be with us, rather than as, so far, largely against us? New thinking on 'evolutionary epidemiology' leads authors such as Paul Ewald to pose challenging questions for the future.[2] Why have some organisms evolved to become so harmful while others have not? Is there scope to use the principles of natural selection to identify where the new threats lie and to selectively target these for intervention at the genetic level?

More rigorous policing of the use of anti-microbials will be one essential strategy in depriving the 'bugs' of future opportunities to develop resistance. Abandoning the indiscriminate and questionable use of antibiotics will become increasingly important; for example rifampicin, used routinely as 'prophylaxis' to eliminate carriage of pathogenic A, B and C strain meningococci among the contacts of meningococcal disease, also kills benign strains capable of inducing protective immunity.

Ewald and others propose that with continuing advances in genetic engineering it is possible to foresee situations where evolutionary pressure could be used to out-compete virulent organisms and prevent them gaining sufficient ground to become established. Benign live strains of organisms could be introduced rapidly in populations at risk to allow natural immunisation to occur, so filling the niche that some more pathogenic strain is trying to occupy. The experience of swine flu in the USA suggests that this is not beyond the bounds of the plausible.

Perhaps the future strategy for humankind's 'Bug Wars' could be one named 'Mesopotamia revisited'. In this strategy Ewald and others suggest we need to find ways to move from the traditional approach of protecting individuals against pathogens by targeting the individual microbes (the hunter paradigm), to a new situation where we 'domesticate' the microbes, so that we can live with them in a mutually beneficial way (a pastoral paradigm). Fiction? Time will tell.

If we are to move into a new and more optimistic era, based on exploiting the potential of 'evolutionary epidemiology', perhaps this new era needs a new symbol to act as its standard.

The ancient symbol of medicine (the staff of Aesculapius – a serpent entwined around a rod – see Figure 10.2) has its origins (according to legend) in ancient Mesopotamia (all roads seem to lead to Mesopotamia, a particular irony given the early-21st-century re-emergence of that region's importance as modern-day Iraq). In settling down to a pastoral and agrarian lifestyle, the Mesopotamians

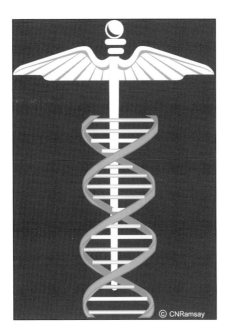

Figure 10.2 The staff of Aesculapius:
a modern-day version

were exposed to parasites, including the particularly odious guinea worm, the cause of dracunculiasis. The life cycle of this worm starts with exposure to the larvae by drinking contaminated water. The larvae migrate through the skin, eventually developing as an adult worm. The mature worm migrates towards the skin surface in order to expel a new generation of larvae. The intense itching caused by this migration leads the victim to scratch and break the skin surface, so allowing the larvae to escape into any water used to bathe the affected limb, thereby perpetuating the life cycle. The traditional ancient remedy for this infestation was to extract the worm by teasing it out very slowly over days or weeks, using a stick to wind it on. Those early healers specialising in this technique were said to display a symbol of a worm (or serpent) wound round a rod, hence the staff of Aesculapius. The rod, therefore, symbolised the leading-edge technology of the day. The intertwined double helix of DNA provides us with a symbol for a new era, one where genetics represents the leading edge technology and the newest tool to aid in mankind's unceasing efforts to conquer communicable disease.

Notes

1   J. Lederberg, 'Cell genetics and hereditary symbiosis'. *Physiology Review* 32 (1952): 403–30, 405.
2   P. W. Ewald, *Evolution of Infectious Disease* (New York: Oxford University Press, 1994).

REFERENCES

Garrett, L. *The Coming Plague: newly emerging diseases in a world out of balance*. London: Virago Press, 1995

Lockie, C., Walker, E. et al. *Travel Medicine and Migrant Health*. London: Churchill Livingstone, 2000

Morse, S. S. (ed.) *Emerging Viruses*. Oxford University Press, 1993

Roizman, B. (ed.) *Infectious Diseases in an Age of Change: the impact of human ecology and behaviour on disease transmission*. Washington DC: National Academy Press, 1995

Tait, H. P. *A Doctor and Two Policemen: the history of Edinburgh Health Department 1862–1974*. Edinburgh: Edinburgh Health Department, 1974

11. Statistics in public health

Sheila M. Bird

Unashamedly, my account of statistics in public health has a distinctly Edinburgh bias.

The account begins in a library, in the days when professors expected to find their students there. Aberdeen University's then-professor of statistics, David Kerridge, came to find me in King's College library to tell me that there was a research assistantship in medical statistics at the University of Edinburgh, which he thought I should apply for. Thus, in 1974, I joined Walter Lutz's Medical Computing and Statistics Unit where Dr Stuart Pocock was research fellow. He subsequently took me on as his first PhD student.

The ethos of the Medical Computing and Statistics Unit was that it was efficient for statisticians to spend three-quarters of their time on study design – a prioritisation that today's analytical arsenal has not displaced. Ergo I developed a tenacity for study design which earned me the nickname of 'ogre' from a professorial collaborator whose instinct for minimisation of study size contrasted with my arguments for its aggrandisement. Meanwhile, Pocock was working on group sequential designs for clinical trials,[1] which allowed orderly early stopping, and on the now widely used method of randomisation known as minimisation.[2]

My tutorials on critical reading of papers in leading medical journals to the diploma class in public health led to a joint publication on the misuse of statistics in the *British Medical Journal* (*BMJ*) with two students, Drs Jones and Rytter.[3] This was a critical assessment of articles in *BMJ* from January to March 1976. In an otherwise news-blighted January 1977 this paper made the headlines and led to my first nervous exposure to statistics in the public eye of television news.

Two other substantive issues from 1974 to 1976 in Edinburgh were equally formative for my practice of statistics. The first was the high non-participation rate in a voluntary behavioural and occupational risk factor survey linked to blood samples for health care workers in the aftermath of hepatitis B deaths in

1972 at Edinburgh's Royal Infirmary.[4] Health care workers' fears about deductive disclosure explained their unwillingness to participate, which taught me that surveys in closed institutions need to be designed with the safeguarding of participants as signal priority, a lesson that, much later, Willing Anonymous Salivary HIV and hepatitis C (WASH–C) surveillance studies in prisons capitalised on.

The second concerned statistical analyses of Edinburgh's Western General breast cancer series of 3,922 patients. Breast cancer exemplified three major departures[5] from Cox's recently published, seminal work on proportionality of hazards.[6] First, there were different times to peak hazard according to tumour stage at the time of diagnosis; second, regression effects, such as of tumour size, waned in the second decade of follow-up; and third, there was cross-over of hazards associated with menopausal status – occasioned, we conjectured, as pre-menopausal women entered the menopausal phase and subsequently became post-menopausal. Event times for these transitions had not been recorded and so could not be analysed as time-dependent covariates.[7] The second and third problems were accommodated by fitting proportional hazards models in distinct epochs of follow-up,[8] which allowed covariate effects to differ as time evolved.

Transplantation

In the early 1980s we imported proportional hazards in distinct epochs of follow-up from breast cancer to transplantation statistics. There, it had major application in identifying Human Leucocyte Antigen (HLA) and other influences on graft failures in the first or first three months;[9] during the remainder of the first year; and beyond one year. Follow-up epochs were determined jointly by statistical (approximately equal numbers of graft failures) and subject matter considerations (such as operative mortality and early sequelae of sub-optimal immunosuppression). Beneficial tissue matching of donor to recipient[10] was defined by such analyses, and served as the basis of cadaveric kidney exchange in the United Kingdom for nearly 10 years until the need to take older donor age into account, and the corroboration that no mismatches at HLA-DR and HLA-B but two HLA-A mismatches constituted a favourable match, led to revised organ exchange rules in the late 1990s.[11]

The statistics in transplantation offer two valuable reservations about the wider public health's obsession with league tables and inappropriate 'naming and shaming' of institutions or individuals. First, centre effects on kidney graft survival[12] had been a) analysed, b) published, and c) followed-up on throughout the 1980s and early 1990s, when outcomes improved and centre-heterogeneity diminished. In publications, centres were labelled (A, B, C, etc.) but not publicly identified; individual centres knew only their own identifier (which did not alter between years) unless others (such as the centre ranked top this year) chose to self-identify. In addition, periodically, 'three wise men', professionals in transplantation, visited typically eight selected centres spanning the performance range to assimilate and publicly report to colleagues aspects of good and to-be-avoided practice for the enlightenment of all. All this was done without loss of face and with remarkable overall improvement in outcomes in a new, rapidly progressive, cooperative and competitive, analysed and performance-attuned specialty. Second, and in stark contrast, adverse publicity surrounded the report by the Commission for Health Improvement on heart transplantation at St George's Hospital in London,[13] despite the investigation having been instigated by the hospital itself. Disappointingly, the report failed to comment on excellence elsewhere, which, in statistical terms, was more remarkable than the recent downturn in outcomes which St George's had begun to investigate.

The last of my transplantation reflections reverts to study design for the 1989–1990 confidential audit of all deaths in intensive care units in England and Wales,[14] for which Mrs Edwina Currie, to whom I had appealed beyond her civil servants, gave the go-ahead. At the time of the confidential audit, intensive care units were being blamed for the shortage of cadaveric donor organs: transplant coordinators averred that families to whom they spoke were willing, and parliamentarians were debating 'required request' legislation to force intensive care staff to ask the family of a brainstem dead patient about organ donation. There was therefore great sensitivity amongst intensive care units, whose willing cooperation was essential if the confidential audit was to succeed. Therefore, to protect intensive care units and so engender their cooperation, a public health intermediary was enlisted per region, through whom the confidential audit forms were distributed to, and returned by, the region's intensive care units. Thus, although the statistical centre had assigned label D to East Anglia, I did not know which of the intensive care units D1, D2, etc., was Addenbrooke's Hospital. All my communications – for example, about missing audit forms, which were serially numbered, or about logical errors in completion of a particular form – with the intensive care unit at Addenbrooke's Hospital (Dx) were forwarded to it by its regionally trusted intermediary. The good offices of these hard-working intermediaries ensured that compliance with the confidential audit was over 95% and that the to-be-corrected rate in audit forms was reduced from over 10% in the first quarter to under 3% thereafter. Within three months, the confidential audit had shown that, in 95% of brainstem dead patients, the family was asked about organ donation.[15] There was therefore no need for 'required request' legislation. But the refusal rate by families was 30%, as in annual Gallup surveys, and the transplant coordinators' perception was biased because intensive care staff did not refer on to them families from whom refusal had been elicited. The confidential audit quantified the various potentials for cadaveric organ donation of kidneys, liver, heart, lungs and corneas;[16] and, even then, it identified that substantial increase in living-related kidney donation would be needed to meet patients' needs.

HIV immunology

HIV immunology brought me back to Edinburgh in the late 1980s to work with most remarkable colleagues, among them the immunologist with whom I was later married. Scotland owes its internationally unique national CD4 database, which is now maintained by the Scottish Centre for Infection and Environmental Health,[17] to the inspirational founding by the late Dr A. Graham Bird, then head of Edinburgh's HIV Immunology Unit, of the Scottish Immunology Laboratories' CD4 database,[18] which allowed Scotland's working parties on AIDS projections to make predictions not only of AIDS incidence but also of the earlier endpoint of severe HIV immunodeficiency, so-called CD200 case, which we defined by the earlier of two consecutive CD4 counts under 200.[19]

Dr Ray Brettle's Medical Research Council-funded work with the Edinburgh City Hospital HIV cohort – a research cohort of mainly injection drug users – was internationally recognised but, as importantly, accorded singular recognition by this ancient and distinguished university in its award of the gold medal to Dr Brettle's MD thesis. At least half of the injectors in the Edinburgh HIV cohort had a narrowly defined HIV seroconversion interval (i.e. of less than 24 months) thanks to the retrospective HIV testing of stored sera from HIV-diagnosed patients, which was conducted with characteristic thoroughness by regional virol-ogist Dr Sheila Burns[20] and which demonstrated unambiguously that Edinburgh's injection-related HIV incidence had peaked dramatically in autumn 1983 and early 1984. The late Dr George Bath made a major contribution to this endeavour by master indexing (initial of first name, soundex of surname, gender, date of birth) blood samples which had been received for HIV testing from the genitourinary medicine (GUM) clinic and which were hitherto identified by GUM clinic number only; and Drs Brettle and Roy Robertson exchanged master-indexed lists of their patients to identify overlaps without risk of inadvertent disclosure of patient identities. Master indexing, which resolved a Medical Research Council-identified problem of probable repeat-counting of HIV diagnoses in Edinburgh – where clinicians had rightly made patient confidentiality paramount to encourage self-referral for HIV testing – now applies to HIV and hepatitis C diagnosis registers throughout the UK. Finally, I pay tribute to immunologist Dr John A. Habeshaw, formerly in the Department of Pathology at Edinburgh University, whose theories about HIV pathogenesis led to the hypothesis that HLA–B27 would be associated with slow HIV progression, which we confirmed in Edinburgh's HIV cohort,[21] just as the association of HLA–A1, B8, DR3 with rapid HIV progression had previously been reported in Edinburgh's haemophilia cohort.[22]

HIV epidemiology in prisons

The above work, and much else,[23] came under the auspices of MRC–BIAS, the Medical Research Council's Edinburgh-based biostatistical initiative in support of AIDS/HIV studies in Scotland for which Gore, Bird, Brettle and Goldberg were grant-holders. Over five years, MRC–BIAS was staffed by a regiment of able statisticians: Raab, Fielding, Ross, Hutchinson and Lewis. Also part of the HIV research at MRC–BIAS was HIV epidemiology in prisons. This four-part programme was inspired by the remarkable governor of Edinburgh prison, Mr John Pearce, who posed to Graham Bird the question of when Edinburgh prison would begin to see severe HIV disease among its inmates.[24] In 1990 we put forward a four-part programme on HIV epidemiology in prisons. The first part was to come up with a study design (now known as WASH [Willing Anonymous Salivary HIV] surveillance linked to a self-completion questionnaire about risks for blood-borne virus transmission) to measure HIV prevalence (how many prisoners are HIV infected, including undiagnosed infections) and prisoners' risk behaviours (how did they become infected: sexually or by injection drug use, including inside prison).[25] Second, if HIV prevalence was found to be much higher than was known about by prison doctors, then blood samples might be required to assess CD4 counts and infer recent HIV seroconversions – fortunately, this was never an issue in the Scottish Prison Service, which had promoted confidential HIV testing by inmates to address their (not the prisons') need to know about HIV status.[26] Third, a WASH-incidence study design was required to measure HIV (or hepatitis C) seroconversions in prison[27] and this has since been implemented at Shotts prison in Scotland. Finally, the question of whether being in prison affects HIV progression and mortality had to be addressed.[28]

To be ethical, the WASH methodology required prisoners' willing cooperation, which was facilitated by requesting a saliva (rather than a blood) sample. Anonymity was for prisoners' protection. Deductive disclosure was further guarded against by inviting all inmates to participate and by allowing each prisoner to choose for himself an envelope (from a bag of about 50 envelopes) in which he found a pair of sealed labels. Under each seal was the same number, but neither the prisoner nor anyone else knew what that number was. The prisoner placed one of the sealed labels on the salivette containing his saliva sample and the other on his self-completion risk factor questionnaire, which was then folded into the envelope. Saliva samples were analysed at a regional virus laboratory, which informed the statistical centre about the serial numbers of any that tested HIV antibody positive so that the linked risk factor questionnaire (but not the prisoner who had volunteered it) could be identified. Saliva samples and self-completion of risk factor questionnaires in privacy ensured high volunteer rates, not only in Scottish prisons but also when the WASH methodology was implemented in other European countries (see Figure 11.1). The first WASH study was conducted at Edinburgh prison in 1991[29] and its major findings have been replicated in all prison jurisdictions:[30] about one-third of adult male prisoners have a history of injection drug use; over half the injector inmates report having injected inside prison at some time; and the majority of HIV antibody positive samples are from men with a history of injection drug use (40/43 in Scotland; 145/173 in WASH-C surveillance under the auspices of the European Network for HIV and Hepatitis Prevention in Prisons).

We used the behavioural data from the 1996 WASH studies at two Scottish prisons (Lowmoss near Glasgow and Aberdeen) – which showed that inside injectors injected on average only six times in four weeks – to estimate that random mandatory drugs testing (rMDT) of prisoners (see Figure 11.2) probably identified only one in two inside users of heroin[31] because heroin stays in the urine for only three days and testing was not fully operational at weekends. As punishment for

Where?	Volunteer rate & Qs	% IDUs	% inside	HIV+ve saliva [IDUs]
91–96 Scotland	85% 2286	32%	58% 411/714	43 [40]
England & Wales	81% 2798	29%	30% 195/660	9 [4]
Ireland	88% 1205	42%	45%+ ?/480	24 [18]
EC Network	75% 3027	32%	46% 406/880	171 [145]

Figure 11.1   Major WASH results: males

this publication, we were banned for three years from conducting studies in Scottish prisons. Operationally, however, the Scottish Prison Service now accepts that the prevalence of inside users of heroin is best estimated as twice the percentage who test opiate positive. Underestimation had potentially serious consequences for prisoners' health because it could have led the Scottish Prison Service to underestimate, and hence be underfunded in respect of, inmates' need for drug rehabilitation services during imprisonment.

Dr A. Graham Bird anticipated that there should be a salivary test for hepatitis C antibodies and so, from the date of WASH surveillance at Glasgow's Barlinnie Prison in September 1994[32] onwards, we asked for the approval of the ethics committee and the prisoners to retain saliva samples for eventual salivary testing for hepatitis C carriage,[33] with results as shown in Figure 11.2: half our injector

Where & IDUs		Injector-inmates' HepC prevalence	95% CI
94/96 Scotland	536	49%	45%–54%
England & Wales	659	30%	27%–34%
Ireland	509	80%	76%–84%
EC Network	542	52%	48%–57%

Figure 11.2   WASH–C: male injector-inmates and hepatitis C antibodies in saliva

inmates are hepatitis C carriers compared to only 3% of prisoners who reported that they had never injected.

- AIDS/HIV=>   **WASH =>** injector prevalence
- Inside risks: **injecting, tattoos, sexual** [bleach, *needle exchange,* condoms]
- **ABC of Hepatitis:** immunization, bar **C**
- Outside risks: **overdose deaths** & crime
- Drugs: **? mandatory** testing => **rehabilitation**

Figure 11.3 Prisons' decade of data

Figure 11.3 summarises the prisons' decade of data: studies of HIV prevalence in prisons quickly focused attention on injector prevalence amongst prisoners and their vulnerability to blood-borne transmission inside prison, primarily from the sharing of unsterilised equipment for injecting, but also from tattooing and from unprotected intercourse. In 1991 Scottish prisoners had no access to harm reduction measures:[34] sterilisation tablets, hepatitis B immunisation, hepatitis A immunisation for hepatitis C carriers, and methadone substitution as well as drugs rehabilitation services, condoms and clean needles. The first four of these, together with throughcare from prison to community for drug-dependent inmates, are now offered to Scotland's prisoners. Meanwhile, in the late 1990s, attention began to focus on outside risks: both overdose deaths soon after release from prison and the acquisitive crimes committed by injectors to pay for drugs.[35] Injectors, mostly unemployed, spend over £300 per week on drugs. Black-market values mean that injectors may steal between two and five times that amount per week. As a consequence, they serve a multiplicity of short prison sentences. Based on male injectors in the Edinburgh City Hospital HIV cohort during the period 1983–1994,[36] there was an eight times higher risk of overdose death in the fortnight following release from prison than at comparable other times at liberty. Bird and Hutchinson[37] used database linkage to follow up for mortality 19,486 male ex-prisoners aged 15–35 years who were released from Scottish prisons in July to December 1996–1999 after an incarceration of 14+ days. Figure 11.4 shows that of 57 drugs-related deaths, 34 occurred within a fortnight of release (relative risk of drugs-related death in the first fortnight = 7; 95% confidence interval from 3 to 16 times higher risk), so that the high relative

DEATHS	1st 2 weeks	Subsequent 5 fortnights	RELATIVE RISK (95%CI)
Drugs-related	34	23	**7** (3 to 16)
Other causes	3	18	**0.8** (0.2 to 2.4)

Figure 11.4 Drug-related deaths in fortnight after release from prison

risk first identified by Seaman and colleagues persisted in the harm reduction era of the late 1990s. Bird and Hutchinson estimated that one in 200 adult male injectors dies within two weeks of release from prison: are judges aware? Since 1997 the Scottish Prison Service has provided prisoners about to be released with an excellent illustrated leaflet that warns about the loss of drug tolerance during incarceration and how to avoid the risk of overdose on release. Other prison-based initiatives are clearly needed, and these could include a randomised trial of naloxone, the heroin antidote, for injectors on release.

Prion diseases

Besides HIV and prisons, Edinburgh is also central to the public health implications of prion diseases because it hosts the National CJD Surveillance Unit, which on 20 March 1996 announced that the UK had 10 cases of a new variant of Creutzfeldt–Jakob disease (vCJD) which was characterised by novel neuro-pathology and young age at onset,[38] and is now known to have been caused by the bovine spongiform encephalopathy (BSE) agent.[39] Cooper and Bird quantified UK dietary BSE exposure to BSE by birth cohort to establish whether differential dietary BSE exposure per se could explain the young age of vCJD patients.[40] It does not,[41] as age-dependency in vCJD susceptibility appears to be necessary to explain the age distribution of vCJD cases in the 1940–1969 and older birth cohort. Based on dietary exposure alone,[42] Cooper and Bird predicted that 58% of vCJD cases would be in males. Probably bloodborne vCJD transmission[43] may alter that expected gender distribution, however.

Other jurisdictions impact on the public health. Study design and sound statistical method need to become sine qua non in those jurisdictions, as in medicine, in order to properly safeguard the public health.

Drug treatment and testing orders

Let me turn now to criminal justice trials and the standards of evidence for criminal justice interventions for drug-dependent offenders. Drug treatment and testing orders (DTTOs) have been introduced as a sentence which diverts drug-dependent offenders from prison into rehabilitation with the objective of reduction in both drug dependency and drugs-related acquisitive crime. Do DTTOs work for injectors? Are they cost-effective? In terms of evaluation, the Australians are a leap ahead, because there offenders are randomised between prison and DTTO, whereas in the UK there has been neither randomisation nor appraisal of cost-effectiveness – judges have not even been asked to pronounce the alternative prison sentence that an injector would have received had he not been deemed eligible for DTTO.

My methodological focus for the 21st century therefore embraces other jurisdictions – such as the criminal justice system – which impact on the public health and for which sound statistical method is as necessary as in clinical medicine. In particular, I envisage expanded non-nominal database linkage of registries by use of a master index for probabilistic matching of blood-borne virus registries, for registers of drug treatment clients, for children who have truanted or been excluded from schools, for children in care and for registries relating to criminal justice and prisons. I look forward to the application of infectious disease methodologies to injection drug use, itself a behaviour which is transmitted from person to person. In particular, there is need to measure injector incidence among young offenders[44] (a group that is currently and appropriately the target of a World Health Organization initiative on healthy prisons) and to count injector initiates per injector because the injector epidemic will not cease until its reproductive number R_0 is below 1. Achieving fewer than one injector-initiate per prevalent injector should be a key public health goal, together with off-injecting as the surest way to reduce hepatitis C incidence, to ensure that hepatitis C carriers are eligible for anti-viral treatment and to reduce drugs-related deaths. Drugs-related deaths would also be reduced if the heroin antidote were made available to injectors, just as adrenaline is available for persons with peanut allergy who are at risk of anaphylaxis. Reducing addictions, which are chronic relapsing remitting conditions, needs a sustained, incremental research programme grounded in properly designed, unbiased and apolitical evaluation of new interventions, whether under the auspices of home or health departments, and whether north or south of the border.

Notes

1   S. J. Pocock, 'Group sequential methods in the design and analysis of clinical trials'. *Biometrika* 64 (1997): 191–9.

2   S. J. Pocock and R. Simon, 'Sequential treatment assignment with balancing for prognostic factors in the controlled clinical trial'. *Biometrics* 31 (1975): 103–15.

3   S. M. Gore, I. G. Jones and E. C. Rytter, 'Misuse of statistical methods: critical assessment of articles in *BMJ* from January to March 1976'. *British Medical Journal* 1 (1977): 85–7.

4   C. J. Burrell, R. W. Tonkin, E. Proudfoot, G. Leadbetter, P. Cowan, L. Lockerbie, S. M. Gore, W. Lutz and B. P. Marmion, 'Prevalence of antibody to Hepatitis B surface antigen among staff in an Edinburgh hospital'. *Journal of Hygiene* 78 (1977): 57–68.

5   S. M. Gore, S. J. Pocock and G. R. Kerr, 'Regression models and non-proportional hazards in the analysis of breast cancer survival'. *Journal of the Royal Statistical Society* (Series C) 33 (1984): 176–95.

6   D. R. Cox, 'Regression models and lifetables'. *Journal of the Royal Statistical Society* (Series B) 34 (1972): 187–220.

7   Ibid.

8   Gore, Pocock and Kerr, 'Regression models'.

9   W. R. Gilks, B. A. Bradley, S. M. Gore and N. H. Selwood, 'Immunogenetic and clinical factors affecting renal transplantation: a rigorous analysis of data recorded by the UK Transplant Service'. *Transplantation* 42.1 (1986): 39–45; W. R. Gilks, S. M. Gore and B. A. Bradley, 'Analysing transplant survival data'. *Transplantation* 42.1 (1986): 46–9.

10   W. R. Gilks, S. M. Gore and B. A. Bradley, 'Renal transplant rejection: transient immunodominance of HLA mismatches'. *Transplantation* 50 (1990): 141–6.

11   P. J. Morris, S. V. Fuggle, R. Johnson, M. A. Belger and J. D. Briggs (on behalf of the HLA Task Force of the UK Transplant Support Service Authority), 'Factors influencing outcome of primary cadaveric renal transplantation in the UK'. *The Lancet* 354 (1999): 1147–52.

12   W. R. Gilks, 'Some applications of hierarchical models in kidney transplantation'. *The Statistician* 36 (1987): 127–36.

13   Commission for Health Improvement, *Investigation into heart and lung transplantation at St George's Healthcare NHS Trust* (London: The Stationery Office, 2001).

14   S. M. Gore, D. J. Cable and A. J. Holland, 'Organ donation from intensive care units in England and Wales: two-year confidential audit of deaths in intensive care'. *British Medical Journal* 304 (1992): 349–55.

15   S. M. Gore, C. J. Hinds and A. J. Rutherford, 'Organ donation from intensive care units in England'. *British Medical Journal* 299 (1989): 1193–7.

16   S. M. Gore, R. M. R. Taylor and J. Wallwork, 'Availability of transplantable organs from brain stem dead donors in intensive care units'. *British Medical Journal* 302 (1990): 149–53.

17   Scottish Centre for Infection and Environmental Health, *HIV and AIDS Surveillance in Scotland: review of the epidemic to December 1994* (Glasgow: Scottish Centre for Infection and Environmental Health, 1995).

[18]   CD4 Collaborative Group, 'Use of monitored CD4 counts: predictions of the AIDS epidemic in Scotland'. *AIDS* 6 (1992): 213–22; CD4 Collaborative Group, 'CD4 surveillance in Scotland: perspectives on severe HIV-related immunodeficiency'. *AIDS* 11 (1997): 1509–17.

[19]   G. M. Raab, S. M. Gore, D. J. Goldberg and C. A. Donnelly, 'Bayesian forecasting of the human immunodeficiency virus epidemic in Scotland'. *Journal of the Royal Statistical Society* (Series A) 157 (1994): 17–30.

[20]   S. M. Burns, R. P. Brettle, S. M. Gore, J. F. Peutherer and J. R. Robertson, 'The epidemiology of HIV infection in Edinburgh related to the injecting of drugs: an historical perspective and new insight regarding the past incidence of HIV infection derived from retrospective HIV antibody testing of stored samples of serum'. *Journal of Infection* 32 (1996): 53–62.

[21]   A. J. McNeil, P. L. Yap, S. M. Gore, R. P. Brettle, M. McColl, R. Wyld, S. Davidson, R. Weightman, A. M. Richardson and J. R. Robertson, 'Association of HLA types A1–B8–DR3 and B27 with rapid and slow progression of HIV disease'. *Quarterly Journal of Medicine* 89 (1996): 177–85.

[22]   C. M. Steel, C. A. Ludlam, D. Beatson, J. F. Peutherer, R. J. G. Cuthbert, P. Simmonds, H. Morrison and M. Jones, 'HLA haplotype A1 B8 DR3 as a risk factor for HIV-related disease'. *The Lancet* 1 (1988): 1185–8; S. M. Gore, S. J. Hutchinson and R. P. Brettle, 'Study requirements for investigating HLA-associated progression of HIV disease, and review'. *Quarterly Journal of Medicine* 92 (1999): 609–617.

[23]   K. L. Fielding, R. P. Brettle, S. M. Gore, F. O'Brien, R. Wyld, R. Robertson and R. Weightman, 'Heterosexual transmission of HIV analysed by generalized estimating equations'. *Statistics in Medicine* 14 (1995): 1365–78; R. P. Brettle, A. J. McNeil, S. Burns, S. M. Gore, A. G. Bird, P. L. Yap, L. MacCallum, C. S. L. Leen and A. M. Richardson, 'Progression of HIV: follow-up of Edinburgh injecting drug users with narrow seroconversion intervals in 1983–85'. *AIDS* 10 (1996): 419–30; S. J. Hutchinson, S. M. Gore, D. J. Goldberg, D. L. Yirrell, J. McGregor, A. G. Bird and A. J. Leigh-Brown, 'Method used to follow-up previously undiagnosed infections in the HIV outbreak at Glenochil prison'. *Epidemiology and Infection* 123 (1999): 271–5.

[24]   A. G. Bird, S. M. Gore, D. W. Jolliffe and S. M. Burns, 'Anonymous HIV surveillance in Saughton Prison, Edinburgh'. *AIDS* 6 (1992): 725–33; A. G. Bird and S. M. Gore, 'Inside methodology: HIV surveillance in prisons' [editorial comment]. *AIDS* 8 (1994): 1345–6.

[25]   S. M. Gore, A. G. Bird, S. M. Burns, D. J. Goldberg, A. J. Ross and J. Macgregor, 'Drug injection and HIV prevalence in inmates of Glenochil prison'. *British Medical Journal* 310 (1995): 293–6; S. M. Gore and A. G. Bird, 'Cross-sectional Willing Anonymous HIV Salivary (WASH) Surveillance studies and self-completion risk factor questionnaire in establishments of the Scottish Prison Service'. *AIDS News* [Supplement to the Weekly Report (Answer)] 95.39 (1995): 1–4; A. G. Bird, S. M. Gore, S. J. Hutchinson, S. C. Lewis, S. Cameron and S. Burns (on behalf of the European Commission Network on HIV infection and hepatitis in prison), 'Harm reduction measures and injecting inside prison versus mandatory drugs tests: results of a cross-sectional anonymous questionnaire survey'. *British Medical Journal* 315 (1997): 21–4; S. M. Gore, A. G. Bird, S. O. Cameron, S. J. Hutchinson, S. M. Burns and D. J. Goldberg, 'Prevalence of hepatitis C carriage in Scottish prisons: Willing Anonymous Salivary Hepatitis C surveillance linked to self-reported risks'. *Quarterly Journal of Medicine* 92 (1999): 25–32.

26   S. M. Gore, J. Basson, A. G. Bird and D. J. Goldberg, 'Uptake of confidential, named HIV testing in Scottish prisons'. *The Lancet* 340 (1992): 907–8.

27   S. M. Gore, A. G. Bird and S. M. Burns, 'HIV epidemiology in prisons: anonymous voluntary HIV surveillance with risk factor elicitation', in A. Liebling (ed.), *Deaths in Custody: caring for people at risk* (London: Whiting and Birch Ltd, 1996), pp. 114–42; S. M. Gore and A. G. Bird, 'Study size and documentation to detect injection-related hepatitis C incidence in prison'. *Quarterly Journal of Medicine* 91 (1998): 353–7.

28   S. R. Seaman, R. P. Brettle and S. M. Gore, 'Mortality from overdose among injecting drug users recently released from prison: database linkage study'. *British Medical Journal* 316 (1998): 426–8.

29   Bird et al., 'Anonymous HIV surveillance'.

30   S. M. Bird, M. Rotily and A. G. Bird, 'Inside methodologies: for counting blood-borne viruses and injector-inmates' behavioural risks, with results from European prisons'. *Howard Journal of Criminal Justice* 41 (2002): 123–36.

31   Bird et al., 'Harm reduction measures'; S. M. Gore, A. G. Bird and J. S. Strang, 'Random mandatory drugs testing of prisoners: a biased means of gathering information'. *Journal of Epidemiology and Biostatistics* 4 (1999): 3–9.

32   A. G. Bird, S. M. Gore, S. Cameron, A. J. Ross and D. J. Goldberg, 'Anonymous HIV surveillance with risk factor elicitation at Scotland's largest prison, Barlinnie'. *AIDS* 9 (1995): 801–8.

33   Gore et al., 'Prevalence of hepatitis C carriage'.

34   A. M. Gore and A. G. Bird, 'No escape: HIV transmission in jail. Prisons need protocols for HIV outbreaks'. *British Medical Journal* 307 (1993): 147–8.

35   A. J. Hutchinson, S. M. Gore, A. Taylor, D. J. Goldberg and M. Frischer, 'Extent and contributing factors of drug expenditure of injectors in Glasgow'. *British Journal of Psychiatry* 176 (2000): 166–72.

36   Seaman, Brettle and Gore, 'Mortality from overdose'.

37   S. M. Bird and S. J. Hutchinson, 'Male drugs-related deaths in the fortnight after release from prison: Scotland, 1996–1999'. *Addiction* 98 (2003): 185–90.

38   R. G. Will, J. W. Ironside, M. Zeidler, S. N. Cousens et al., 'A new variant of Creutzfeldt–Jakob disease in the UK'. *The Lancet* 347 (1996): 921–5.

39   A. F. Hill, M. Desbruslais, S. Joiner, K. C. L. Sidle, I. Gowland and J. Collinge, 'The same prion strain causes vCJD and BSE'. *Nature* 389 (1997): 448–50; M. E. Bruce, R. G. Will, J. W. Ironside, I. McConnell, D. Drummond, A. Suttie, L. McCardle, A. Chree. J. Hope, C. Birkett, S. Cousens, H. Fraser and C. J. Bostock, 'Transmissions to mice indicate that "new variant" CJD is caused by the BSE agent'. *Nature* 389 (1997): 498–501.

40   J. D. Cooper and S. M. Bird, 'UK dietary exposure to BSE in beef mechanically recovered meat: by birth-cohort and gender'. *Journal of Cancer Epidemiology and Prevention* 7 (2002): 59–70; J. D. Cooper and S. M. Bird, 'UK dietary exposure to BSE in head meat: by birth-cohort and gender'. *Journal of Cancer Epidemiology and Prevention* 7 (2002): 71–83.

41   J. D. Cooper and S. M. Bird, 'Predicting incidence of variant Creutzfeldt–Jakob disease from UK dietary exposure to bovine spongiform encephalopathy for the 1940 to 1969 and post-1969 cohorts'. *International Journal of Epidemiology* 32 (2003): 784–91.

42   Ibid.

43   C. A. Llewelyn, P. E. Hewitt, R. S. Knight, K. Amar, S. Cousens, J. Mackenzie and R. G. Will, 'Possible transmission of variant Creutzfeldt–Jakob disease by blood transfusion'. *The Lancet* 363 (2004): 411–2; S. M. Bird, 'Recipients of blood or blood products "at vCJD risk": we need to define their rights and responsibilities and those of others'. *British Medical Journal* 328 (2004): 118–9.

44   Bird, Rotily and Bird, 'Inside methodologies'.

THE FUTURE

12. Genomics: impact on public health
Harry Campbell

In June 2000 an announcement was made of the partial completion of the Human Genome Project. In February 2001 results were published showing the sequence of three billion base pairs in which approximately 40,000 genes are located. The focus now lies in understanding genetic variation in humans and how this variation influences health and disease. The high expectations are illustrated by a vision of future genetically based individualised preventive medicine described by Francis Collins, a leading geneticist.

> John (23 years) works through an interactive computer programme at his GP surgery that explains the benefits and risks of genetic tests. John agrees to 15 that provide risk information for illnesses for which preventive strategies are available and declines a further 10 for which there are no validated preventive interventions. A cheek swab DNA specimen is sent off for testing and results come back in one week. John's counselling session with a genetics nurse focuses on conditions for which his risk differs from the general population by a factor of more than two. John has reduced risk of prostate cancer and Alzheimer's disease and increased risk of coronary artery disease, colon and lung cancer. Confronted with the reality of his own genetic data, he arrives at that crucial 'teachable moment' when a lifelong change in health-related behaviour, focused on reducing specific risks, is possible. A prophylactic drug regimen based on John's genetic data can be precisely prescribed to reduce his cholesterol level and risk of coronary artery disease to 'normal' levels. His risk of colon cancer is addressed by annual colonoscopies starting at age 45. His substantial risk of contracting lung cancer provides the key motivation for him to join a support group of people at genetically high risk of serious complications of smoking and he successfully kicks the habit.[1]

I will briefly review what the advances in knowledge of the human genome might achieve in the near future in the following areas:

- single-gene disorders

- complex disorders

  - communicable diseases

  - non-communicable diseases

- pharmacogenetics.

I will then consider some public health aspects of advances in genomics and the impact of these advances on world health.

Single-gene disorders

These can be considered as conditions with a 1–2% lifetime prevalence in contrast to complex disorders (multifactorial), many of which have a greater than 60% lifetime risk. Five thousand inherited diseases which result from mutations in a single gene have been identified. Their global prevalence is approximately 10 per 1,000 births. Although rare they are often severe, needing lifetime treatment. These include conditions such as inborn errors of metabolism, inherited haemo-globin disorders, cystic fibrosis and haemophilia.

The genetic basis of approximately 1,500 of these conditions has been identified in the past 10 years. This has in turn led to the development of reliable, cost-effective (DNA) tests for diagnosis and these are used in detecting carriers for prenatal diagnosis and in population screening. For example, one in seven of the world's population carry a mutation which results in thalassaemia. Control programmes now have the potential to greatly reduce birth prevalence and a successful example can be found in Cyprus.

In summary, diagnosis, prevention and, to a lesser extent, management of inherited diseases caused by single defective genes has progressed enormously due to genomic advances.

Communicable diseases

Major progress has been made towards sequencing the genome of more than 30 bacteria and parasites which are important human pathogens and over the next five years a further 100 will be studied. Completed genome sequences have been identified for organisms responsible for tuberculosis, leprosy, cholera, plague, typhoid fever, meningitis (haemophilus influenzae type B, pneumococcus), food poisoning (E. coli) and diarrhoea (campylobacter). Work on the genome sequence of the organisms that cause malaria, anthrax, leishmaniasis, sleeping sickness and Chagas' disease are under way. This may be of more immediate benefit to global health than the Human Genome Project, certainly in developing countries. Examples of the impact in this field include the development of new vaccines against HIV and tuberculosis, which are under evaluation; new improved diagnostic methods for dengue fever and leishmaniasis; new treatments against drug-resistant forms of malaria; and molecular methods to improve surveillance of pathogen spread and drug resistance across the globe.

In summary, new diagnostic agents, vaccines and therapeutic agents are likely to become available against communicable diseases in the next few years and this should lead to a significant public health impact in proportion to the ability of health systems in developing countries to implement these new approaches.

Pharmacogenetics ('the right drug for the right patient')

The aim in this field is to apply pharmacogenetics to medicines to identify patients who are most likely to obtain maximum benefit and least likely to experience a serious adverse event. Two specific areas of application have been identified: adverse event pharmacogenetics and efficacy pharmacogenetics.

Patients may have altered ability to respond to drugs and to drug efficacy or greater risk of drug-related adverse events from polymorphisms in genes encoding drug targets and encoding drug metabolising enzymes involved in drug clearance mechanisms or in adverse event mechanisms.

The general strategy is to recruit patients with and without adverse effects and then type 200,000 single nucleotide polymorphism (SNP) markers in each patient in order to identify SNPs associated with adverse events. This will require the production of 'SNP chips' based on SNPs which confer no information on risk of disease (since this would complicate their use in practice). The aim would be to predict adverse effects before drug prescription. Thus a doctor would make a diagnosis and base subsequent prescription on the results of the 'SNP print', which would give a read out of all effective treatments and their safety profiles for that patient. This would allow doctors to identify patients at risk of adverse effects before a patient takes a drug. This would act to enhance medicine safety profiles, make more informed treatment decisions, increase doctor–patient confidence in safety and thus encourage compliance.

This has, therefore, the potential to save lives and valuable health care resources by identifying populations who will respond to treatments. It could limit occurrence of adverse effects of treatment – a major cause of ill health. As the molecular basis of many of these pathways is likely to be less complex than those of complex disease (see below), it is more likely that they will be tractable to study, and thus progress with current technology and approaches is more likely in the near future.

In summary, clinical pharmacogenetics is likely to be a reality in the next five years. It will start slowly due to high initial start-up costs to generate SNP assays but will then accelerate, driven by regulation and strong commercial incentives.

Non-communicable diseases

> The incidence of cancers and chronic diseases in a particular popula-
> tion is largely determined by its environment and lifestyle, and not by its
> particular genetic make-up.[2]

Despite this perceptive statement by Rose, heritability for many of these conditions is moderately high (although this declines with age – implicating generalised ageing processes that are much less influenced by genetic variation). The aim of genetic research in this field is to identify the different genetic variants involved in variable susceptibility to environmental agents or effects of ageing, better understand pathogenesis and hence develop completely new approaches to prevention and therapy.

However, success is likely to be governed by the underlying genetic architecture of complex disease. This is often conceived of as what is known as the common disease/common variant model. In this model genetic risk for common diseases is due to (a few) high frequency alleles. Support for this model is found in the common alleles which have been identified as risk factors for Alzheimer disease (*APOE epsilon 4*), breast cancer (*BRCA2* N372H), Crohn's disease (*NOD2* 3020insC), type 2 diabetes mellitus (*PPARG* Pro12Ala and *CAPN10* 112/121), venous thrombosis (*F5* R506Q) and AIDS (*CCR5 delta 32*).

However, a competing model is the multilocus/multiallele model. In this there are many alleles at many loci and the genetic risk for common diseases is conferred by (very many) very low frequency alleles. Once again, there is empiric support for this model. The LDLR gene (coronary heart disease) has over 700 variants, the BRCA 1 and 2 genes (breast cancer) each have over 400 variants, MSH2 and MLH1 (colorectal cancer) have over 400 variants and the HBB gene (haemolytic anaemia) has more than 100 variants.

Finally, it may be that the genetic basis of some common complex diseases is the result of genes which have evolved to resist infection and periods of famine during a limited reproductive lifespan (common disease/fixed variant model). This suggests that conditions such as coronary heart disease, type 2 diabetes and many cancers are almost inevitable with current environmental exposures, and genetic factors will play little role in their aetiology except to modify age of onset.

If the multilocus/multiallele model is found to be the dominant biological model, then progress in understanding the genetic basis of complex disease will be slow. It may be important to adopt strategies to enrich for genetic effects, for example by looking for a family history (familial cancers); early onset (familial cancers, ischaemic heart disease); severe disease (recurrent depression); disease subgroup (HLA-matched diabetics); less affected sex (SLE, pyloric stenosis); high prevalence group (type 2 diabetes in Mexican Americans); population isolate; low environmental risk (COPD in non-smokers) or sub-clinical phenotypes such as HDL cholesterol, bone mineral density or blood pressure. Although these may result in the study of rarer and atypical cases, the study of their genetic basis may be tractable in the near future and insights into key pathological pathways can come from such investigation. For example, most of the insights into the pathological mechanisms of Alzheimer's disease have come from the study of the rare early onset familial form.

Another response to complexity has been to assemble vast collections of DNA and environmental data. Thus, BioBank UK[3] seeks to recruit 500,000 individuals. The aim is to rely on 'Mendelian randomisation'[4] to limit confounding and so aid identification of small 'causal' effects. However, there is concern that these variants with small effects may have little importance. Their effects will be too small to support screening and they will be unlikely to be involved in key physiological pathways.

One of the most important tools for a better understanding of the function and pathology of human genomes is the study of animal genomes. There are important similarities between mouse and man in terms of large DNA segments, anatomical structures/physiological processes and many diseases (disease animal models).

In summary, dissecting aetiology of complex disease is a huge long-term challenge. Breakthroughs in cancer and new treatments for chronic diseases are far less certain in the next few years. The major contributions are likely to be through elucidating molecular mechanisms of disease leading to new drug treatments or prevention strategies (in the medium term). The complexity of the genetic basis of disease (typified by very many small and interacting genetic effects) may make the vision of personalised medicine based on genetic profiles an unrealistic goal in the short term. Thus, in terms of the vision of genetically based individualised preventive medicine described above, this may be technically feasible in the near future but is unlikely to result in accurate disease risk prediction since the nature of risk in common multifactorial disease is too complex. Ethical issues, such as the definition of adequate informed consent and rights of access to genetic information within families and by employers, insurance companies and the police, are still to be resolved fully.

Finally, any screening should have a preventive principle – to identify not just increased risk but reversible risk. The long lag between the discovery of a new genetic risk factor and the elucidation of the molecular pathways and subsequent development of an effective intervention means that there will be many instances of long periods between discovery of genetic risk, which permits increased risk to be identified, and the availability of an effective intervention to reduce the risk.

Rose described a 'prevention paradox' whereby a preventive measure that brings large benefits to the community may offer little to the individual. Conversely, a genetic test that benefits a minority of high-risk individuals may have little impact on the burden of disease. However, the concept of genetically based individualised preventive medicine as described above seems to point to a new paradigm that incorporates elements of both population-based and 'high risk' disease prevention strategies (with everyone being found to be at increased genetic risk for some conditions).

Public health aspects of advances in genomics

Classical models of disease prevention: primary, secondary and tertiary prevention

Prevention of disease has classically been considered in terms of primary, secondary and tertiary prevention. What impact will the ability to define genetic risk have on these levels of prevention?

Primary prevention aims to prevent disease before it occurs. Current examples at present would include carrier detection and prenatal counselling for rare fully penetrant and lethal single-gene and chromosome disorders. In the future it has been proposed that there may be a new approach to primary prevention of chronic disease whereby there will be identification and interruption of environmental cofactors that lead to disease among those with susceptible genotypes. However, most common complex diseases are multifactoral and very heterogeneous, and no single gene is likely to account for a significant attributable fraction of cases. It will, therefore, be very important to consider gene–gene and gene–environment interrelationships, and at present these are poorly understood.

The development of novel primary prevention measures may require improved understanding of disease aetiology. This in turn will not come directly from new knowledge concerning genetic susceptibility but rather through further scientific investigation into the function of the proteins coded by newly identified genetic factors. Thus genetic discovery is the start rather than the endpoint, and it may take many years for new preventive measures to be developed.

Secondary prevention aims to target clinical manifestation of disease by early detection and intervention during the preclinical phase of disease. A current example would be new-born screening for metabolic disorders with resulting early intervention. In the future, advances in molecular epidemiology will result in earlier identification of disease pathology at the stage of preclinical disease or even earlier at the stage of early biological effect. However, there will still be a need to define effective interventions since the concept of screening is not one of assessing risk factors but of reversible risk (as discussed above).

Tertiary prevention aims to minimise the effect of disease by preventing complications and clinical deterioration. A current example would be antibiotic prophylaxis in patients with splenectomy to prevent serious bacterial complications. In the future, the identification of genetic factors that predict prognosis or response to treatment or the likelihood of adverse effects with specific treatments should be possible, and indeed recent advances in pharmacogenetics suggest that this may be one of the first areas in which advances in genetic technology will impact on clinical practice.

Overall, the increasing understanding of aetiology and the mechanisms of pathogenesis of disease should lead to increasing opportunities to shift towards primary prevention.

Classical models of disease prevention: behaviour, environmental and clinical strategies

Public health programmes can also be considered in terms of those that focus on behaviour prevention, environmental exposure prevention or clinical prevention strategies.

Behaviour prevention strategies aim to educate people about individual risk and then to bring about behavioural change to eliminate, reduce or change their exposure to that risk factor. In the future, education and behaviour modification may be targeted to people with differential genetic susceptibility to specific environmental risk factors. However, it is by no means certain at present that this approach will be effective. There is little evidence to support the hypothesis that being able to express individual risks more precisely will increase the motivation of people to change their health behaviour. Indeed, concern has been expressed that genetic risk might be perceived as unalterable and this may promote nihilism and reduce motivation to change behaviour. If it cannot be shown clearly that giving individuals information about genetic risk is effective in promoting positive behavioural change, then it may actually be detrimental to their health to provide this information.

Environmental prevention strategies aim to change the shape of the exposure outcome curve. If the disease occurs only at high exposure, the aim is to prevent high individual exposure. However, if even low-dose exposure carries some risk, the aim may be to reduce population exposure (for example, total emissions of an airborne pollutant in the environment). If there is uncertainty about which is more appropriate, the latter policy is safer. In the future, it will be possible to identify people within the population who are particularly susceptible to environmental exposure because of genetic factors. Many current strategies are geared to the population as a whole and are not geared to addressing specific genetic differences between individuals (although some may be more sensitive to adverse effects of intervention). There is a risk of the shift of attention from the risk factor to the disease. This may result in less societal pressure to take action to reduce population exposure to an environmental hazard and may result in stigmatisation and discrimination against individuals with the susceptibility genotypes.

Clinical prevention strategies deal with prevention in a health care setting. Current examples include cervical or breast cancer screening programmes or family-based prevention through genetic counselling. Traditional methods – based on, for example, family history, blood lipids, blood pressure or dietary assessment – are often weak predictors of disease risk. In the future genetic tests may reduce misclassification of risk factor status and improve the predictive value of risk assessment. However, as described above, this will be at the expense of a reduced population attributable fraction and thus reduced impact on the burden of the disease in the community.

In each of these strategies any genetic information given to individuals will need to be accompanied by adequate counselling. Individuals need to understand the probabilistic nature of risk, and it is important that they be aware of the level of potential adverse effects as well as potential health benefits. There is a danger that the high technology associated with genetic testing will be seen as a 'higher level of evidence' when, in fact, it will only deliver probabilistic information on disease risk.

Genomics and world health

The report of the World Health Organization (WHO) advisory committee on health research pointed to a number of key principles that need to be widely disseminated. An over-optimistic picture of genetic research has emerged. The potential medical applications of genomics suggest they will lead to major advances in clinical practice, but it is difficult to predict when this will happen. This over-optimism has the potential to distort spending for health and research priorities. Any benefits that result from genomics research will be irrelevant to countries that do not have a functioning health care system in place. Therefore, advances in genomics for global health care must be assessed with respect to their relative value in the practice and delivery of health care compared with the costs and efficacy of current approaches to public health, disease control and provision of basic preventive medicine and medical care. It follows that conventional, tried-and-true approaches to medical research and medical practice must not be neglected while the medical potential of genomics is being explored. Research priorities in genomics should address health needs of poor populations and clinical advances from genomics should be distributed fairly among the world's population, otherwise the gap in health care between rich and poor countries of the world will widen.

It is important not to let genomic research result in further inequities in access to benefits of research. The concentration of research funding in industrialised countries – and increasingly in the private rather than public sector – fuels this concern. It will be important that some international organisation acts to monitor how research priorities are decided in order to counterbalance their likely direction against problems of the largest 'markets' driven by profit incentives and to promote a process by which intellectual property and benefits of genomic research are shared globally. It will also be important to guard against bio-prospecting a country's biological resources for useful genes. One step towards this is the Convention on Biological Diversity, which requires prior consultation with communities, benefit sharing with local communities, assessment of affordability and efforts to promote the accessibility of the eventual products of research.

In conclusion, it is impossible to predict how genomics will change the health and health services in the medium to long term. In these circumstances we need clear principles that will guide policy making. 'We may not know where we are going but we should decide how we will travel.' Some key policy issues will include:

- open debate on aims of genetic services

- evidence-based services governed by need

- aim to reduce rather than increase inequity

- national health services responsive to interests of all, not just pressure groups

- national health services to lead industry and not the reverse.

Genomic advances may illuminate our understanding of the molecular processes governing health and disease and serve as a basis for the development of new prevention and treatment strategies through links with biotechnology and pharmaceutical companies. However, they will need to be set in a framework of ethical public health action if the benefit of this knowledge is to be realised.

ACKNOWLEDGEMENTS

I would like to acknowledge the excellent WHO publication *Genomics and World Health*.[5] I have drawn from this in some sections of this paper.

Notes

[1]   F. S. Collins, 'Shattuck lecture: medical and societal consequences of the Human Genome Project'. *New England Journal of Medicine* 341 (1999): 28–37.
[2]   G. Rose, *The Strategy of Preventive Medicine* (Oxford: Oxford University Press, 1992).
[3]   A. Wright, A. Carothers, and H. Campbell, 'Gene-environment interactions: the BioBank UK study'. *Pharmacogenomics Journal* 2 (2002): 75–82.
[4]   G. Davey Smith, '"Mendelian randomization": can genetic epidemiology contribute to understanding environmental determinants of disease?' *International Journal of Epidemiology* 32 (2003): 1–22.
[5]   World Health Organization Advisory Committee on Health Research, *Genomics and World Health* (Geneva: World Health Organization, 2002.

13. A Public Health Act for the 21st century?

Helen Zealley

Now is the moment for a leap into the future, to see if we can establish the same foundation for the future that the giants of yesterday provided for us. I have been asked to explore the possibility of a Public Health Act for the 21st century. I ask you to join me on three separate journeys during which today's public health legislative framework was analysed with a view to determining what is needed for the future.

Review of public health legislation

The first journey began in 1998 following the centenary of the 1897 Public Health (Scotland) Act – a masterpiece of legislation based on the principle of 'protection from nuisance' (principally communicable diseases) – which has stood the test of time and as we enter the 21st century still provides the framework for action when new or unexpected health hazards arise which have not been covered by subsequent legislation or regulations.

This journey involved a 'short-life' working group established by the then Scottish Office Department of Health to review public health legislation in Scotland and make recommendations to update and augment it. As ever with such a working group we were inundated with paper. The most important papers were the 1897 Act itself and, because we were anticipating devolution and the incorporation of the European Convention on Human Rights (ECHR) into all our legislation, a summary of the ECHR legislation.

We also reviewed the impact of the new Food Standards Agency as well as the implications of the data protection requirements and, with the help of a public health historian, the history of public health legislation since 1897. We looked at an English review of the law on communicable diseases, recent public health legislation in New Zealand and, in the light of a recent outbreak of food poisoning on a ship off the west coast of Scotland, we explored the fiscal responsibility for health protection on the high seas. And, of course, we sought – yet again – to clarify the respective responsibilities for outbreak control between the local authority (LA) and the National Health Service (NHS).

We identified that public health law is that which seeks to prevent the external environment exercising, either directly or indirectly, a deleterious effect on human health whether in the shorter or longer term, and concluded that Scottish communicable disease legislation was fragmented, out of date and in need of updating and consolidating. In our discussions we agreed a framework for the future, taking account of the ECHR, and we even achieved agreement between the LA and public health representatives about outbreak control, although the exact responsibility for control in prisons and certain other institutions remained to be clarified.

By the end of 1999 a draft consultation document was being prepared – and there, fellow travellers, we must leave this journey. For various reasons – particularly the steady build-up of pressure for legislative time in the first session of the Scottish Parliament – our work had to be put on hold. However, I am assured that our journey was not in vain and that now is the time to urge that the files be dusted off and prepared for legislative action following the 2003 Scottish election.

Healthy Public Policy Network

Journey number two also began in 1998 following the change of government in London and in anticipation of the Scottish Parliament. The newly established Scottish Council Foundation drew together a broad mix of academics and practitioners to form a Healthy Public Policy Network (HPPN) to develop ideas for healthy public policies.

Much less paper was produced on this journey. Instead, we engaged in active and stimulating discussion about the factors that influence health, the poor health status of Scotland and the steps we could take to influence the new Scottish Parliament to introduce health-oriented legislation. We focused particularly on the Evans–Stoddart model of health[1] and explored the potential for broad spectrum legislation which would address the wide range of influences that impact on health. However, because we were less than optimistic that the new Scottish

Parliament would be ready to embrace such a complex challenge as a first step, we agreed to develop a policy paper which would, hopefully, inform and educate the new parliamentarians about Scotland's poor health status and the factors that influence it.

And so was born *The Possible Scot*,[2] a short, very readable report describing Scotland's comparative health experience and incorporating a specific analysis of the 'Scotland effect': the extent to which the health experience – i.e. the early deaths – of the people of Scotland at all levels of the social spectrum is worse than that of their counterparts south of the border. It included a summary of the influences on health, in particular identifying that 'lifestyle is not the key issue but that more attention needs to be paid to wider structural influences, especially the impact of wealth on health – or rather vice versa, the association of poverty with ill health':

> The Possible Scot will be nurtured in a stimulating but safe physical environment and a supportive social environment free from violence or abuse. He or she will acquire a first class education that includes the development of life skills such as empathy, assertiveness and the creative use of leisure. As they grow, Possible Scots will be valued in society, irrespective of differences that may be apparent at birth or later in life. In turn, the Possible Scot will make a productive contribution to the lives of others, valuing their differences. Freedom from major disease and impairment through adult life, combined with a sense of well-being, will enable the achievement of personal and collective ambitions. Where illness or impairment exist, a society committed to providing support and removing barriers will maximise the potential for living a full life. Possible Scots will have concern for themselves, for others and for future generations and this will be reflected in their lifestyles.[3]

We indulged in some new thinking about government – dreaming, as we could in anticipation of a new Executive, that it would be truly possible to achieve 'joined-up' government initiatives; and suggesting new approaches to involving the people of Scotland in the development of policy for transport and housing, of life skills for children and young people, and of welfare reform and income redistribution.

Our discussions concluded with practical proposals for area regeneration and budgeting to achieve the changes we proposed; ideas for managing and monitoring the changes; and an outline agenda for the future.

Four years on, and coming to the end of the first term of the Scottish Parliament, we can ask to what extent these ambitious dreams have been realised. Not very far. The biggest disappointment is the extent to which the critically important 'joined-up' or 'cross-cutting' government appears to be a will-o'-the-wisp – something that many seek to achieve but no one manages to pin down. Indeed, in 2000, the network undertook an audit of the Scottish Executive's initial programme for government to assess the extent to which it was likely to achieve the late Donald Dewar's ambitious goal 'to end health inequality'. We took each of the commitments in the executive's programme – and, because certain UK legislation has an important impact on health in Scotland, also included relevant UK-wide policies. Each policy was scored from +5 to –5 against each of the health influences identified in the Evans–Stoddart model.

Three main messages emerged from this audit:[4]

- Very few people, including the executive itself, ever review the potential impact of their cumulative legislative programme – on anything, let alone health.

- While every department in the Scottish Executive was found to be making some (mostly modest) contribution to the overall goal of reducing health inequality, the network estimated that the biggest contribution was coming from UK tax and benefit and employment legislation, followed by UK and Scottish social justice legislation targeted at children and young people.

- While the overall impact of the legislative programme was marginally positive, there was a striking impression of a fragmented programme that was full of good initiatives but lacking a coherent strategic focus.

So the big message – to the Scottish and the UK Parliaments – is that 'joined-up government needs to move beyond rhetoric and become a reality'.

UK Partnership for the Health of the People

Finally, the third of my journeys takes us to London and the Nuffield Trust, where, following an earlier meeting of public health leaders in Christchurch College, Oxford, the trustees had agreed to establish a UK Partnership for the Health of the People, with a remit to build a case for, and undertake detailed preparatory work towards, a 'UK Health of the People Bill'.

Like my other two journeys this one also began in 1998, but with a slightly different background. First, this was the 150th anniversary of the (English) Public Health Act 1848, which had led to the establishment of the formerly overarching Board of Health. The other key background features were the relatively recent change of UK government, the anticipated establishment of devolved governments in Scotland, Wales and Northern Ireland, and expectations surrounding the new millennium. Again the partnership comprised a broad spectrum of health policy analysts, academics, statisticians and practitioners and, importantly, its work was driven by a small project team. In reporting on this journey I am indebted to the Nuffield Trust and to the project team members who undertook most of the work: Dr Stephen Monaghan, Dr Dyfed Huws and Marie Navarro.[5]

As with the Scottish Healthy Public Policy Network, the partnership engaged in extensive and stimulating debate – not only in the meetings but also over a generous dining table (courtesy of the Nuffield Trust) and, for the two Scottish participants, during our subsequent walk to the sleeper home. The discussions covered:

- the comparatively poor health status of the UK population and the unacceptable extent of inequalities

- the wider determinants of health

- the processes by which new legislation is developed

- the context within which the 1848 Act had been developed and the principles on which it was based

- the increasing loss of trust in government and its agencies, and

- the context in which this UK-wide initiative to develop a new public health legislative framework would be developed, including reference to:

  - the impact of EU legislation since the incorporation of a public health remit in the Maastricht and Amsterdam treaties

  - the European Convention on Human Rights

  - the World Health Organization (WHO) and its overarching 'health for all' philosophy, and

  - the implications of devolution, also with reference to the Good Friday Agreement for Northern Ireland.

We sought to review the scope of existing legislation on the wider determinants of health we had identified. However, this was a Herculean task. We therefore identified four exemplar health topics to provide us with a framework from which we could identify the scope for legislative change. The exemplars were selected to represent health challenges where the UK performs poorly in comparison with the rest of the EU, and where major gaps in inter-sectoral cooperation had been identified:

- the health of children

- accidents and injury

- teenage pregnancy, and

- communicable diseases.

In practice even these proved to be too broad in their scope and the project team focused more specifically on:

- child-pedestrian road traffic accidents

- domestic fire injuries

- alcohol misuse and road traffic accidents

- unintended teenage pregnancy, and

- communicable diseases.

In addition the project team reviewed the scope of the public health function at local and national levels; the actual and potential impact of devolution; alternative legal frameworks in the UK (such as the Audit Commission, the Greening Government Initiative and the Food Standards Agency); and the public health framework in a number of other countries.

The team's analysis task proved to be enormous. First, for each exemplar they sought: to identify the evidence for effective health policy intervention; to review the existing legal framework and powers provided by legislation of the EU, the UK, England, Wales, Scotland and Northern Ireland; to identify strengths, weaknesses and gaps; and to propose changes by relating the weaknesses and gaps back to the evidence.

Finally, from all the exemplars, the team concluded that, despite the massive volume of detailed legislation and regulation, there was a complete absence of a coherent approach to population health protection and improvement.

They identified that specific issues need to be addressed concerning:

- The government (UK, Wales, Scotland, Northern Ireland) –

  - there is no focal point or ministerial responsibility for the cross-cutting issues that influence the public's health

  - there is no coordinated monitoring of health

  - no one has a statutory duty to monitor health and advise

  - the departments of health, and the committees that shadow their work, focus primarily on the NHS and pay little attention to public health.

- The chief medical officers –

  - they have very few statutory functions and have no current duty to act 'to protect the public health' or to report on health status

  - they have a duty to advise other government departments but no requirement to make this advice public.

- The health organisations and directors of public health –

  - they have no explicit duty to protect and improve health or to report on the health of their population

  - they have increasing opportunities and a duty to collaborate with others who have a more direct impact on health, especially local authorities, through health improvement and community plans.

- The local authorities –

  - with the exception of the Greater London Authority, they have no duty to bring about health improvement or to undertake health impact assessments of their own policies and programmes

  - they have no statutory duty to engage the local director of public health in the work of the local authority at senior officer level.

The team also identified that responsibility for various aspects of public health is spread across a multitude of 'national' public bodies – covering, variously, the UK, Great Britain only, England only, Wales only, England and Wales only, Scotland only or Northern Ireland only – and that there is growing scope for duplication, for inconsistency and for black holes to get worse as the four separate UK parliaments (or three depending on whether Northern Ireland is or is not devolved) introduce different legislation to address the same public health problems. Interestingly, the dilemma surrounding confusion over responsibility for communicable disease control – a dilemma with which we had recently tussled in Scotland – reflected similar ambiguity throughout the UK, as demonstrated by the Philip's Enquiry into BSE and vCJD in 2000. The same dilemma is increasingly being identified as a cause for concern in an era of potential bioterrorism.

In addition, the team identified that most of these public bodies act without seeking public health advice and that none has a remit, independent of government, to scrutinise the public health function of national or local public bodies – let alone report on this to the public. Moreover, many of their remits overlap – and also overlap with those of local organisations, and particularly local authorities – resulting in a lack of clarity about responsibility. The Food Standards Agency – at that time newly established following extensive consultation – proved one exception, with its carefully structured national and devolved responsibilities, its independence from government and a requirement for openness. Another exception was the Public Health Institute for Scotland (PHIS) with its remit to work with the Information Services Division of the Scottish health service to create a new public health information base that would draw together the disparate national statistics relevant to health and include an epidemiological interpretation.

The team was also optimistic that the imminent restructuring of the NHS in England, with its nine regional directors of public health, would overcome some of the gaps they had identified. However, the team concluded that there was also scope for confusion between the role of these directors, that of the chief medical officer for England and that of the four regional directors of health and social care – and we noted also that none would be independent of government. In addition, the partnership as a whole expressed formal concern that the associated devolution of statutory functions for health improvement and protection to primary care trusts could compromise the public health function in England because of the relatively small populations and (unlike Scottish health boards) their lack of an explicit remit as 'public health organisations'. Indeed, these concerns gave an added sense of urgency to the task of identifying an appropriate future legislative framework to protect the health of the people in the 21st century, a framework that would be rational, simple and effectively coordinated between the many different players.

So how can this be achieved? And what were we able to learn from others?

The partnership looked at structures that had been developed recently in a number of other countries, particularly those where responsibility is split between a federal/national level and a state/devolved tier of government. We were particularly impressed by the Australian Commonwealth and State agreements for health information combined with an Australia-wide public health partnership – as well as by the Catalonian 'right to health protection'. We also had to admit that the UK's pragmatic approach to piecemeal legislation and regulation had, over the past 50 years or so, created a confused muddle when compared with, say, the disciplined French system of codification. In addition, our problems were compounded by the growing lack of trust in central government.

Our goal was therefore to propose a system that provides for the UK:

- a clear definition of the public health function – ensuring that this is broad enough to cover such health influences as

  - transport

  - the planning of industrial developments

- a definition of roles and responsibilities – clarifying who is responsible for what

- a rational legal framework based on

  - a general human right to public health – balanced between the rights of the individual and the common good

  - the precautionary principle.

After lengthy discussion the partnership was agreed that the focal point for any new UK legislation must be an independent public body with a statutory duty of care for population health, including:

- a duty to collect and disseminate relevant health information

- a duty to undertake and publish health impact assessments across a wide range of policy making

- a duty to advise publicly on appropriate action

- a duty to act as the champion of the people.

We suggested that this body be designated a 'commission/board/agency for the health of the people'. Its independence would need to be assured and it would need to be adequately resourced to fulfil its functions competently and openly.

Although, for the sake of rebuilding public trust, the partnership has stressed the importance of a statutory body that is independent of government, it was also clear that there is a critical leadership role for government at all levels – UK, devolved and local. This needs to be demonstrated by the establishment of explicit ministerial responsibility for public health, linked to a clear framework for protecting the health of the people across all relevant government departments and supported by authoritative public health expertise. Clearly the relationships between the UK and devolved governments will be important and may, at times, provide for tension. Despite my strong support for the Scottish Parliament I have for a long time recognised that there would be value in an overarching UK (but not English) framework for public health – with coordinated health surveillance data and health information – even if we introduce different statutory approaches to achieve health improvement.

The project team's final task was to explore possible models for our proposed independent commission/board/agency. Indeed, as a nation, the UK has an amazing range of organisational structures – executive, regulatory, advisory and consultative – from which to choose. The Audit Commission, the various regulators, the environment agencies, the Greening Government Initiative, royal commissions and the Food Standards Agency were all examined in some detail. Of these the Food Standards Agency seemed to provide the best model for a 'UK health of the people commission', with its explicit UK–devolved government relationship; its public health support; its clear role to provide impartial and transparent scrutiny; and its remit to advise government as a whole rather than any specific department.

And so, as we come to the end of my third journey, we can look back and see that – yet again – we have identified very specific concerns about the existing UK framework for protecting the public's health. More importantly, by enabling a small project team to undertake the necessary research, the Nuffield Trust has allowed the partnership to identify a way forward that could address the problems that were found on all three journeys. A summary of this final journey and the proposal to establish an independent commission is being presented to parliamentarians as the 'next step' towards a 'UK health of the people Act' for the 21st century – one that will be practical, focused and implementable.

But how will this address John Last's big challenges – ecosystem destruction; fossil fuel addiction; HIV/AIDS and sex; and tobacco addiction. A paradigm shift for the 21st century requires that all public health practitioners need to be aware of these wider challenges to the health of people throughout the world and to the health of future generations. They need to understand and believe that the work they are doing is important; to define the action required to achieve the necessary changes; and to act locally, nationally and globally as advocates for change by being brave, making contact with power and 'using the moments' that arise.

By working together, and with others, it is to be hoped that we can achieve a legislative framework that will allow all little 'Possible Scots' to grow into global 'Possible Humans', protected from the threats of today and tomorrow in the same way that we have, for so long, been protected by the foresight of our forebears.

Notes

[1]   R. G. Evans and G. L. Stoddart, 'Producing health, consuming care', in R. G. Evans, M. L. Barer and T. R. Marmor (eds), *Why are Some People Healthy and Others Not? The determinants of health of populations* (Berlin and New York: Walter de Gruyter, 1994).
[2]   Healthy Public Policy Network, *The Possible Scot* (Edinburgh: Scottish Council Foundation, 1998).
[3]   Ibid. 43.
[4]   A. Cook, *Promise and Practice: will government policy improve our health?* (Edinburgh: Scottish Council Foundation, 2000).
[5]   Nuffield Trust, *UK Partnership for the Health of the People Project: Draft Final Report* (2002) (unpublished).

14. The future of public health practice
Peter Donnelly

What constitutes public health practice? It conforms to a standard definition of public health which would encompass the art and science of prolonging life and improving health through the organised efforts of society. In practical terms, modern public health practice in this country involves three things:

- health protection

- health recovery

- health promotion.

Health protection involves traditional public health functions and some new ones, including communicable disease control, emergency planning, immunisation and vaccination, and the planning, supervision and evaluation of screening programmes for, for example, breast cancer and cervical cytology.

Health recovery refers to the work undertaken by modern public health departments in relation to the planning, provision, evaluation and review of the quantity and quality of health service provision in the National Health Service (NHS). Other terms for this are applied epidemiology, health services research or simply numerate and intelligent health services management, but I like the term health recovery because it focuses on the purpose of the service – to recover health – and, as a concept, it seems active rather than passive. It emphasises patient contribution and indeed patient autonomy and minimises the possibility of medicalisation and dependence.

Health promotion – by encompassing health education, health improvement, the reduction of health inequalities and community development – seeks to make real the desire to improve the health status of a defined population through a series of targeted actions taken in concert with other agencies, voluntary organisations and the public.

	Health protection	Health recovery	Health promotion
Underlying Science			
Background norm			

Figure 14.1 Matrix on health protection

One way of considering this further is through the use of a matrix (Figure 14.1). Along one axis, we have health protection, health recovery and health promotion. Down the other we have underlying science and background norm. 'Underlying science' speaks for itself and has been well covered elsewhere in this publication. 'Background norm' requires that we all work against a prevailing ethical, legal and philosophical background. Its origin is complicated, shifting; and, over time, shifting quite profoundly. But its influence is near all-pervasive. Occasionally brave souls will stand out against such background norms and will effect a change. William Wilberforce's 16 years of opposing slavery in the House of Commons is one example. But such foresight and courage is given to few; the vast majority, often without realising it, work within established paradigms.

I have included it in my matrix because trying to anticipate what the prevailing norms may be 25 years from now, whilst difficult, is at least as important as trying to anticipate technological advances in underlying public health science and forming an understanding of alterations and developments of public health practice.

Eric Schlosser's *Fast Food Nation* looks at the fast-food industry, particularly in the United States of America.[1] It examines the industry's impact not only on diet but on American society in general, through working practices, planning applications, agricultural reform, etc. Crucially, his book also helps us to see into the future in terms of public health practice. Some of the large corporations to which he refers are now much more powerful in their global impact than many nation states. Because of their influence and wealth they are immune to most legislative strictures and many norms of the free market, and respond only to organised consumerism. The fast-food nation provides one alternative, and somewhat dispiriting, view of the future – but let's try an alternative and perhaps more optimistic mental image.

Most of us have an image of the earth as a beautiful sphere of green and blue suspended in what appears an otherwise dark and inhospitable universe – the picture taken for us by *Apollo* spacecraft and widely distributed by the National Aeronautics and Space Administration (NASA). Many credit the growth of the environmental movement to the power of that single, repeated graphical image.

When you see how small and apparently insignificant the earth appears in the void of space, it is understandable that people do indeed begin to think in terms of sustainability, of caring for the planet and looking after future generations. My hunch is that 25 years from now the prevailing norm will be that we will have rediscovered the importance of quality of our food.

Health protection

In future the fast-food nation may seem like an embarrassing episode of our past, a time when we simply lost focus of the fact that food is more than fuel. I say I predict this; perhaps I should say I predict this in my more optimistic moments. But there is something that may drive this that ties us back to another box in our matrix. Developments in terms of the underlying science of health protection – involving the use of DNA technology to trace exactly pathways of infectivity and thereby apportion legal accountability – may make it harder for some within the fast-food industry to hide behind legalistic defences which tend to find epidemiological proof insufficient in a strictly legal sense. Once one can track back individual incidents of ill health and infection through delivery, and possibly mishandled food preparation, to inadequate hygiene at slaughter houses and meat-packing facilities, and ultimately back to individual producers, then you have a very powerful consumer drive that even the new nation states of the multi-national food conglomerates cannot ignore.

Yet, in another way, such individualistic rights-driven demands for increasingly effective health protection may cut across other traditional public health and health protection initiatives. Much of public health, after all, depends on the balance between individual and collective rights. One classic example is immunisation. Arguably the single most effective personal policy in terms of protecting your own health is to be the only individual in a society who remains un-immunised. You are then effectively protected by the well-established herd immunity conveyed by others, whilst yourself not suffering the small but inevitable risk of any immunisation or vaccination procedure. How does an increasingly litigious society cope with such a balance of rights? Perhaps not very well.

And whilst I, therefore, would be optimistic about the rediscovery of real food and the pursuance of better standards of hygiene by those in the food preparation industry, I don't think the future is as bright for immunisation and vaccination as many would have us believe.

Ideally, I hope that we will find a vaccine for awful diseases such as meningitis B. When it comes I will be delighted to have it if appropriate and to take the decision on behalf of my children that they too should have it. But over the long run is the future of immunisation secure? Not unless we can adopt a radically different way of engaging the public, which, put simply, means that parents need to work out if that is something that they wish to be done to them and their children and not just something they feel they should do just because we are telling them it is a good idea. In short, we need to help people put the tiny risk of immunisation in perspective and help them place it in the mental box of voluntary and acceptable risk rather than that of risk which is external and imposed. My message, therefore, is that we need not fear the consumerism exemplified by potential improvements in the fast-food industry; rather, once it is properly understood, we need to harness it in order to drive improvements in the uptake, effectiveness and safety of vaccines and other interventions.

I will complete my matrix on health protection by discussing improvements in the underlying science. We need to understand more about the true basis of prophylaxis. Every time I am on call, I am uncomfortable that what we recommend as prophylaxis for meningitis is not as grounded in epidemiological fact and understanding as it could be and that while rules of thumb have a utility, we can and should do better. In 25 years from now I believe we will.

So health protection will see technical advances. Its everyday practice will be increasingly multidisciplinary and involve nurses, other health care professionals and, in my view, some multidisciplinary public health practitioners from non-clinical professions; and the background environment will be driven by litigation and by a rights-ruled culture of an individual nature. Vaccination programmes will be difficult to run and maintain unless they are fundamentally different in their philosophy.

Finally, in health protection, imagine another – this time rather disturbing – image. We have all seen the appalling but strangely compulsive way in which the twin towers of the World Trade Centre imploded and slowly collapsed, killing over 2,500 innocent people. That mental video is one that we can all replay. Imagine now, however, that the World Trade Centre is full, not of 2,500 innocent workers going about their daily business but of 2,500 equally innocent children from the developing world, many of them from sub-Saharan Africa, and watch with me in horror as you play forward that video of the towers collapsing and killing all of those children not once but twice – and not twice only, but twice every day, of every week, of every year. It is a truly horrific and depressing vision. It is, however, a reality in that it approximates to the number of young children in the developing world who die needlessly from communicable disease. If ever there was a need for a contrary and alternative view of the future, it is best summed up in that alarming mental image – one for which I cannot claim originality but which has been conjured up by Ian Banks,[2] one of Scotland's best contemporary writers. Surely here is opportunity. Malaria, tuberculosis and, increasingly, HIV and AIDS are amenable to treatment. Financially, the world can afford it – we only lack the collective political world to make it happen. If that can be assembled, then undoubtedly colleagues in health protection will find their expertise at a premium for the best possible reasons as we move forward to 2027 – 25 years from now.

Health recovery

Turning now to health recovery, let me give you a rather more light-hearted video to play in your mind. Imagine going into a local travel agency to book a holiday. There is a long queue before you can speak to the young woman sitting behind the desk. When you do finally get to talk to her she is clearly harassed, tired and distracted.

She nevertheless conscientiously takes a note of your request but says she cannot give you a date for your holiday; however, she will choose one for you and once she has she will write to you at sometime in the future, telling you where you will be going, who you will be going with, what exactly is going to happen to you – and by the way that might be sometime off. You leave feeling rather disappointed but when six weeks later you do get notification of your holiday, which is to commence nine months hence, you are dispirited to find it is not the place you thought you were going to. Your humour is even more challenged when the day before you are due to go on holiday it is postponed, apparently because the airline pilot was unexpectedly scheduled to do something else, or because there wasn't a plane available or the hotel beds were still occupied by the previous week's holidaymakers. The situation gets worse when this happens two or three times, until eventually you conclude reluctantly that the whole process of going on holiday isn't worth it because you are going to need another holiday to recover from the trials and tribulations of arranging the first one.

Perhaps you can see the parallels in the way in which we sometimes treat people in the NHS who have a legitimate need for elective surgical procedures. I am not making a cheap point in that I know that those who work at the clinical interface try extremely hard in difficult circumstances to make this huge and bureaucratic system work. I know because I have been there myself and tried to do it. My point is simply this: that if in any other sector of industry we treated people in the way the NHS treats them, we would long ago have gone out of business. And if I look 25 years to the future, or frankly even five or ten years to the future, I think such an approach to our customers, our patients, our clients, our fellow citizens will be totally unacceptable.

Furthermore, I think that the way we choose to tell them what we choose to tell them will also become rapidly and quaintly outdated. Within a few years, outcome statistics for procedures and acute health events will, of necessity, be in the public domain and at that point interpretation will become everything.

Those involved in public health practice will, therefore, have to become interpreters of data par excellence. We will have to get smarter at explaining and balancing risk, at putting into context options and alternatives for treatment, and, overall, at treating patients and the public as if they are important and valued partners whose views and comments really matter, not simply individuals who will have to make do with what we can give them because in some outmoded paternalistic way we can decide what they receive.

The alternative is too unpalatable to consider, because it would surely involve those with the financial and intellectual wherewithal paying and negotiating their way out of that system into a superior consumer-focused alternative, thereby leaving those most in need of health care with least access, slower access, less responsive access – in fact even no meaningful access. So public health's role in health recovery (or if you don't like my terminology, the provision of health services) will continue and, indeed, increase. We will be the interpreters of evidence, the explainers and balancers of risk – the advocates for those who otherwise will suffer inequalities of access to service. We will review, audit, evaluate and clinically govern and if we don't – then God save the NHS. These efforts will have to be underpinned by further technical advances in risk analysis and risk communication. In particular, some of the technical advances we need involve synthesis rather than further reductionism. As a teaching methodology, case studies (in the business school rather than clinical sense) have much to offer. But how do we research things as complicated as the policy and communication strategy surrounding BSE and CJD? Here I think standard scientific methodology has limitations, and rediscovering the importance of academic scholarship – or even emulating the methods of quality investigative reporters – may be the answer. It is, for example, interesting to note that in recent years the Faculty of Public Health Medicine has turned to investigative journalists to deliver two of its keynote lectures at its annual scientific meeting.

In 2001 Isobel Hilton gave an interesting and thought provoking DARE lecture on the relationship between the pharmaceutical industry and the developing world.[3] In 2002 Jeremy Laurence of *The Independent* challenged on mental health legislation and practice.[4] Perhaps we also need to learn from the great populisers of scientific thought such as Stephen Jay Gould, Richard Dawkins and Matt Ridley.[5]

Health promotion

Let me turn now to health promotion. Interestingly, it is perhaps in this area where I think some of the biggest changes may occur over the next 25 years. Undoubtedly, we need to know more – not necessarily more about where ill health is (although there are some interesting developments in geographical mapping and the study of intervention in real and meaningful communities); rather, we need to know more about what works, how exactly it works and how we can break into the seemingly endless generational cascade of socio-economic deprivation and ill health that besets our urban communities, particularly in Scotland. Interestingly, and as an aside, Scotland – and Edinburgh in particular – does not really have an inner-city problem; rather we have had an outer-city problem that is largely focused upon poor-quality peripheral housing estates, barren of facilities and opportunity. But, returning to health promotion, one change in practice that must occur is that we must somehow shake off this idea that it is all too difficult to make a difference. We must be as prepared to perform-ance manage improvement in health as we are to performance manage waiting lists. We must be courageous enough to target our services at those truly in need. We must come to realise that every health visitor (or public health nurse – a much better term!) who spends time in a middle-class household that perhaps does not really need her or his intervention is doing it with our agreement and blessing and is helping to perpetuate patterns of deprivation and ill health by not being in those places where he or she really could make a difference.

So let me conjure up another mental image, again not at all pleasant, but one that I think is instructive. It is not so very long ago that one could see in South Africa or in the southern states of the USA signs barring people of colour from accessing beaches, restaurants, lavatories, transport, etc. Imagine those signs scattered liberally around our health care facilities, only instead of saying 'whites only' they say 'no poor communicators'; or perhaps they say 'clever people only', or maybe 'priority for the articulate'. You may laugh and you may think that this is ridiculously far-fetched, that 25 years from now we will surely not have such signs. My response is that there will be no need for such signs – and indeed there is no need for such signs now because, in effect, that is what we are doing.

In the United Kingdom, the likelihood of coming forward to get timely treatment for your heart disease and your cancer probably depends as much on your ability to advocate your way through the system as on expectations built through life experiences – perhaps also on the relationship that you have with your general practitioner and your ability to describe to him or her your signs and symptoms. These factors may be as important as your underlying disease. We have suspected this for years. But we don't tackle it because it is hard; it is sensitive; it involves loading resources into deprived areas; it involves the coordinated efforts of society (to pick up on the textbook definition of public health) to remove the invisible barriers that make so many of our fellow citizens sick. Now you can call me a naive optimist, but I genuinely think that, 25 years from now, by the time I and many of you have retired, it will seem as false to us, as appalling, as unfair, as outrageous, to discriminate against the poorly educated and inarticulate as it does, in 2002, to discriminate against people on the basis of race. And just as with

Raj Bhopal's help we are moving in Lothian to tackle the unwitting but pervasive racism that besets the health service, so we must also tackle the institutional nature of health inequalities – whether they be of access or of outcome.

Now in the other five boxes in my matrix (Figure 14.1) I have tried to be objective. I have tried to decide what I really think might happen. But in this sixth box – the one that deals with the background norm in terms of the philosophical, ethical and legal framework for the future of health promotion – I really don't feel the need or the desire to be impartial or objective. I think, collectively, we just need to state what we want to happen and – utilising the expertise of all the people we have heard from earlier in the day – commit ourselves to making good health, and the lifetime opportunities that go with it, a meaningful right for every citizen of this small nation of ours and for every citizen of an increasingly small world. Such a commitment could create a future worth inheriting and a public health inheritance worth passing on.

Notes

[1]   E. Schlosser, *Fast Food Nation: what the all-American meal is doing to the world* (Harmondsworth: Penguin, 2002).

[2]   I. Banks, *Dead Air* (London: Abacus, 2003)

[3]   I. Hilton, 'Whose drugs are they anyway?' DARE Lecture 2000, Faculty of Public Health Medicine, Annual Scientific Meeting, 2000. DARE (Doctors Awards Redistribution Enterprise) is a charitable organisation set up a number of years ago, after a pay award, in line with the review body's recommendation, was awarded to doctors while other health staff were paid less than recommended. A group of doctors protested against this action and established DARE. It is funded by the doctors through a four-year covenant system, based on the pay rise they would have received if they received the lesser pay award.

[4]   J. Laurance, 'Pure madness: how fear drives the mental health system' [King's Fund Lecture] (Faculty of Public Health Medicine, 2002) (online at http:///www.fphm.org.uk).

[5]   J. S. Gould, *Wonderful Life* (London: Vintage, 2002); R. Dawkins and L. Ward, *Climbing Mount Improbable* (Harmondsworth: Penguin, 1997); M. Ridley, *The Origins of Virtue* (Harmondsworth: Penguin, 1997).

REFERENCES

Chin, J. (ed.) *Control of Communicable Diseases Manual* (17th edn). Washington DC: American Public Health Association, 2000

Donaldson, L. J. and Donaldson, R. J. *Essential Public Health* (2nd edn). London: Petroc Press, 2000

Gardner, K. and Chapple, A. 'Barriers to referral in patients with angina: qualitative study'. *British Medical Journal* 319 (1999): 418–21

Last, J. M. (ed.) *A Dictionary of Epidemiology* (4th edn). Oxford: Oxford University Press, 2001

Mandell, G. L., Bennett, J. E. and Dolin, R. (eds) *Principles and Practice of Infectious Diseases* (4th edn). New York and Edinburgh: Churchill Livingstone, 1995

Morgan, M, 'The Doctor–Patient Relationship', in G. Scrambler (ed.) *Sociology as Applied to Medicine*, pp. 47–76. Edinburgh: Harcourt Publishers, 2000

Naumann, P. and Vessey, J. A. 'Teaching patients self-advocacy'. *American Journal of Nursing* 102.7 (2002): 24A–24C

Strategic Action Plan on Minority Ethnic Health: being fair for all in the NHS in Lothian, January 2003–2008. Lothian NHS Minority Ethnic Health Group, 2003

Thomas, H. *The Slave Trade: the history of the Atlantic slave trade, 1440–1870.* London: Macmillan, 1998

Tod, A. et al. 'Barriers to uptake of services for coronary heart disease: qualitative study'. *British Medical Journal* 323 (2001): 1–6

Epilogue: towards transdisciplinary public health

Margaret Reid and John Last

Public health has always been made up of an amalgam of disciplines. The notion that public health is multidisciplinary nonetheless remains contentious, because there have been some persisting uncertainties about which disciplines are at the core of the field and which are peripheral. In the early decades of the 19th century the core disciplines were engineering, biology and social science. Public health was concerned with identifying and solving public health problems by way of sanitation and social science, including politics. Medical input was placed at the heart of public health by Edwin Chadwick, who greatly influenced the drafting of the Public Health Act 1848, and wrote into that act the medical officer of health as the lynchpin of the new boards of health. Thereafter, public health in the United Kingdom became a medical specialty that until recently was dominated by the input of physicians.

In the USA, public health, especially in academia, remained largely non-medical until about the 1920s. Even after that some schools of public health continued to be led mainly by scientists whose background, education and research expertise were in disciplines such as biostatistics, sanitary engineering or behavioural sciences. The situation is somewhat like this in Scotland in the early 21st century: three of the four academic departments of public health sciences are led by people from disciplines other than medicine.

It is useful and productive to move beyond debate about core and peripheral disciplines, beyond the very notion of a multidisciplinary approach, to the problems of modern public health. We should consider public health as a transdisciplinary activity, as a field that transcends conventional disciplinary boundaries – and the territoriality and petty squabbles that sometimes arise between and among groups who consider themselves as belonging to this discipline or that. The problems of modern public health are complex and multifaceted, embracing ideas and beliefs from so many fields of scholarly activity that they demand new ways of thinking, and the integration of all these ideas, beliefs and concepts in the quest for solutions that work.

This concept is a subtext in many of the papers that were presented at the centennial celebration of academic public health in Edinburgh and are gathered in this anthology. Those who spoke drew upon many disciplines, including epidemiology, statistics, social sciences, microbiology, genetics, medicine, chemistry and public administration. Most speakers stepped outside the boundaries of their own disciplines to address their topics from several perspectives.

The reductionist approach to problem solving has served humanity well for several hundred years, but in this new century the most troubling problems and the potential solutions are too complex to hope that the reductionist approach will continue to work.

Consider, for example, the challenge of the social, economic, political and public health problems that inevitably accompany violent armed conflicts. In central and west Africa this cluster of problems has caused close to a million deaths annually for several decades, and many millions more are maimed and permanently disabled. For the most part, United Nations agencies and non-governmental organisations have attempted to deal with this tragic situation in a piecemeal fashion. Yet it can be viewed in a holistic manner as a massive public health problem that could be approached from a transdisciplinary perspective. Communal violence often has roots in tensions between ethnic groups, which lead to mutual suspicions that evolve into confrontations, hatreds and escalating violence. It is at its worst when opposing groups seek to occupy the same space. Aside from the obvious toll of premature death, maiming and injury, entire communities suffer physical, mental and emotional illnesses that can persist for generations, fed by a constant diet of reinforcing narratives, the propaganda of folklore. Meantime, the essential societal infrastructure of public health and curative medical services and education deteriorates. Few public health problems exceed this in magnitude and scope, and few lend themselves so well to a trans-disciplinary approach.

When a companion volume to this is compiled 100 years from now to celebrate the 200th anniversary of academic public health in Edinburgh, the perspectives of all those who contribute will surely be devoid of an association with single fields of scholarly activity. Instead, all will belong to the overarching scholarly field of public health sciences. This prediction we make confidently, knowing we won't be here to see it fulfilled, but rather wishing that we could be.

List of centenary conference participants

Munir A Abu-Helalah	Dundee	Scotland
Lee Adams	Bo'ness	Scotland
Rob Aitken	Edinburgh	Scotland
Freda Alexander	Edinburgh	Scotland
Isobel Alexander	Edinburgh	Scotland
Leslie Alexander	Haddington	Scotland
Linda Alston	Edinburgh	Scotland
Amanda Amos	Edinburgh	Scotland
Katy Anderson	Galashiels	Scotland
Niall Anderson	Glasgow	Scotland
Froso Argyri	Edinburgh	Scotland
Kathryn Backett-Milburn	Edinburgh	Scotland
Rani Balendra	Glasgow	Scotland
Angus Bancroft	Edinburgh	Scotland
Mike Barfoot	Edinburgh	Scotland
Tom Bell	Edinburgh	Scotland
Muriel Berkeley	Aviemore	Scotland
Raj Bhopal	Edinburgh	Scotland
Roma Bhopal	Edinburgh	Scotland
Sunil Bhopal	Edinburgh	Scotland
Marianne Biggart	Edinburgh	Scotland
Colin Bird	Edinburgh	Scotland
Shelia Bird	Cambridge	England
Rosa Bisset	Edinburgh	Scotland
Eric Blackadder	Pittenweem	Scotland
Rob Blake	Edinburgh	Scotland
Andrew Boddy	Glasgow	Scotland
Jim Bond	Edinburgh	Scotland
Stewart Bonnington	Edinburgh	Scotland
Elaine Boyle	Edinburgh	Scotland
Margaret Bree	Glasgow	Scotland
Elizabeth Brotherston	Edinburgh	Scotland
Sandra Brown	Edinburgh	Scotland

Florian Burckhardt	Munich	Germany
Rachel Burrow	Edinburgh	Scotland
Ann Burt	Edinburgh	Scotland
Christopher Byrne	Southampton	England
Shona Cameron	Edinburgh	Scotland
Christine Campbell	Edinburgh	Scotland
Harry Campbell	Edinburgh	Scotland
Ian Dugald Campbell	Edinburgh	Scotland
Andrew Carnon	Dumfries	Scotland
Maggie Carson	Edinburgh	Scotland
Vera Carstairs	Melrose	Scotland
Harden Carter	Dunfermline	Scotland
Roseanne Cetnarskyj	Edinburgh	Scotland
Lyn Chalmers	Edinburgh	Scotland
Alec Chisholm	Macclesfield	England
Michael Clapham	Linlithgow	Scotland
Richard Clark	Dalkeith	Scotland
Vicki Clark	Dalkeith	Scotland
Kirsty Coey	Edinburgh	Scotland
Paul Coey	Edinburgh	Scotland
Richard Cooke	Edinburgh	Scotland
Neil Craig	Glasgow	Scotland
Peter Craig	Edinburgh	Scotland
Julia Critchley	Edinburgh	Scotland
John Crofton	Edinburgh	Scotland
Iain Crombie	Dundee	Scotland
Sarah Cunningham-Burley	Edinburgh	Scotland
Sara Joy Davies	Edinburgh	Scotland
Gillian Dennis	Edinburgh	Scotland
Claire Devlin	Edinburgh	Scotland
Maria Dlugolecka-Graham	Bonnyrigg	Scotland
Martin Donaghy	Glasgow	Scotland
Joan Donnelly	Edinburgh	Scotland
Peter Donnelly	Edinburgh	Scotland
Shelley Dorrans	Edinburgh	Scotland
Anne Douglas	Edinburgh	Scotland
Margaret Douglas	Edinburgh	Scotland
Darren Downing	Edinburgh	Scotland

Dave du Feu	Linlithgow	Scotland
Jo Dumville	Edinburgh	Scotland
Marguerite Dupree	Glasgow	Scotland
Tim Dyke	Cupar	Scotland
Sharon Edmunds	Edinburgh	Scotland
Victoria Elliott	Edinburgh	Scotland
Brian Ellis	Cousland	Scotland
Rob Elton	Edinburgh	Scotland
Wilma Elton	Edinburgh	Scotland
Steve Engleman	Edinburgh	Scotland
Tracey Farragher	Edinburgh	Scotland
Mireille Ferrandon	Edinburgh	Scotland
Colin Fischbacher	Linlithgow	Scotland
Sally Fischbacher	Linlithgow	Scotland
Paul Fleming	Jordanstown	N. Ireland
Gillian Fletcher	Edinburgh	Scotland
Patrick Forrest	Edinburgh	Scotland
Catherine Forwell	St Andrews	Scotland
George Forwell	St Andrews	Scotland
Gerry Fowkes	Edinburgh	Scotland
Andrew Fraser	Edinburgh	Scotland
Geraldine Fraser	Edinburgh	Scotland
Helen Frew	Edinburgh	Scotland
Jayawant Fuke	Dundee	Scotland
Mary Fulton	Edinburgh	Scotland
Louise Gallagher-Marsh	Edinburgh	Scotland
Margaret Gilmore	Edinburgh	Scotland
Dermot Gorman	Edinburgh	Scotland
James Gould	Edinburgh	Scotland
Nikki Gould	Edinburgh	Scotland
Barbara Graham	Edinburgh	Scotland
Cecil Graham	Edinburgh	Scotland
Angus Grant	Edinburgh	Scotland
Elizabeth Grant	Edinburgh	Scotland
Deborah Green	Edinburgh	Scotland
Jamie Green	Edinburgh	Scotland
Laura Grossman	Edinburgh	Scotland
Laurence Gruer	Glasgow	Scotland

Nana Gruer	Glasgow	Scotland
Rosamond Gruer	Edinburgh	Scotland
Jennifer Guise	Edinburgh	Scotland
Nick Guise	Edinburgh	Scotland
Sachin Ashok Gupte	Edinburgh	Scotland
Bruce Guthrie	Edinburgh	Scotland
Julie Hall	Edinburgh	Scotland
Eisa Hamid	Edinburgh	Scotland
Lisa Hanna	Edinburgh	Scotland
Erika Harding	Edinburgh	Scotland
Nadine Harrison	Edinburgh	Scotland
Elizabeth Harstad	Stavern	Norway
Herlof Harstad	Stavern	Norway
Miranda Harvey	Edinburgh	Scotland
Victor Hawthorne	Ann Arbor, Michigan	USA
Allan Hay	Edinburgh	Scotland
Jenny Hay	Edinburgh	Scotland
David Heaney	Edinburgh	Scotland
Anthony Hedley	Pokfulam	Hong Kong
Wilma Hepburn	Edinburgh	Scotland
Jane Hislop	Glasgow	Scotland
Bridget Hoeldke	Hamburg	Germany
Dorothy Horsburgh	Edinburgh	Scotland
Helen Hughes	Edinburgh	Scotland
Sonja Hunt	By Haddington	Scotland
Fintan Hurley	Edinburgh	Scotland
James Inglis	Edinburgh	Scotland
Helen Irvine	Glasgow	Scotland
Katie Jack	Edinburgh	Scotland
Kerry Jardine	Edinburgh	Scotland
Kathy Jenkins	Edinburgh	Scotland
Phil Johnston	Edinburgh	Scotland
Alan Johnstone	Edinburgh	Scotland
Gordon Jones	Edinburgh	Scotland
Kirsty Jones	Edinburgh	Scotland
Peter Jones	Edinburgh	Scotland
Roland Jung	Edinburgh	Scotland
Aileen Keel	Edinburgh	Scotland

Mike Kelly	London	Scotland
Robert Kendell	Edinburgh	Scotland
Helen Kettle	Edinburgh	Scotland
Sandra Kiauka	West Drayton	England
Celia King	Edinburgh	Scotland
Hazel King	Edinburgh	Scotland
Rachel King	Edinburgh	Scotland
Shem Kiptoon	Edinburgh	Scotland
Rebecca Kiptui	Edinburgh	Scotland
Robin Knill Jones	Glasgow	Scotland
Iveta Krupova	Edinburgh	Scotland
Gillian Kynoch	Linlithgow	Scotland
Susanna Lacey	Edinburgh	Scotland
John Murray Last	Ottawa	Canada
Wendy Last	Ottawa	Canada
Yuen Kai Lau	London	England
Ann Lawlor	Edinburgh	Scotland
Julia Lawton	Edinburgh	Scotland
Mandy Lee	Edinburgh	Scotland
Morag Leitch	Edinburgh	Scotland
Kirstin Lindberg	Edinburgh	Scotland
Mignon Ling	Alexandria	Scotland
Linda Lockerbie	Edinburgh	Scotland
Walter Lutz	Edinburgh	Scotland
Dennis McCaffery	Edinburgh	Scotland
Michael McCloskey	Edinburgh	Scotland
Finlay MacCorquodale	Edinburgh	Scotland
Kenneth MacDonald	Glasgow	Scotland
Lesley MacDonald	Cupar	Scotland
Sheena MacDonald	Edinburgh	Scotland
Elizabeth McEwan	Huntly	Scotland
James McEwen	Huntley	Scotland
David Macfadyen	Isle of Skye	Scotland
Patrica Macfadyen	Isle of Skye	Scotland
Kathleen McGill	Glasgow	Scotland
Kelly McGorm	Edinburgh	Scotland
Cecilia MacIntyre	Edinburgh	Scotland
Sally MacIntyre	Glasgow	Scotland

Haylis MacKay	Lauder	Scotland
Judith MacKay	Kowloon	Hong Kong
Neil MacKay	Lauder	Scotland
Ian McKee	Edinburgh	Scotland
Douglas MacKenzie	Edinburgh	Scotland
Isobel MacKenzie	Edinburgh	Scotland
Phil MacKie	Edinburgh	Scotland
Brian McKinstry	Edinburgh	Scotland
Gordon McLaren	Cupar	Scotland
Sheila MacLaren	Edinburgh	Scotland
Una MacLean	Edinburgh	Scotland
Daniel McQueen	Edinburgh	Scotland
Christine Maguire	Edinburgh	Scotland
Claudia Martin	Edinburgh	Scotland
Moyra Anne Masson	Edinburgh	Scotland
Lucy Matheson	Scotland	Scotland
Margaret Maxwell	Edinburgh	Scotland
Jonathan Meenagh	Edinburgh	Scotland
Paula Midgley	Edinburgh	Scotland
Keith Millar	Glasgow	Scotland
Hamilton Milligan	Hartlepool	England
R. M. Mitchell	Edinburgh	Scotland
Rory Mitchell	Edinburgh	Scotland
Sarfraz Mohammed	Edinburgh	Scotland
Boyd Moir	Edinburgh	Scotland
Scott Morris	Glasgow	Scotland
Marion Morton	Edinburgh	Scotland
Rod Muir	Edinburgh	Scotland
Rebecca Mullan	Edinburgh	Scotland
Brian Murray	Edinburgh	Scotland
Gordon Murray	Edinburgh	Scotland
Kenneth Murray	Glasgow	Scotland
Lilian Murray	Glasgow	Scotland
Lorna Murray	Glasgow	Scotland
Mary Murray	Edinburgh	Scotland
Scott Murray	Edinburgh	Scotland
Farshid Namdaran	Edinburgh	Scotland
Gina Netto	Edinburgh	Scotland

George Nuki	Edinburgh	Scotland
Chijioke Ogbu	Dundee	Scotland
Timothy O'Shea	Edinburgh	Scotland
Antionette O'Toole	Edinburgh	Scotland
Elizabeth Owen	London	England
John Wyn Owen	London	England
Geoffrey Palmer	Edinburgh	Scotland
Margaret Palmer	Edinburgh	Scotland
Jane Parkinson	Glasgow	Scotland
Odette Parry	Edinburgh	Scotland
Andrew Payne	Edinburgh	Scotland
George Peat	Macclesfield	England
Suzanne Penfold	Aberdeen	Scotland
Prodromos Petridis	Edinburgh	Scotland
Catherine Plant	Manchester	England
Stephen Platt	Edinburgh	Scotland
Frank Popham	Edinburgh	Scotland
David Porter	Edinburgh	Scotland
Mike Porter	Edinburgh	Scotland
Janette Pow	Dundee	Scotalnd
Robin Prescott	Edinburgh	Scotland
Satpal Puri	Glasgow	Scotland
Aimie Purser	Edinburgh	Scotland
Susan Quin	Edinburgh	Scotland
Gillian Raab	Edinburgh	Scotland
Snorri Rafnsson	Edinburgh	Scotland
Colin Ramsay	Glasgow	Scotland
Margaret Reid	Glasgow	Scotland
Mark Reynolds	Edinburgh	Scotland
Robin Richardson	Edinburgh	Scotland
Rudolph Riemersma	Edinburgh	Scotland
Andrew Riley	Melrose	Scotland
Graham Robertson	Edinburgh	Scotland
Judith Robertson	Edinburgh	Scotland
Roma Robertson	Edinburgh	Scotland
Wendy Rogers	Edinburgh	Scotland
Sheena Ross	Edinburgh	Scotland
Igor Rudan	Edinburgh	Scotland

Simona Scarparo	Edinburgh	Scotland
Graeme Scobie	Glasgow	Scotland
Graham Scott	Melrose	Scotland
Thomas Scott	Edinburgh	Scotland
Anne Scoular	Glasgow	Scotland
Chris Seiler	Edinburgh	Scotland
Edmund Seiler	Edinburgh	Scotland
Mary Shaw	Bristol	Scotland
Christine Sheehy	Edinburgh	Scotland
Susan Shepherd	Edinburgh	Scotland
Lorna Sibbett	Edinburgh	Scotland
Emma Sklaroff	Edinburgh	Scotland
Stanley Sklaroff	Edinburgh	Scotland
Alice Smith	Edinburgh	Scotland
Felicity Smith	Edinburgh	Scotland
Kate Sommerville	Edinburgh	Scotland
Polly Sommerville	Edinburgh	Scotland
Colin Soutar	Edinburgh	Scotland
Theocharis Stavroulakis	Edinburgh	Scotland
Markus Steiner	Hamburg	Germany
David Stevenson	Edinburgh	Scotland
James Stevenson	Edinburgh	Scotland
Jenny Stevenson	Edinburgh	Scotland
David Stewart	Coleraine	N. Ireland
Edith Stewart	Edinburgh	Scotland
Keith Stewart	Edinburgh	Scotland
John Stirling	Edinburgh	Scotland
Catherine Strang	Edinburgh	Scotland
Graham Sutton	Pontefract	England
Mark Taylor	Aberdeen	Scotland
Dorothy Thom	Edinburgh	Scotland
Alison Thompson	Musselburgh	Scotland
Ian Thompson	Musselburgh	Scotland
Marjory Thomson	Edinburgh	Scotland
Pauline Upton	Stirling	Scotland
Gillian Usher	Jedburgh	Scotland
Richard Usher	Jedburgh	Scotland
Stuart Usher	Jedburgh	Scotland

Jan Utkilen	Straume	Norway
Liv Utkilen	Straume	Norway
Zacharoula-Maria Valai	Edinburgh	Scotland
Raul Valdivia	Edinburgh	Scotland
Marlene van Wijk	Edinburgh	Scotland
George A. Venters	Edinburgh	Scotland
Douglas Walker	Edinburgh	Scotland
Drew Walker	Dundee	Scotland
Jacqueline Walker	Dundee	Scotland
Matthew Walker	Edinburgh	Scotland
Shona Walker	Edinburgh	Scotland
Anne Marlee Wallace	Edinburgh	Scotland
Hester Ward	Edinburgh	Scotland
Chris Warner	Edinburgh	Scotland
Pam Warner	Edinburgh	Scotland
Wilma Warwick	Edinburgh	Scotland
Jennifer Watkins	Edinburgh	Scotland
Penny Watson	Edinburgh	Scotland
Voirrey Watterson	Edinburgh	Scotland
Belinda Weller	Edinburgh	Scotland
David Weller	Edinburgh	Scotland
Jo White	Edinburgh	Scotland
Rosalind Wight	Edinburgh	Scotland
Sarah Wild	Edinburgh	Scotland
Linda Williams	Edinburgh	Scotland
Lucy Williams	Edinburgh	Scotland
Diane Willis	Edinburgh	Scotland
Jim Wilson	Edinburgh	Scotland
Susan Wiltshire	Edinburgh	Scotland
Mark Woolhouse	Roslin	Scotland
Sally Wyke	Edinburgh	Scotland
Ranjan Yajnik	Pune	India
Gulnur Yaman-Dent	Edinburgh	Scotland
Andrew Zealley	Edinburgh	Scotland
Helen Zealley	Edinburgh	Scotland

Index